The Unholy Union

The Unholy Union

✦

Church and State

Al Hamilton, missionary recruiter

cover illustration by Twila Schofield

iUniverse, Inc.
New York Lincoln Shanghai

The Unholy Union
Church and State

iUniverse books may be ordered through booksellers or by contacting:

iUniverse
2021 Pine Lake Road, Suite 100
Lincoln, NE 68512
www.iuniverse.com
1-800-Authors (1-800-288-4677)

ISBN-13: 978-0-595-40572-5 (pbk)
ISBN-13: 978-0-595-84937-6 (ebk)
ISBN-10: 0-595-40572-X (pbk)
ISBN-10: 0-595-84937-7 (ebk)

Printed in the United States of America

I AM MUCH AFRAID THAT
SCHOOLS WILL PROVE TO
BE—GREAT GATES OF HELL
UNLESS THEY DILIGENTLY
LABOR IN EXPLAINING THE
HOLY SCRIPTURES,
ENGRAVING THEM IN THE
HEARTS OF YOUTH.
I ADVISE NO ONE TO PLACE
HIS CHILD WHERE THE
SCRIPTURES DO NOT REIGN
PARAMOUNT. EVERY
INSTITUTION IN WHICH
MEN ARE NOT
INCREASINGLY OCCUPIED
WITH THE WORD OF
GOD MUST BECOME
CORRUPT.

Martin Luther

"…And you shall be hated
by all nations, because of me…"
Matt. 24. 9.

Contents

Reprinted From Star-Bible Tract Corp. Tx-

✦

RELIGIOUS CONTROVERSY

By Alexander Campbell

Many good men whose whole lives have been one continued struggle with themselves, one continued warfare against error and iniquity, have reprobated religious controversy as a great and manifold evil to the combatants and to society. Although engaged in a real controversy, they knew it not; but supposed that they only were controversialists who were in debates and discussions often. Had they reflected but a moment, they would have discovered that <u>no man can be a good man who does not oppose error and immorality in himself, his family, his neighborhood, and in society as far as he can reach</u>, and that he <u>cannot</u> oppose <u>it successfully</u> only <u>by argument, or, as</u> some would say, <u>by word and deed—by precept and by</u> example.

<u>There</u> can <u>be no</u> improvement without <u>controversy.</u>

Improvement <u>requires and presupposes</u> change; <u>change</u> is innovation, and innovation always has elicited opposition, and that is what constitutes the essentials of controversy.

<u>Every man who</u> reforms his own life has a controversy with himself. And, therefore, no man who has not always been perfect, and always been in company with perfect society, can be a good man without controversy. This being conceded, (and who can refuse to concede it?) it follows that whensoever society, religious or political, falls into error; or rather, so long as it is imperfect, it is the duty of all who have any talent or ability to oppose error, moral or political, who have intelligence to distinguish, and utterance to express, truth and goodness, to lift up a standard against it, and to panoply themselves for the combat.

But yet, plain and obvious as the preceding remarks may be, many will contend that religious controversy, oral or written, is incompatible with the pacific and contemplative character of the genuine Christian, and promotive of strifes, tumults, and factions in society, destructive of true piety towards God and of benevolence towards man. This is a prejudice arising from the abuses of controversy. Admit for a moment that it were so, and what would be the consequence? It would unsaint and unchristianize every distinguished Patriarch, Jew, and Christian enrolled in the sacred annals of the world. For who of the Bible's great and good men was not engaged in religious controversy! To go no farther back than the Jewish lawgiver, I ask, What was his character? I need not specify, Whenever it was necessary, ail—yes, all the renowned men of antiquity were religious controversialists. Hoses long contended with the Egyptian magi. He overcame Jannes and Jambres too, Elijah encountered the prophets of Baal. Job long debated with the princes of Edom. The Jewish prophets and the idolatrous kings of Israel waged a long and arduous controversy. John the Harbinger, and the Scribes and Pharisees, met in conflict. Jesus, and the Rabbis, and the Priesthood, long debated. The Apostles and the Sanhedrim; the Evangelists and the Doctors of Divinity; Paul and the Skeptics, engaged in many a conflict; and even Michael fought in "wordy debate" with the Devil about the body of Moses; yet who was more meek than Moses—more zealous for God than Elijah—more patient than Job—more devout than Paul—more benevolent than John?

If there was no error in principle or practice, then controversy, which is only another name for opposition to error, real or supposed, would be unnecessary. If it were lawful, or if it were benevolent, to make a truce with error, then opposition to it would be both unjust and unkind. If error were innocent and harmless, then we might permit it to find its own quietus, or to immortalize itself. But so long as it is confessed that error is more or less injurious to the welfare of society, individually and collectively considered, then no man can be considered benevolent who does not set his face against it. In proportion as a person is intelligent and benevolent, he will be controversial, if error exists around him. Hence the Prince of Peace never sheathed the sword of the Spirit while he lived. He drew it on the banks of the Jordan and threw the scabbard away.

We have only to ask how we inherited so many blessings, religious and political, contrasted, with our ancestors same five hundred years ago, to ascertain of what use controversy has been, and how much we are indebted to it. All was silent and peaceful as the grave under the gloomy scepter of Roman Pontiffs under the despotic sway of the Roman hierarchy until Luther opened the war. The Roman priesthood denounced the "ruinous errors" and "damnable heresies" of Luther, the "deadly influence..." of the tongue and pen of the hierarch; but they fasted, and prayed, and denounced in vain. No "crocodile tears over the souls of men"; no religious penances for "the church in danger"; no invocation of "all who loved Zion"; no holy co—operation of "the friends of evangelical princi-ples," could check the career of this reforming Hercules. Bulls of excommunica-tion. assailed him as stubble would Leviathan in the deep. "He feared no discipline of human hands." All was impotent and unavailing. The fire then kin-dled, though oft suppressed, yet burns. Jer. 20:9, 23:29

The controversy begun by Luther, not only maimed the power Of the Roman hierarchy, but also impaired the arm of political despotism. The crown, as well as the miter, was jeopardized and desecrated by his Herculean pen. From the con-troversy about the rights of Christians arose the controversy about the rights of men, Every blow inflicted upon ecclesiastical despotism was felt by the political tyrants.

Religious controversy has enlightened the world. It gave new vigor to the mind; and the era of the Reformation was the era of the Revival of Literature. It has enlightened men upon all subjects—in all the arts and sciences—in all things—philosophic, literary, moral, and political. It was the tongue and pen of controversy which developed the true solar system ~ laid the foundation for the American Revolution—abolished the slave trade—and which has so far dis-enthralled the human mind from the shackles of superstition. Locke and Sidney, Milton and Newton, were all controverts and reformers, philosophers, literary; re ligious and political. Truth and liberty, both religious and political, are the first fruits of well directed controversy, Peace and eternal bliss will be the "harvest home", Let the opponents of controversy, or they who controvert controversy, remember, that had there been *no* controversy, neither the Jewish nor the Chris-tian religion could have ever been established; nor had it ceased could the Refor-mation have ever been achieved. It has been the parent of almost all the social blessings which we enjoy.

If, indeed, all mankind were equally in love with truth, equally rational, equally intelligent, and equally disinterested, we might have only to propose a change for the better, and all would embrace it. But just the reverse of this is the true history of society, He is but little experienced in the human heart—he knows but little of the world, who imagines that what appears clear, wise, and useful to him, appears so to all; or that it is only necessary to support truth and goodness by unanswerable arguments, to render them universally triumphant. The more clearly and forcibly an unpopular truth is argued, the greater will be the dislike to it by all who are interested in representing it to be an error. Melanc-thon was for a time the subject of an illusion of this sort. He once told Luther that so clear were his apprehensions, so deep his convictions, and so forcible 'his arguments, that he could soon convince all Germany of the truth of the Reformation principles. He became an itinerant, and commenced a campaign against the priesthood. On returning from his first tour Luther said to him, "Well, Melancthon what speed?" "Alas!" replied the young reformer, "old Adam is too strong for young Melancthon."

A little experience will convince the most astute that the clearness and force of argument will not subdue opposition. It very frequently provokes the greater resentment. The adversaries of the Messiah are proof of this. So were the aristocrats in the late Virginia Convention. Orpheus could, by his music, as easily have caused the oaks to follow him, as could the republicans, by their arguments and demonstrations, have caused the oligarchs in power to consent to extend equal rights and immunities to the proscribed casts in this commonwealth.

When error has but a single ally in the corruptions of the human hearts, it is very formidable; but how strong when pride, passion, and interest become its auxiliaries! To overcome these, reason and logic must be strong indeed, and rhetoric most persuasive. Pride, ambition and selfishness, are all powerful allies of error. Hence double, triple, and quadruple the evidence necessary to convert a layman, will not often convince a priest. The pride of the understanding is the most invincible of ail sorts of pride, and more especially when religion is the problem. A bigoted skeptic, a prejudiced sectary, and an interested priest, are more without the pale of reason, are more beyond the reach of controversy, than the errorists of any other school. But while error lives, and falsehood has an auxiliary upon earth, controversy will be necessary, and argument indispensable.

When controversy proceeds from benevolence it will be more successful and less injurious to the comfort of them who are engaged in it. But when argument and debate are dictated by resentment, prompted by pride, or controlled by the lust of power, the hearts of the combatants must be polluted, and their passions inflamed. The wrath of man never did, and it never can, affect the righteousness which God requires; nor can it promote the happiness of man. When we love truth for its own sake, and when our efforts to maintain it proceed from brotherly kindness and love to all men, then we will plead its cause with force and with success; and then, and then only, wil 1 we be sanctified and blessed in the work. But a controversy for opinion, or for truth, instituted by vanity, by the pride of understanding, or the lust of under the banners of error, There are honest differences of opinion, and men equally sincere and virtuous on both sides of every question. This must never be lost sight of, It is nevertheless true that our great models, the Prophets and Apostles; nay, the Savior himself, though often mild as the genital influence of Spring, were sometimes severe and surly as the Winter's blast. At one time, and amidst one class of opponents, they were as gentle as the balmy zephyrs on beds of violets; at another time, and amidst other opponents, they were 1 like the mountain storm roaring through the cliffs. Soft and persuasive were their words and arguments to those who appeared honest in their convictions, but severe and tart were their reproofs to such as appeared obstinate in error. Hence Paul, who instructed his son Timothy to imitate him in all things, admonished him to instruct some opponents "with all meekness," and "sharply to rebuke and confute" others. So did Peter and Jude in their epistles. "Make a difference", says Jude, between those "who are complainers, who walk according to their own lusts, whose mouths speak great swel l ing words, and admire men's persons for the sake of gain"—"have compassion upon them." (I Cor.4:19-21).

The following pages, are the compilation of a series of class lectures that were given at Central Christian College of the Bible in Moberly Missouri in 2003, and 2005, as part of a missions class assignment. They were prepared for students who plan to travel abroad and share their faith in roles of 'tent makers' teachers of English or as those serving with missionary ministries. After more than 30 years of mission work, 15 of which were in Africa, and several years in other locations, and 6 months as a volunteer for Voice of the Martyrs in Sudan Africa, and many years of recruiting missionaries, these presentations reflect the views that came about as a result of such involvement with foreign cultures, and study of the persecuted churches in many countries.

The subjects and insights are presented with the purpose in mind to share what I believe God has given me to understand and therefore, present to youth of America (who look today upon a country (USA) and a world that has changed much and will continue to race toward it's destined end), who seek to serve God by serving others, with the intent of proclaiming the Gospel of Christ as the Lord commanded. Repetition of material is due to change of students attending some lectures and not having advantage of different lectures on those various subjects.

Sincerely,
In Him who is in us who believe.

Al Hamilton

1

Introduction to Unholy Union

In the present evil world, (age) as the Bible states, (Gal. 1.4), the observant person will see the continual increase in wickedness and uncontrolled hatred, of nation against nation, and kingdom against kingdom. Some of us who have been given many years already, can recall when this 'broken dam' of social acceptance became the cause of a flood of discontent.

When the 'increase of intensity' that was found to be prevalent in all walks of life, from sports to the 'work place' then to the happy little home of the average American citizen, we could see something coming down the 'pike' which could not be stopped or controlled. **It was the introduction of the philosophy of the 'extreme'.** There seemed to be no limit to the desire to win, to be first, to be unafraid, ("No Fear" signs in vehicles and on 't' shirts). The **'me' generation** had created a monster that it could not control. In recent articles you will find revelations of the frustrations and surprise that accompanied the 'dawning' of the light—which finally revealed to the age of the 'boomers' that it was a big mistake to promote the 'self esteem' agenda of the 70's 80's and 90's.

Many of those who now lead in corporate America, or teach in the public schools, have recognized this mistake. As one article entitled it, "the bubble has burst," (recent USA Today News article). One person who has now graduated from a University, believes that he was led down the path of the 'yellow brick road' but it led to disappointment and despair. A recent and timely, book (regarding partnership), identifies this dilemma, it is by Jonathan Tish, and deals **with 'we' as opposed to the 'Me'** of that popular but misdirected age of narcissism we see around us. But that 'me' generation, will not die easily, and it has already affected a great deal of the thinking in all levels of American society. It has not finished its course. Sadly to say, the 'me' generation is still with us, it has carved out a home in the brains of most people who still want the power of selfishness and greed.

Those of us who write articles or express ideas and concepts which find a more biblical basis, are often ridiculed or ignored. Many of us who direct the attention of the American public, and especially the so called 'God fearing' church members of America, to matters of fact which reveal this 'monster of narcissism' for what it really is, are often called cynical. This is one reason the statement earlier quoted by George Bernard Shaw in a recent news paper from California, is so powerful and so important. This great man had the insight and brilliance to clearly depict the present condition in his statement, as follows,

> "The power of an accurate observation
> is often called cynicism—by those who
> do not have it."

I have found that in an effort to remind people, (especially young college age youth, with whom I work in my calling), of the serious nature of this 'special ness' and extremely exaggerated view of one's personal worth, as opposed to one's humble, (Lk.17. 10) usefulness, that the educated elite who hold the key of 'worldliness wisdom' in our religious circles as well as the social center of American life, become most abrasive and contrary.

It is not without (selfish) reason that America's monolith of educators cringe when I, or those who think as I do, (and this number is not small), speak of the deceitful displacement of spiritual matters which is prominent today. For this reason, the following articles will not be welcomed by the average 'right wing' religious zealots or the 'left wing' liberal, indulgent pacifists of the present generation. However, opposition never stopped the prophets of old, from speaking as they were led to speak. (EZ. 33. 33). As Apostles of Christ the Lord, stated to those who refused to believe their message, "since you judge yourselves unworthy of everlasting life, behold, we go to the Gentiles." (Acts 13. 46). There have always been those who fear truth—since evil prevails in selfish desires, even among believers. Acts 20. 27-31.

Al Hamilton

2

AMERICA and the AMERICAN

In our present social order, and in the present society that makes up the United States of America, we have two components which comprise the country known as America.

We have the citizen and the government. Although the government is based on the constitution which was designed to create a nation of the people, by the people and for the people, there has arisen in recent years a great chasm between the two, the American as a citizen and the country called America.

We have the citizen, who fights in wars that are not his/her own, for principles of freedom and justice. We have the business man/woman who provides jobs for others and yet whose labor has as a goal, the purpose to increase wealth for his/her business and family primarily. We also have the professional who works in a field that requires skill, expertise and training, so that other citizens who depend upon the services and materials that they can supply will be available.

All of the above combines to make a strong community and social order for progress and development of the human condition in the present world. The person who is an American, with strong religious convictions, representing, about 85% of the population, I would guess, does not see the America that much of the rest of the world sees. The American citizen, on the average is one who believes in God, and even this is a broad description from which to work in trying to discover identity. To truly and correctly identify the average American becomes more difficult as years go by. If we break it down into social identity, spiritual identity and political identity we would have an even more difficult task. Our dilemma here is mostly due to the multiplicity of social identities that each person in America relies upon for a description of their citizenship. The Christian American wants a description that provides their religious belief as a dominate feature of their social status. The politically minded American wants the right people in public office, so that his entire social existence is peaceful and pleasant. The Working Class citizen of America wants job security, high wages and all the

3

benefits that accompany such status. There seems to be no end to the array of components that dominate the individual perception of life in America, held by the individual citizen in America. There is as much diversity in identifications for describing citizenry as there are adult people in the country. There are polls taken continually for trying to identify the whims and fancies of the entire society. The sectors of society, even when divided as consumer and provider of services, are so versatile and changeable at all levels, that the entire American society seems to be a road that has a beginning but no end.

Since it is so impossible to describe the person we call, an American, with any degree of uniformity or commonness in areas other than their citizenship, I would like to dwell only on this one issue of what I would call, Life as an American citizen who is a Christian by faith and practice.

A Christian who is an American citizen, has been able to move in a circle of freedom and opportunity that few other countries afford their citizens. But in this circle of 'comfort' and 'ease' there is perhaps the greatest danger of all for people of strong Biblical convictions. The Bible states…that in this world the Believer in Christ will have persecution. This statement was first made by Jesus who also said, to His followers, they should be of good cheer, for He has Himself overcome the world. This means the believer can live in this world and not be overcome by it, since the world was overcome already by the Commander in Chief, the Lord of the Believers. Jesus overcame the world, by not yielding to the temptation (Matt. 4) to be under the control of the god of this world, (Satan), or be a part of this world's carnal and narcissistic way of life. Jesus 'parted the water' here too, when He showed by life and teaching, that the Kingdom from above was different than the kingdoms of this present evil world (Gal. 1. 4). This is the great example, and clear message, that these two kingdoms are not only different but opposed to one another. Now we must choose how we shall live. Satan showed one way, and Jesus showed us *the way.*

The American who is also a Christian, needs to know how to live in a country that accommodates his/her belief system, without showing complete agreement with it. This is the challenge of the hour. To live in America and in that social order without being led down the wide path of '**world love**' but be a witness to truth, justice and Biblical principles, in a land of tolerance toward evil, and tolerance toward good. This is more of a dilemma than most people are aware of. The Devil is limited, he can use evil, and he can take a thing you intend for good and make it turn out bad. That is what the Devil does, he intends for all things to work against God and against man's purpose to be with God and to serve God. Evil only has power to produce evil results. But God can take an evil thing and use it for good. He took the crucifixion of His Son, Jesus Christ, and brought from this death, eternal life for those who believe in Jesus as their Savior and Lord. A Christian in America can use the world around him, his social conditions and the society, with all of its technology and information, etc. for the purpose of reaching people for Christ. Even if the technology of the world was meant for the people who belong to this present age and the enjoyment of those who do not know God, the followers of Christ can use the things of the world for the purpose of God (Lk. 16 1-11). This is also illustrated in the account of Moses in Exodus, before Pharaoh of Egypt, when the magicians of Pharaoh copied the miracle of Moses and made their staffs turn into serpents. But the staff of Moses, overcame and devoured the serpents of Pharaohs magicians. The power of God is greater and will always overcome the power of the enemy.

The gates of Hell cannot prevail against the Church, the true Ecclesia of Christ. The social order or government of men cannot overtake or overpower the church either. The people of God can use the present advancements and technology that mankind has been allowed to discover, and use for the advancement of personal and social development, as an avenue to fulfill the Great Commission of Christ. To go into all the world with the Gospel of Christ to make disciples.

Only God can use an experience or intent of wicked men to do harm, (such as persecution) and turn it into a good thing, for His Name to be glorified.

In the Old Testament book of Genesis, chapters 46-50 and verse 20 of chapter 50, we have the perfect example of how God can take what people can mean for evil, and use it for good, and even for His good plan and purpose. All who know about the Bible, and know something about what the Bible says about God and His way, can now understand (Eph. 5.17, Eph. 4. 14-32) how to live right, and how God can use what is intended by the enemy (Satan) to be for our destruction, and turn it to our salvation. One of the greatest principles of the Kingdom of God, and one of the greatest lessons in life, is the lesson that God can take man's evil intentions, and deeds and bring about a good outcome from that same experience or intent.

If America as a country seems to have turned a corner and become a nation of all religions and all kinds of immoral activity, it still has 'bits and pieces' which can be utilized for advancing the Gospel to others around the world. The bits and pieces may be in technology, or fields of communication which will only enhance the rapid deployment of Christian soldiers. The country was prepared for the churches use, as a launch pad or a resource for the Saints of God to take advantage of. As in the days of Lot's deliverance from Sodom, perhaps the Lord has said, "if there be 10 righteous in the city, I will spare the whole city for the 10's sake. "The salt remaining in America, those who are true to Christ and pray for the world, are the ones who may be the reason, the country has not already been destroyed. The Christian citizens of America, who can devote money, time and skill into advancing the Gospel world wide, must be taking giant steps in all haste, to fulfill the ministry that we have been given, as people of God.

In the early years of America's history, when the framers of the constitution sought the blessing and guidance of the God of Heaven, for the establishment of the country, there was a strong moral element in their intentions. These men who signed the constitution, knew that they represented a people who had faith of some measure in the Lord Jesus Christ. They also had strong convictions about the Holy Bible, as the true and lasting Word of God. From this premise and assumption, we know that these men, would never have accepted the idea of 'legalized abortion' nor would they have accepted a legal position of what today is called, 'same sex marriage.' This would have been seen as old fashioned Sodomy. Now in these present days we look back and see a different America, in our 'rear view mirror' just as the present church in America, sees a church in the past, and in other countries around the world, that looks a little different from themselves. Today the church sees extravagance, narcissism, and affluence looking back at itself in the mirror. The country, America, sees immorality and just plain sin looking back at itself in the mirror. Things which were not present in the beginning of the country, now test the original purpose and intent of the founders of the country. If we were to test these differences by Holy Scriptures, to see what God thinks of our present political and social values, we would have to look at the books of God written to His people, Israel, by the prophets of God.

To give my point, a frame of reference, look at the 18th chapter of Ezekiel. 'If the righteous, turn from their righteousness, and commit iniquity, and die in that iniquity, for this iniquity they have done, they shall die. And if the wicked turns from wickedness and does what is lawful and right, in that (present sate of right living) they shall save their soul alive. This is a principle, of how God deals with the righteous, and the wicked. Is it not also true therefore, that if a nation which at one time, had the blessing of God upon it, turns from righteousness, to work iniquity, it shall face His wrath, and no longer see His favor? Our call to America, and any people group, as a church is a call to repentance. Though America once, with high moral standards and respect for the laws of God, had blessings from God and was able to achieve great things in the world, it now faces a time of ensuing wrath. Ez. 18. 26, 27 makes it very clear what the future holds for America, if this country pursues this present goal of pleasing the wicked as well as the righteous. Light and darkness cannot dwell together.

There is a lesson and warning also for the religious community in this country. If the churches lean into the standards of immorality in the country, they too, shall reap what they sow. Our task as messengers of Christ, is to warn the unruly, to reprove, rebuke and exhort with all longsuffering and doctrine. Let us not fail our Master in these most serious days when evil increases. (Matt. 24. 1-12; 21,22).

If the American Christian, fails to take full advantage of the talents placed within his hands, we can expect to face serious consequences. The country that was not used by the Church to spread the Gospel world-wide, may lose its blessings and tools, and become only a dark cloud on the horizon of history. But if the church will use, to the fullest extent, the advantages and inventions this modern society has seen develop in recent years, God may grant more years to the success and freedom that America as a country has experienced since its beginning. The church plays a greater part in the Country's future than it probably realizes. For it is God who promotes (Ps. 75. 6,7) not man, the judge of all the earth shall have the last word, and the last vote.

3

AMC
Articles of Major Concern
vol. 1 doc. 2

♦

5-15-04

Title: First Christian Church—Incorporated
American owned and operated

Many events in the present days, which have 'exploded' upon the world and upon the major 'political powers' of the world, have affected the total fabric of modern society. Not only has the Western World, or all modern and developed countries found conditions of war and struggle to be a puzzle without all the pieces, that must still, somehow be put together, but the developing and under-developed nations of the world are also entangled in this chaotic, political subterfuge as well.

It was enough that centuries of war, dictatorship and a hundred other causes, including natural disasters in more extreme measure than usual, and cruelties of mankind carried out against itself, was the norm. But since the announcement of 'terrorism' as a worldwide threat to human existence has become the biggest 'Dragon' breathing the most fire upon all it comes in contact with, **no country or nation is safe**. When people (including children), become enamored with suicide bombing, as a way to 'make things better' or to prove some religious or political point, a new kind of danger is present. This new kind of 'real and present' danger has taken on a role of rather extraordinary proportions. It is religious, it is political, it is ethnic, it is an enemy that looks like one of the 'beasts' described in the book of Revelation. It does not take on any one identity, but has the appearance of many kinds of fierce and destructive powers, all or any one of which, would be more than an army or nation of even great political influence and military power could out-wit.

An enemy that can't be described as all religious, or all political, or even located in any one geographic center, is not the usual foe, but is still, a formidable adversary. It is very obvious that in these last days (1 Tim. 4.1, 2 Tim. 3.1, ff) the final battles will be religious ones. It is the opinion of many of the believers who have studied the Scriptures, that a war which has religious views and religious prejudice as the root cause for its very existence, is not going to be called to a halt because of political pressure. No amount of social or economic, crisis, will be motivation for 'a round of talks', and no degree of interest in unity and human dignity can bring religious factions, whose basic belief justifies extermination of the opposition, to see any reason for abandoning their cause. Today the people labeled as 'terrorists' are people who have placed less value on human life, including their own, than they have on their 'religious' views.

So how will such an enemy in the world today—do battle?

It is my (educated?) guess, that the senior partner, in this war of the worlds, the real enemy of mankind, has a plan that may have been unnoticed by those who sit in the seats of the nations governing bodies. Those in political positions will not quickly recognize the fact that **the church was told, "we wrestle not against flesh and blood, but against principalities and powers, and spiritual wickedness in high places**." (Eph. 6. 12). Those in Washington, as well as those who govern the leading powers of the world, may have overlooked some serious facts about the strategies that the real enemy of man, who sees war as a spiritual battle against all that is Good and that is Holy, will employ. If the Prince of this world, the Ruler of darkness, wants to do battle with the Lord Almighty of Heaven, in these last days, what better way than to rally his forces of evil, and attack the very strongest center for resources, that the Lord Jesus has on earth? Since the church in America is a wealthy church, Satan could attack the country of America and try to weaken the offensive strategy of the Lord's people there. If America and pro-Christian people of all the 'Western World' can be neutralized, or rendered impotent, a great victory for evil will surely be the result. Why not wage an attack on the 'Elect' of God, in the land where great resources of people and money could be set against his cause in a moment's notice? Now such an attack upon Christians who are in America, Great Britain, and such countries, in some obvious form of armed conflict would not be deceiving enough or strategically smart.

However, if America, a major source of Christian influence and resources, can be brought to its knees, the enemy will think of himself as quite a wise strategist, and the Great Commission purpose of the Lord of Heaven and earth, will be threatened. Jesus sent His people to the whole world, and His command is that all nations of the world should hear, and therefore have opportunity to receive salvation in Christ. As a matter of fact this purpose will finally be fulfilled, (Matt. 24.14,—Rev. 7.9).

Now the battle which America finds itself engaged in, against all this 'terrorism' creates world disorder and chaos and stands as evidence that the enemy has made his move. To take out the strength of God's holy people in America (as a major player in this world battle), it would be necessary to weaken the churches' defense and to reduce the offensive moves of the church, which are moves toward the fulfillment of the great commission.

The battle has come to the home field. While the saints of God around the world, (in over 70 countries), suffer for the Lord by simply being Christians, the politically free countries of the world seem oblivious to the plight of these courageous brothers and sisters in Christ. One voice, the mission known as 'Voice of The Martyrs', established by Richard Wurmbrand, in 1967, continues to carry news of the current events that authenticate the horrific and inhuman treatment, measured out by anti-Christian governments. We are told that over 100,000 people die for the Lord Jesus, at the hands of persecutors around the world, every year. Since the Sept. 11, 2001 disaster in N.Y. City, people in the United States are beginning to see that an enemy of democracy, freedom and Christianity has dared to step on the Eagle's talons. Now we can see the degree of the seriousness of terrorism, we see attacks by religious groups, (whose faith, religion and government principles differ from most Western nations), know no boundaries. Much of the rejection, and hatred that has been aimed at Christians around the world, outside of the 'Western World' has come to a new 'playing field.' **America has now been attacked by those who hate Christianity, Judaism and any form of government that harbors the same.**

It must have appeared to the majority of Americans and those in free lands, which are sympathetic with the principles that America is governed by, that this attack in New York on Sept. 9. 11, was aimed only at the political, social and economically based ideals of the United States. But it is my belief, that there is much more revealed in the openly defiant and cruel attack upon the 'land of the free' and the 'home of the brave'. Free enterprise, democratic form of government and freedom to make religious and other personal choices in life, were not the only (or perhaps even the major) target of the 'big bad wolf'—the so-called militant

Islamic groups. Many of these freedoms are enjoyed around the world by other nations. **But what does America have** which has been politically controlled and threatened in other 'less free' and less tolerant nations?

What is it that America as a nation holds dear, but also exhibits as one of the most popular exports in the world? <u>Christian teaching, and</u> thereby, freedom of religious expression, is the answer to that question. It is very obvious that freedom of religious expression is an open ticket for people of any religious persuasion in America, and therefore travels with any American passport. It just so happens, that the 85% Christian population of America has the wealth and means to travel the entire globe, and carry it's message with great 'gusto' and with technical rapidity and skill. Christianity is the dominant religion of the land.

Now if the great enemy of the Lord Jesus Christ, the enemy of all the chosen elect of God, wants to 'take out of circulation' the messengers of 'grace,' those who carry the Good News of salvation in Jesus, how would he get a 'strangle hold' on these who serve God in this way? If Satan and his angles want to slow down, or at least discourage the continual spread of the Gospel to all parts of the world, would he not strike a blow at the 'large camp of his enemy'? It is true that there are more missionaries coming from S. Korea, S. America and other countries now, than at any time In modern history. But in America is a large source of financial strength and personnel for the accomplishment of this task that Jesus gave His church. Sooner or later the old serpent, the Devil, was bound to strike a blow at a Christian base of operation, from which location comes much of the church's efforts for world evangelism.

This theory is not likely to be so unwelcome to the minds of most believers in America, **but what I am about to suggest will not be so well received**. Perhaps this attack in New York by terrorists, was seen to be a strike against the country only, and an attack against all that **America** stands for in the minds of extremist Islamic factions. But perhaps it is also being used by the 'senior partner' in evil, as a means of slowing down the progress of the evangelistic efforts of the Lord's people. Why not hit America? Such a blow will make many Christians feel less attentive to world wide needs of souls who are presently without the Gospel, and turn the attention of many 'church members' inward, and surely slow the progress of mission efforts. The 'old serpent' Lucifer is not dumb, he is a liar and the father thereof, but he is a formidable foe, just look at how he has cleverly attacked since the beginning. Satan appeared as a harmless beast of the field, and deceived the woman whom God had given to man as a helper, and a companion. **Satan struck at man's weakest point, that which man <u>loved the most, his wife</u>. Take on an opponent at his point of weakness and you have a chance to**

overcome his strength. Jesus promised blessings upon those who overcome the world, and overcome the enemy. So this is an obvious announcement that **a battle rages.**

Now, the not so welcome suggestion!

If we accept **the fact of the 'war'** the church of Christ is engaged in on this planet, let us notice how war time strategy is a more superior approach to battle than a peace time strategy. The American church has moved in its mission, as if there was no hurry to fulfill it. It only makes sense that someone who knows they are in a serious battle, will engage in war time strategy not a peace time strategy. But Christians in America are funny, they are a 'brand' of Christian not used to battles like those that are raging in other lands, against courageous souls of saints who suffer and die willingly for Jesus, souls who have never known political freedom. The American Christian cries 'uncle' or runs home to 'mama', (who by the way, for many, is the declaration of Independence), a type of political—single parent who was provided for all citizens of the country.

I believe that the church in America has become soft, and American Christians have become preoccupied with inner, or 'in country' social issues, fighting for prayer in school, and many other little fires that only concern those in the 'brave new world' of liberty and justice for all, as if the church with 'peace time' political strategy, might find the government of America willing to appease its 'Christian' citizens. In this little war that American Christians fight, within their borders, few of them have any idea of the 'big picture' so they spend effort, time and money on matters which cannot compare with the hunger for the Word of God that many suffer in the 'unreached' and persecuted places of the world.

The church in America does face many issues, and always has and always will, issues which can be attended to with clear conscience and even attended to with support of Bible verses. But the Great Commission of the Lord did not leave any room for considerations which allowed the free choice to work the works of God 'at home or abroad' as convenience might dictate. But rather the spreading of the Gospel to the entire world is the only marching orders the body of Christ has been given, and no creature is to be left out, this command is paramount. If the American church is leaving someone in the world out of the picture, by it's continual extravagance and 'over spending' on it's own 'in country' interests, then the American church is guilty of **failing to carry out to it's ability and its potential, in this generation, the very command of the Lord.**

Forbid, that a missionary should 'overspend' or not wisely use his resources in his field of labor, **but if the American congregation buys extra land for its building**, (which is the opposite of what those in Acts 2, were doing, they were surrendering property not hoarding it), this is very acceptable today. We call this 'great stewardship' when churches 'think' ahead and borrow money for property they 'may' soon need. But if a missionary does the same thing, he is extravagant or using 'poor' stewardship principles in the use of mission money.

The mission committee speaks with forked tongue, they want to do mission work at home, often **telling the told, feeding the spiritually full**, or continue placing 90% of its emphasis on one country alone, (and this is often done, though never admitted) at the expense of cutting out the souls who have never heard for the first time who Jesus really is! Notice where the largest amount of the budget of an American (mega?) church goes, this will identify the major emphasis and the heart's desire, (where the treasure is, there will the heart be also).

If a person in America has a hard time finding a Bible, and is seeking the Lord, or if a person In this country, spiritually lost or not, has a real hunger for the Gospel message, do you think it would be difficult for that person to find a place of prayer, or a book about salvation, or to find some way to discover the truth about Jesus? Certainly not! Pastors often say (trust me I have heard it for 30 years) "we can do both" we can reach people in America and those who hunger for the Word in other lands as well. But if this is true, **why has it not been done with the same financial expenditure and the same or equal distribution of trained Bible teachers**? Do you have one preacher per church, and one missionary overseas? I think not! *Statistics make liars of those who would think there is equality of personnel in Christian ministry world wide.*

Today, 90% of all trained Christian evangelists are in America which comprises a population of about 5% of the world. Hello out there in church pulpit, are you listening? I challenge you to show me which of these figures is not true. If it is true, then how can churches continue this selfish direction without shame and remorse? Check out 2 Tim. 3. 1-7, 1Tim. 4. 1, 2Thess. 2, 1Thess. 5.15, I doubt that I need to cite more passages, which deal with our duty to one another, to warn, reprove and rebuke, with all longsuffering and doctrine, and of course in meekness to instruct one another.

The Unholy Union

I have called this section the unholy union, because it identifies the problem as I see it. The church in America became so enamored with the freedoms and the privileges which were privy to the citizens of the country, that it became difficult to see a difference between the church and the country. *The idea of 'God and country' is evidence of this phenomenon, and the church in America became an incorporated entity*, just like any business corporation, with by-laws and all. But if you take time to compare the church of the Lord in America with the church in persecuted lands around the world, ie. Sudan, N. Korea, China, to mention only a few, **you will see a vast difference in many ways**. Churches undergoing persecution do not have a 'Disney park' persona, with a message like "we have a good program for you and your family" etc. etc. The Lord's church in persecuted countries faces suffering daily and has only basic essentials, and the book of Heb. (13. 2-3) says, to consider ourselves as one with this kind of brotherhood. I believe that I will not need to take that comparison further.

Back to the battle field. Consider this: If the enemy of God's Kingdom, would strike a blow against the church in America, would he not hit the easy target first? When the church in America became weak (and I think it has), by continued emphasis on self (2 Tim. 3. 2), the church became its own worst enemy. Now that the church in America was weakened by its connection to the country, the enemy could strike at the country and put fear even in the church. Here is why,- this continual emphasis on 'church growth' failed to tell us or failed to announce that this emphasis really meant—growing inward. It sounded good, and very noble, but in reality it became a 'watch word' for stacking up, rather than spreading out! So it was easy for Satan to use the American church against itself, because Satan knew that selfishness was not of God, and that enough funds, resources and personnel spent on one country would limit the amount of outreach around the world. Even in chess, a person is no fool, who surrenders a pawn to gain a queen. Satan had much of the world under false religions and political ideologies that are godless, so he controlled much of it already. **The way to maintain that control would be to hold back evangelistic efforts by believers with great resources, so they could not find their way to the front line of battle.**

But this was not difficult, since the wealthy American church was centered on its own development anyway. So I think Satan left the church in America to its own devices, for many years, while he whittled away at the rest of the world. Why not, he had a queen, (95 % of the world) and one small country (a pawn) of 5 % who loved themselves, and their freedoms, their extravagance, and their narcissistic life styles anyway, more than the lost souls of the world, could be left alone for a time, **so let the American church have America, this was not much concession as far as number of souls is concerned**. So for years the USA church was like a pawn to the Devil. And when the terrorists came to N.Y. they were not trying only to take down a political system, **their real target is the church of the Lord Jesus.** Since the church is powerful in America, or has been in ages past, the real target is the power of the Gospel of Christ in the country, not just the country itself. And since America and the church in America walk hand in hand, if you take out the country, and try to reduce it to confusion and chaos, or even get it preoccupied with internal affairs, there is some victory.

The real enemy wants the church, it just so happens that the **incorporated church** will fall with the country, because it (the church) is so joined to the nation, (notice verses which speak of a falling away—in 2 Thess. 2. 3) if you take out the car, the trailer will go with it. *It is quite obvious to this writer, that the enemy's plan to bring disaster to the American system, is really an attempt to hurt the work of the church.* Too bad the church and country (God and country') were so closely connected. It is sad, but perhaps all to true, that there is this unholy union today in America between church and state. And remember we are **Jesus' bride and should never have courted the world, but it sure looks to me like the church and America have been having an affair while the Master was away.** Perhaps this is why the churches in the book of Revelation are told to repent, and the church of Laodicea (which looks all to familiar right now), was so deceived, about it's real condition, that Jesus told her to repent and overcome this enemy who tries to win the Lord's bride! We must overcome, by the Blood of the Lamb, the word of Testimony, and by **not loving our own lives, even unto death!** Right now, the church in America is so in love with itself, and so enamored with its own growth(?) within the country, its own financial strength, you could recognize the Laodecian church of Revelation by just looking in the mirror.

Christians who love others, and all lost people of the world, have no time to think of themselves, therefore they can die bravely for Jesus. Christians who love themselves, have no time for others, and they fear whatever economic distress may come upon the world, and upon their land. Any disaster of war, terrorism or whatever will shake their faith. James 2. 5 states, that it is the poor people (as the world sees them), who, if they are rich in faith in spite of their poverty, are the ones whom GOD has chosen to be heirs of the kingdom. Not many books written on that subject by the great and popular Pastors of today. The real subjects worthy of time and attention are being lived out by the saints of God who suffer in the persecuted countries of this world. These are men and women of God, and children as well, who have no time for 'flag' waving or for complaining about the price of school lunch, nor do they worry about which university to attend, or what vocation(?) they should select when they become 17, these are the heroes, **they are the teachers, and we who live in America should be their students**. These material and physical concerns of Christians in America, are not the matters that face the **real Christians** of our generation. Those who can die well for Jesus, who enjoy the fellowship of their suffering in His suffering, are saints of God who never did think of themselves first, or last or at all. **Jesus was and is, their only thought. To get real, is so necessary in order to get right!**

So do we really want to join their number? Then we must get busy and make some change in emphasis, from self to others, from here (in this land) to somewhere beyond these borders. Let us show the world our faith, by our deeds, not our books, seminars, lessons, tapes, conventions and hundreds of 'plastic' images of religion. I recently saw 'T' shirts with the words, "I want to be like Jesus" printed on them. I wonder how serious the people are who wear these shirts, my suggestion to some of them was, **if you want to be like Jesus, then go and die for someone who lives far from your home, that's what Jesus did. Lets get real, or we will never get right!**

A.W. Hamilton, Missionary

4

Biotech—Church

✦

The Lukewarm Brotherhood
Rev. 3. 16—Lk. 16. 13-31

In the U.S. News & World Report, May 31, 2004 edition, on page 62, there appeared an article by James Pethokoukis, which revealed the most modern thought on present day science, as it relates to man's effort to advance in Biotechnology. Renowned scientists now carry on a deadly debate, as the author of the article stated, with ethicists, as the National Science Foundation studies the societal impact of technology. The article awakens the sleeping minds of those who live in modern and highly advanced societies. While most of the world today, deals with issues such as 'survival' and simple basic day to day livelihood, the world of the 'scientifically advanced' and 'economically extravagant' people (about 5% of the world's population), debate issues which make the discovery of electricity look like 'kindergarten—101'.

In this article James Pethokoukis, states—"at the core of the conflict lies a fundamental question: How far should homo sapiens be allowed to go? Nascent technologies like genetic engineering, stem-cell therapy, and neuropharmacology promise not only to cure our diseases but to enhance our bodies, even to turn us all into the Six Million Dollar Man—better, stronger, and faster."

The author also reminds us of present day signs of extreme self-love, (not his term), when he states, "with the proliferation of plastic surgery, for example, or the use of Ritalin by achievement-crazed students hoping to score better on the SAT, enhancement seems to be the wave of the future." I could say more about the very revealing article and how it is a 'photo perfect' presentation of society 's present rage of self-indulgence. But this will be enough background for you to consider with me the serious condition that modern man has found himself in, due to the constant move toward higher, bigger, better and expanded goals in the 'achievement worship' system we now find surrounding us. This fact would not be of great personal concern to those who hold faith in Christ and His word of promise—to come back to planet earth for His 'called out' people, if it were not for the effect this 'mind-set' of Biotech Streamlining of the human condition has had upon the American church.

I am not aware of the influence that society in it's modern, scientific Frankenstein approach to life, has held over other modern countries, but **in the American scene there is an obvious parallel in this Biotech world and the American mega-church religious trend. When science began to lead the way in finding out how to possibly develop ways to make people live longer and with limited ailments, or to cure more ills and have happier and longer life on planet earth,** the American churches were busy at the same time, trying to make each church, bigger, better and more appealing to the people who would listen. It is apparent to the trained eye, that in spiritual matters, according to the Scripture, there is no companionship to be established with the society and it's effort toward love of self, and carnal devotion to things in this present life. 1John 2. 15, 17, 2Cor. 6. 14-18, makes it quite clear, that believers are brought out of darkness into light (Gal. 1. 4) and delivered from the world. **Any influence from the world and the unbelieving is not to have power over the Lord' people**. The church is the light, and any influence i.e. sharing of the Gospel is to be done by the church for the sake of leading people to Christ

Anyone today who is not able to see how American society, and the love of 'country' has had enormous effect on modern American churches, is simply closing their eyes. You can't find two flags flying in the church meeting houses of other countries, because the Lord's people in other countries, especially persecuted countries have no real or social connection to the political system. You can argue this point, but even if there is some alignment with the government of a country by the believers in Christ, there is nothing to compare with the alignment and connection that exists between church members in America and the country itself.

Most Christians who come to America for the first time often wonder about the place that the American flag has in the church houses of this land, I know because I have been asked many times by believers from different countries, why churches in this country fly two flags? You can explain it to your own satisfaction, but try to place yourself in the shoes of the Christian from another land where the country had little or no respect for things of the Lord. Americans easily mention that the basic American principles and founding philosophy is based upon

Biblical principles, but today those basic principles are under the gun, and are fast disappearing from the heart of what the world sees—as the American position. **The flag of the United States stands for freedom and democracy, for truth and justice, in the minds of those who know the history of the country and it's early foundation.** But America is more than just a 'past' social order, it has continued to be a free country, but **now that freedom includes unholy and unbiblical positions.** When do we begin to separate the past from the present? And how is this to be done?

This point is important if we are to understand or at least become aware of the fact that churches in America have done what the scientific world in America and the scientific leaders of other western countries have done, and that is to build a 'tower of Babel' all over again, to try and reach levels of human development which exalt man, but make no effort to seek the Lord God who has created all things for His glory. The American churches have continued to develop plans and schemes which make a larger impact on the modern society of rich members, by enlarging the borders of their garments to impress the society around it, while virtually ignoring the lost sheep of the world who have never been told the Good News.

Enhancement is not just the wave of the future for self centered and self loving Americans, it is also the persona that has swelled the minds and hearts of church members who seek a 'plastic surgery' and Ritalin dosed spiritual—million dollar Christian 'experience' to impress lost people who see right through the façade of Pharisaical religious zealots. If Christians in America really care to serve God (not just impress God, as if they could,) they would seek every lost tribe and tongue of the world, and find a way to bring them the Gospel of Christ. God's word states, "love not in word, but in deed and in Truth." The entire book of James states that respect of persons is a sin, and that the deeds we do, exhibit faith, not a pack of lessons and books about things we already know. **You can't have 2 billion people in this present world who have no knowledge of salvation, and a church in America with the resources and personnel to reach these people, and still claim that this "Ivory Tower of Babel" in America is a church that God is pleased with!**

God has told us what is pleasing to Him. Leaving a soul stranded at your door-step while building bigger and better storage bins is not something that God likes (Lk. 16. 15-31). Business men in this country say that world trade and bigger business opportunities lie at America's door steps in China and around the globe. The churches have followed a lot of big ideas of development based upon 'good ole American know how' but they have failed to pick up on the only thing that even makes sense in the scene of American world-wide expansion, that of reaching out into a global market.

While America fights a battle with terrorism (and you can't whip an ism), with conventional ideas & conventional weapons, giving the American churches, time to spread out all over the earth, the churches rather, continue to seek better, bigger and more advanced means to look like some kind of beauty, in physical extravagance, rather than get their hands dirty in the hard to reach places of the earth for the glory of God and the finding of lost sheep. **Mega church, multi-staff leadership, basketball courts for the children, all of this spells not sacrifice, but spells narcissism. Of course those who need to be teaching others, and need themselves to be taught, probably have a hard time with spelling as well, Heb. 5. 12, Rom. 12. 1-13.**

What the world of scientists we have referred to here, fail to realize is that God already had a plan for a better human, even a new world, wherein dwells only righteousness. God has a plan for a new body, one without ailments, life with no sorrow, and no death. God already plans for His people who come to Him in Faith and obedience, to be like Him, "we shall be like Him for we shall see Him as He is." 1 John. 3. 2. This is the future, and man does not have to create it, because man cannot bring such things to pass. God has the only plan that works. God created man in the first place, and He can make mankind brand new, provide a whole new world, a whole new city and nothing needs repaired, and no one will be sick. Seems like people just need to come to Christ, who is our Lord and Creator, that would eliminate all this unnecessary Biotech—know how, any how. God has allowed us to have doctors and medicine to overcome illness in some measure, and help us on the journey of life. **But to go into a task that only God can perform, only man under the influence of the Enemy will attempt.**

God will also present the church, the real church, His bride, before His throne, faultless (Jude 24) our task is not to improve our looks, as a people of God, but to improve our service as slaves of God. We must be about our Father's business, but we must not pretend to be our own father!

Awh.

Ahead of Your ~ ~ Time

Like the account of "The Court Martial of Billy Mitchell" clearly portrays ~ some men and women see ahead of their time, though the world is really only equipped to take what they see as the reason and rhyme for conditions of their time.

If a person in the world today, has something to do or to say, that does not fit the pattern or scheme of the majority (who know not how to dream), that person is in for a lonely ride, unless that person gives in to the flow of the tide. But those who are like Billy Mitchell, who took on the whole Army and lost, can smile when their work is done. **Because in the loss was the success, he remained true to his passion and conviction that** an Air force must be established as part of American armed forces, he maintained that a war will be coming which is an 'air' war and planes would fly faster than the speed of sound. The court before which he appeared called him insane, and he was indeed discharged from all rank and duties as an Army officer. But he was right. *And that is why history remembers his name*, not the names of his inquisitors. He was a man ahead of his time, but in line with truth and conviction and as most men and women ahead of their time, he could not keep from speaking his convictions, his only regret was the unbelief of his peers. If you don't know this feeling, that he experienced, you haven't really lived.

Now this man called General Billy Mitchell, (you should look into his story and life), was under Court Martial, for having the sense to see ahead, but he was not believed or accepted, so the Army took off his head (in a figure of speech). But his story is quite an example, for those who dare to be different, for those who dare to stand against the tide and tell a dream or story that the days demand be told, Acts 2:17 (dream dreams).

I want to put this kind of history into a different context. For we could speak of the many whose lives brought into focus, new challenges, new ideas, discovery and progress aimed at saving lives and securing peace.

As A.W.Tozer spoke of Leonard Ravenhill, the times demand such a man. A spokesman for truth and action is now in demand, one who is dedicated to effective and decisive change, in order to bring about a return to fulfillment of Biblical purpose and Godly design. If you choose to be such a person, you will be ahead of your time. It will be a lonely road, to have a message from God that no one else wants to deliver. I can remember asking in prayer for such a message, the one that God wants spoken, but cannot find anyone willing to proclaim. Perhaps I was granted my answer to that prayer. For it has been my walk, and my talk to speak of selling buildings, and dispensing with multi-staff, multi-ministry churches, in order to send more laborers into the harvest fields of the world. *Since the world for the most part (90%)* is *outside of the United States, and over 90% of college and seminary trained ministers remain IN the United States, this seemed to be a reasonable request.* I have had the grace of God upon me to walk this talk as well as announce it to the churches. All of four children and my wife and I have served in at least two other countries for over 10 years. The message I speak is not simply from outward observation, but from inward information, which was the result of heavenward invitation.

So I suggest even now, to those who may seek a message closely related to that of the Prophets and Apostles of our Lord, that your journey will be lonely, if you want to please Jesus only. Your path will not be covered with rose petals, like your comrades who please the people and tickle the ears of the saints. *Today there are those weak messengers who fear more the loss of self esteem than the loss of self respect.* There are those who Fear more the *loss of their public's acceptance, than the loss of God's approval.* Many ministers, clergy they may be called by the world, seem to be more aware of the concerns of a depraved society, than the commands of the Living Savior.

The message that the church must, not just 'needs to' change it's emphasis from itself, (*from the narcissistic implant of* personal satisfaction with self described accountability to itself*), and begin to emphasize to the church body that _others_ *around the world must be our priority*, others before self, (Luke 10,Matt. 28:18-20), not just our sideline interest. The American church for example, (and this does describe the church in America, it has become an American church) has ceased to be the Christian Church in America, and it has become an American church. Much like the Church of England belongs to England. This we can tell is true from the view that lost people have of the community of believers. Even an enemy of the Lord's Church, recently on TV and Radio who is a leader of the Islamic religion, stated that the enemy of Islam is the Jewish and American people.

Now in this statement he made reference to *Jewish* people (not the State of Israel but their religious alignment) and in the same sentence used the words *"American"* people. So this indicates that this enemy, (and I am sure, he represents many who think as he does), can see no difference between *American* and the term *Christian.* To most of the world, the term American is synonymous with the term or title 'Christian'. This has come about mainly because of the actions and behavior of the *Christians who live in America* and who give as much or more *allegiance to the 'land of the free and home* of the brave' as they do to the 'Kingdom of God.' To go further with this point is another subject, but the obvious *intertwining of the Christians devotion to the country of America* and all that it stands for, *and the allegiance to Christ the Lord of Lords and King of Kings,* has been so obvious to all of the world, that the Christian church in America has weakened it's position and it's witness to all people everywhere. For this reason, when a messenger of God does come into our arena with a message to turn from self-ism and quit spending money and personnel extravagantly on ministers, more ministers, buildings, programs, educational materials etc. and turn our attention to the whole world into which we were sent by the Lord's command, the ministers and much of the congregation become personally offended and feel personally attacked.

Missionary committees are today discussing, how they can think(?) "outside the box" but they don't mean to apply the term with serious application to the entire world, but rather only to *their own world of the congregations personal and limited—'mission goals'.*

I doubt that we need much evidence that a messenger of God, a prophet for today, would not be welcome, understood nor accepted in the pulpits of our churches today. If this statement is to be contested, then I could site many examples from personal experience which would prove the very fact that tough messages are not well received. I believe that many preachers today however do not need to pray for boldness, I doubt they will say anything that requires boldness. Even when prophets have risen up among us their message is quickly submerged under the flood of comments that 'being negative is not really acceptable to the present congregation of 'I'm ok you're ok' and Schullerism philosophy.

The effort to be an accepted church in an unacceptable time, is no better illustrated than in a recent issue of "Christian Standard", published by Independent Christian Churches and Churches of Christ people. As a matter of fact the issue had three articles on the subject of the command of Baptism as given in the New Testament. I read the issue, and all of the articles on the subject of 'Baptism' with great interest. As I came to the end of that brief study, what appeared to me, (and perhaps I think in a different frame of reference), was the fact that the authors were making great attempts and expending much effort *to explain God, and how God would be 'obligated' to accept those* who seemed to miss the point of the literal meaning of Baptism. What the Bible said about the subject of Baptism was well presented, which happened to be the subject in the first place. What is most obvious is that great pains were taken by all of the authors to make people feel good about themselves who have not correctly understood the meaning of the subject of Baptism.

The word in the original language of Greek, means immersion, or to plunge. And since the Bible explains that baptism (a transliteration of a Greek word) is in water, and means immersion,(Rom. 6:4-6 buried) it would be hard to accept other meanings, without being dishonest to language and to the purpose of language as a means of communication. In any case, the articles dealt with the true meaning of the word, and the Biblical statements which contained that word. But after that clear and accurate presentation, the authors of the articles took great pains to explain how those who do not accept this truth and the plain, simple command of the Lord and His Apostles, as a plain simple command, must also be given a 'wide birth' or allowance for their lack of understanding or acceptance of this simple word and simple command.

Much was said about the fact that 'we all fail, and must be forgiven, so why should we worry about making it look like anyone who failed to practice or obey this word, and this command, would not be received up into glory as if they had followed this command and obeyed this teaching accurately, (my choice of words as I understood the content of the articles). This great discussion about great preachers of the past, is not even the point! *A command of God is God's business.* It is from HIM to all mankind, so our job is to tell it, not excuse everyone who fails for any reason to do it, teach it or even understand it**. The response of others to the meaning of Baptism is not our responsibility, much less our playing field designed for showing how much we know about God and His opinion about His own Word!**

Theologians as we call them, have become so content with writing commentaries on the Bible, and what they think God meant, that many of them have neglected to pay attention TO the Bible. To build a discussion around how God feels about His commandments is like looking at a house and wondering why the architect didn't use some other plan or design. That is not the real question. The question could perhaps be, do we like the house or not, why the design is what it is, really would not change the house since it is already built.

I suggest we spend less time thinking for God and realize that as humans, we do not make the conditions for entrance into the Kingdom of God, Just the decision to be in it or not. And making the decision to follow Jesus is far from making the conditions under which we follow. We only have to make the choice to be in or out of the Kingdom. That leaves plenty of room for discussion but it primarily calls for action. Discuss it all you please, but act upon it we will, if we live long enough be aware of our sins, and of God's purpose for man. Our task in Christ as His ambassadors, is to announce and proclaim the Gospel. Perhaps our great Christian writers and theologians will someday decide to devote their gifts, talents and time to the point of our need and our obvious responsibility to God not to the wishes of our emotions.

Now wouldn't that be good news!

Sincerely,

Albert Hamilton
Servant of the servants of God.

5

Come out from among whom?

✦

2 Cor. 6. 1-18

In the days of the Old Testament as the people of God, Israel, went into the promised land, given to them by the Lord, they were told to occupy the land, (Deut.11. 31, 32-12. 1-4) and destroy the idols and false worship which was foreign to the teachings of the Lord their God who delivered them from the land of bondage. In the New Testament, under the Lord Jesus Christ and His apostles, instruction was given to the church, not to have fellowship (close communion or association based upon agreement in philosophy* my personal explanation) with unbelievers, for light and darkness cannot share the same spot. God who delivered Israel from Egypt did not say to Moses and the nation of Israel, "now you must get along with the nations in Canaan, and do not be prejudiced against them, you must co-exist with idolatry, evil behavior etc. etc". Not on your life!

<u>Strangely enough, in the Dallas Morning News paper Oct. 28, 2003</u>, an article appeared entitled "Fellowship charts course for growth" describing the position of the Oak Cliff Bible Fellowship Church, a congregation of about 7,000. The statement above a photo of some children singing was—"we *don't believe in the separation of God and government.*" And my first thought was, **well, I do!** And I'll tell you why.

There is no doubt that God in Heaven holds all things together, and He will raise up one and put down another, promotion comes not from the East nor from the West, nor from the South, but God is the judge(Ps. 75. 6.). But this same Lord of heaven and earth, told his people in the New Testament to have no fellowship with unrighteousness, for there is no agreement between Christ and wickedness. Therefore my question is this—how can the church, or the fellowship of Christ (called out people) which is the body of souls who have accepted a call to be separate from this present evil world (Gal. 1. 4), having in time past walked (Eph. 2) according to the course of this world,—**have an attachment to that which is what we left behind?**

We know that the country of America is not the church, for you can be an American and not be a Christian or follower of Jesus, and visa versa. It seems obvious to me that there is already a separation of God and government, whether you are talking about the God of heaven and the government of America or any other government.

Recently an operation was performed on twin boys who came from Egypt, who were born joined at their heads. Until the operation in Dallas, Tx. The two had never looked upon each other as separate individuals. To be so joined is abnormal and seriously dangerous to the existence of both. The church or body of Christ can be and is, all over the world, and exists in every country, even the atheistic lands of this world. But the church has one head, even Christ the Lord. The members or fellowship of the believers is a unity of faith world wide, and their communion and faith in Christ unites them world wide though they have for the most part no contact or connection except their common bond in Christian faith. The Christian has citizenship in heaven, and is given the acknowledgement from the Word of God, that God Himself is their King, their Father and He dwells by His Spirit in each heart.

If there is no separation between God and Government, then we have to ask, which government, since Christians in other lands have a different government over their society. Which government will be joined with the Lord God in this world, the American government? The government is full of unbelievers, those who voted in their courts in favor of legalized abortion, and for homosexual men to adopt children. We could go on and on listing the position of the American government on issues that clearly defy and oppose the laws of the God of Heaven. How can a minister of the Gospel of Christ, say he does not believe in separation of God and the government*? **There never was a joining of the two.** The government and church were not born joined at the head, nor in any other way. For even a popular and prominent minister to say he does not believe in the separation of God and government, is like saying "I like the world and I like the church." What part of the world does he like? Or we might ask, if there is no separation of government and church, what does he mean by government? He can mean what he would like the government to be, or we can interpret this any way we like. It is not clear how such a unity can exist between what Paul calls "this present evil world" Gal. 1.4, and America, and the church.

Now such statements about religion and America being joined can be made by politicians, but there will be a problem when a person says I stand for what God wants, and I stand for what the government wants. The Bible says, "Thou shalt worship the Lord thy God and *Him only* shalt thou serve." The American Christian can say, he doesn't believe in the separation of God and government but he better stay home, and cut off his connection with his brothers and sisters in Christ around the world, because they cannot have a connection with America as a government. And if there is no connection there must of necessity be a separation. Hello! Is there anyone at home there in churchland or pulpitville? Let no man separate what God has joined together the Bible says regarding marriage, and we can also gather from that by simple deduction, that no man had better try to join what God has kept separate either. The scripture in Romans 13, refers to civil obedience and this is quite easy for the Christian anyway, since the laws of God in His Word are more demanding than the civil laws of any country. But Romans 13 does not mean that the church has joined Rome or any other government so that the Christians can control people by force and make everyone follow Bible teachings. This is an individual choice to Follow Jesus, and you can't take **unconverted hearts and lives** and make them walk and talk like Christians.

Where would the "with freedom and justice for all" part of the American constitution come in? Does this mean we favor justice for women to have an abortion with sanction of the government since America is a land with laws to give equal freedom to all views, and give the nations blessing to homosexual life style and all other religious positions etc. not to mention freedoms that the Bible in no way condones. The church of the Lord Jesus is certainly not going to have any such laws as America now supports. Jesus stated in Matthew 28, that all authority in heaven and in earth is given unto Him. The Bible also states that God the Father, has given unto Jesus the Son, all authority. This means that Jesus will not allow His followers to follow another God, nor another religious persuasion, His sheep hear only His voice. If this is not a separation than I would like to know what it is. The Romans 13 verses do not join the nation and the Church, it simply explains the behavior of Christians as just persons, who will not be a detriment to society but a blessing to others in society.

There may be a lot of people on the membership role at many large Churches, who have love for the country of America and they have love for the Lord's church, but they had better realize that you can't serve two masters. Jesus said, we must love the Lord our God with all of our heart, and with all of our mind, and all of our strength. The word all means there could not be some part of our heart, soul or strength for something else to be loved equally. This hot pursuit of the churches of America upon the heels of the United States of America must be embarrassing to the Christian brotherhood around the world. I have worked in countries where persecution against believers in Christ is rampant. I can see little family resemblance between that church of the Lord in those lands and the church in America. The reason for this, I believe, is that the church in America forgot that the command of the Lord was to *'overcome the world'—it was no to join the world*. America is part of this present world order, we cannot as believers carry the country everywhere we go, it is excess baggage. Lot's wife was proof of the fact that you can't have your surroundings and nice 'downtown' fellowship with unfruitful workers of darkness and have the direction of God too, our association with the country of our birth, (just as Paul as a Roman citizen) is an advantage when it needs to be, but we are not spiritually joined to it. This means that our association with our nationality **is not** one that affects our spirit and soul, only our physical presence.

To devote our energy as ambassadors of Christ, to 'making the world a better place to live' is a mistake. That is not our commission from our Lord, and it is not therefore our task. The world will always still be the world, to make it a better place, would be like trying to sweep all the dirt off of the earth, you can't because it is all dirt. To be the light of the world, and the salt of the earth, means our influence will be felt as God designs it, but **our hearts** must not belong to a nation, but only to Christ the Lord and His purpose. The persecuted church can teach the church in America many things about such relationships. We pray for America's leaders and the direction the country takes, that we may lead a quiet and peaceable life, but the believer *is an alien* in this present world, *a stranger*, and *pilgrim*, a *foreigner* as the Scriptures teach, and these roles mean we do not belong to this world, and it is not our real home. Our love for a country or nation, cannot be placed 'along side' our love for the Lord God.

We hold 'dual citizenship' on a very restricted basis. We are Christians who live in America, but our new citizenship forbids us to be **joined at the heart** to any present world order. If anyone denies that they have overlooked the entire Bible and history. If there is no separation of the government and God, (as many believe and teach,) then the two must be joined, because the opposite of separation is 'joined'. The twins from Egypt were joined, existing together as one, but having two brains and two bodies. If you can picture the church and the government in such a way, perhaps this is the kind of existence the church at Oak Cliff is talking about. Does this arrangement that the pastor of Oak Cliff refers to mean that there are in his association of church and State two heads, a government head (Washington no doubt) and the head of the church (now who might that be?). It could be Rome and the church of Rome all over again. Or does the Pastor mean that there is no separation of God and government in certain areas?

<u>What **does** he mean</u>? You are either joined to something or separate from it, you can't have it both ways. We can't have our cake and eat it too. If any church is joined to the United States government, are there some parts of the government (like the Supreme Court decisions) that are not joined, or can you separate some of the government and join other parts of it? Sounds to me like you are going to have a creature here, similar in kind of a Frankenstein monster. Some people in Rome did this centuries ago and men like Martin Luther later came on the scene, to announce a recall of church doctrines, and a return to a Biblical perspective. Let's not make that mistake again of getting a 'state' or government into the church. Or are we too late? Our God is a jealous God, and I don't think that any church joined with a country in this world, is His church.

Al Hamilton
Missionary

6

Contend with Horses

✦

Jer. 12. 5
1 Cor. 10. 6, 11.

We can know the value of teachings and events of the ages past. And because we can know the value of these things, we must be wise and understand what the will of the Lord is (Eph. 5. 14-17). We need to see clearly why things of the Old Testament have been plainly recorded for our admonition (1 Cor. 10. 11). It is upon us, this generation, that the responsibility of sending of the Gospel of Christ to all the world (in the final days), falls. Matt. 24.14, states that the Gospel of the Kingdom of God will be preached into all the world for all nations to hear, before the end of all things comes about. Today there are almost 2 Billion souls, (it is estimated) without a knowledge of the Gospel of Christ. I believe that the task has not been adequately approached by churches in America, for some reason. It is obvious that there is no shortage of finances in American churches, nor of personnel among the household of Faith in this 'Land of the Free'.

So I will attempt here to deal with some of the issues which I believe need to be addressed regarding the failure of Christians in America. **If the present generation** of Christians in America, **will be found doing the work of the Master, when He returns**—Matt. 24. 45-51, there will need to be a lot of changes made. There will need to be a change in **emphasis.** Right now you can pass down any street in a large suburb of Dallas, Texas and see a sign on a church building which states as follows—"Family Worship Center," or some other title without the mention of the word—Church. Emphasis is on family, or worship or fellowship, anything that centers on the people. When you see the names you can understand the emphasis or point which stands out as most important. There will also have to be a change in direction. Many churches (especially mega churches), are directing their funds and their efforts inward, toward some kind of inner growth without giving a second thought to other people in the world. A servant as illustrated in Matthew 24, who is found faithfully executing his duties when the Master of the house returns, is one who feeds the others in the house, or meets the needs of the entire household. We have fellow 'household' members around the world who go hungry while the American members of the family fill their already 'fat' spiritual 'family worship centers' to the point of spiritual gluttony.

Old Testament Example and Lesson No. 1
As Jeremiah the prophet complained—the Lord explained!

The concern of Jeremiah was not unlike the case in John 6. 60 when the disciples of the Lord began to find the teachings of Jesus too hard to take or to explain to others. Jesus did not offer some other—'less difficult' teaching, on the contrary, He said, 'if this offends you, what will you do when you see something even more amazing"?—(my paraphrase here). When the Lord told the prophet Jeremiah, 'if you get worn out in competing with men in a foot race, what will you do when I put you up against horses in a race...' it was clear that God's message is not going to change, and it must be delivered accurately and faithfully.

Jesus explained to the disciples, that there is no easy message nor some other way to explain His Kingdom to the people. His words are spirit and they are life (John 6. 63), they cannot be replaced or other words be substituted. Only those who have a heart and desire for doing the will of God, will come unto Him in faith and obedience—John 7. 17.

This is exactly the case with Jeremiah in chapter 12 and verse 5.

The prophet was shown that the fierce anger of the Lord was sure to come upon the disobedient people. In Jeremiah chapter 13. 10, the Lord used the illustration of the waistband that had become good for nothing, saying my people have become good for nothing. It seems to have happened again, the people who wear the name of the Lord, have not honored the God of heaven by obedience to His word, they have declared their own message as if it was from God. The time has come to quit seeking an easy message or an easy task, and face the music. Not the tune we have been hearing from weak and selfish leaders, but the music that comes from the word of the Lord, unedited, unchanged.

The Lord is calling out of the world, a people for His Name who will fit into the Kingdom of God by faith and obedience to His Word. The Lord has given His followers all that is necessary for this 'membership' in His family. He has said that we have all things, provided as His gift to His kingdom people, which are needed for entrance into, and citizenship in God's household. We are laborers in the harvest fields of God when we become citizens of His kingdom. In 1st Corinthians the followers of Christ are told that our faith should not be in the wisdom of men, but in the power of God. (chapter 2. vs. 5). In chapter 2 verses 10-12, Paul states, "...**we have received the Spirit** who is from God that **we may know the things which are freely given to us by God."**

All things, referred to here, I believe, has two parts. The first part of "all things" given to us, deals with <u>our salvation</u>, and the second part deals with <u>our service</u> as His workers-(1Cor. 3. 9). Some things are for our salvation, and some things given to us are for our service to the Lord.

The first part of 'all things' comes from the words of the Lord in 1st Cor. 3. 19-23. "...No more boasting about men! Or as the KJV records it, **"let no one glory in men". All things are yours,** whether Paul, or Apollos or Cephas, or the world, or life or death or the things present **or things to come—all are yours, and you are Christ's and Christ is God's.**

The things that God has given His followers are mentioned in scriptures like—Luke 12. 32, "do not fear little flock, for it is your Father's good pleasure **to give you the kingdom.** He has also given us a **relationship.** We could not have gained access to the Kingdom of God unless the Lord God opened the way for us to come in. We are saved by grace through faith, (Eph. 2. 8), so this relationship with Christ and the Father, are His gift to those who love and obey Him.

In 1st Cor. 2. 12, as quoted above, we have received the Spirit who is from God, **that we might know the things that have been freely given to us by God.** Here are some of the things He has given us **1. A <u>relationship</u>, 2. A <u>King-dom</u>, 3. <u>His Spirit</u>, 4. His <u>Word</u>,** (Jn. 17. 14), **and 5...He has given us a <u>task</u>,** (Mk. 16. 15, 16). These things are what I call part of the "<u>all things</u>". Part 2 involves what it means to have part 1.

In part 2 of all things, lies the basic purpose for our salvation, (from God, not some driving purpose of man). If we see part one as God's gift of saving grace, to His followers or disciples, (which gift creates the relationship between God and man), then we know that the purpose for such a saving relationship is higher than any purpose of man. We know the purpose of God will be to do the work of God, which is only possible through God's power not man's wisdom (1 Cor. chapters 1-4). We also know that it will be for the good of others, not simply a goal for ourselves, to exalt ourselves in our own eyes or in the eyes of others.

Jesus had made it plain in Luke 10, when the disciples came back from their mission, excited that even the demons were subject unto them, that they should not rejoice in that power, but rejoice in the relationship—with the Lord, and that their names were recorded in the books in heaven. Jesus said that greatness is in the humility of a child, not in the pride of a man. He also clarified the importance of humility in Luke 16, vs. 15, when He stated that men highly esteem money, but this kind of thinking is an abomination in the sight of God. It cannot be made more plain, that God values the eternal things, the internal heart filled with justice and unselfishness.

Today the church meetings are filled with pride and **self-esteem, which is the modern term for excessive narcissism. The first three** chapters of 1st Corinthians capture the source of problems arising from pride and exaltation of man. Romans 12 addresses this attitude of high-mindedness with the command to esteem others better than self, and to come down to men of humble estate. Pride brought down the two who fell dead at the Apostles feet in Acts chapter 5. Romans 14.8, states that we are the Lord's, in life and in death. A proud man cannot bring honor to the Lord who humbled Himself to become obedient unto death, even the death of the cross (Phil. 2). If we run against men in a foot race, we should not be weary. God may have even greater odds for us in due time.

Perhaps today in America the church has been put into a competition or race against horses. It is very difficult to compete with the pleasures and entertainment of the world, but the church seems to have taken that challenge. In the purpose of God, the persecuted churches around the world who have no Disney Land to compete with, (nor would they get into such a competition if they could), go on into their ministry of holy living and serving the Lord in the joy of suffering. The American church paper or monthly papers that I have read, look like some kind of advertisement for the 'family happy hour' at the beach, or some kind of smile and be rich appeal. You can't tell a difference between the local paper's advertisement for 'get all you can out of life' bargains, and the local church announcement of a youth picnic. That's because they both cater' to the world's agenda for life. But the word of God says—"woe unto you who laugh now for you shall weep, Luke 6, 1-30. Jesus was known as a man of sorrows, and the joy He brings into a life, is deeply planted in concern for lost souls, in a dying world, because of a hope in the world to come where there will be no crying nor death or sorrow.

What kind of church is this which seems to be completely separated from the Kingdom of God which Jesus revealed and proclaimed? If the saints of God must do battle with principalities and powers, against rulers of darkness and spiritual wickedness in high places, than this is a great description of the days battle. To overcome the lust of the eyes, pride of life and lust of the carnal nature is the battle. We find ourselves contending with and against ourselves. We have met the enemy and it is us. The church or assembly that is filled with tares, which only resemble the true wheat, would be a great force to overcome. What must be overcome is the temptation to join the enemy, where the broad road leads to destruction, because so many more seem to be taking that road than there are on the narrow path that leads into Life. John 17. 2,3 is clear, this is life eternal, that they may know the Lord, the only true God, and Jesus Christ whom He has sent. Don't ask a pastor or minister where he went to school, ask him if he has been with Jesus! (Acts 4. 13).

Issues we must deal with in these last days!

One of the many problems which was 'self inflicted' upon the country of America and the church abiding within it, is the teaching, (now a concept), that everything will come out ok! In a country like America, where decent people, God fearing (to some extent), have been the majority, and therefore decent moral standards are the general rule, <u>children were taught</u> that goodness and truth will always win, sooner or later. Now if we hold this concept, knowing that faith in life, and altruism, are the major players in such a doctrine, we find it comforting to believe and promote this view. Who has not been taught that a person must keep believing in what is right, and what is good even in bad times? Those who represent the majority of America's population, are people who have valued freedom, justice and truth. There are many other such positive and biblical qualities which are too numerous to mention, which have permeated the society, the homes, the schools and business in the United States.

Now we face a time in history, in America, the church and in the whole world, where terrorism and other deterioration of these values makes people question their original and foundational beliefs. Things in the 21st century are not turning out alright when most people do the right things. We can even say now, that people who believe in what is right are no longer the majority. In this present evil world (Gal. 1. 4), (1 John 5. 19), there are over one billion Muslims, nearly one billion Buddhists, and out of a world population estimated to be about 6 billion souls, Christians are not the majority. Since America consists of about 90% Christian belief, these values stated above become dominate, and in a country that finds itself as the world leader in the political and economic world scene, Americans think that other nations should live by the same rules. So the dilemma is this, we have a controlling country with a majority of the people who want to see that their personal and religious values are upheld and distributed 'evenly', we may say, in all the earth, yet we have a world of terror prompted by religious views which do not agree with those of the Americans or the churches in America.

This means that those of us in the churches in America, have a real hard time continuing to believe that terrorism cannot be 'defeated' or at least controlled, since we have always been taught and will not easily give up, the idea that right will finally conquer evil. Such a concept is based upon the fact that finally in the end of all things, God will definitely put down Satan and all evil; and the Kingdom of God shall be established—a new heaven and new earth is promised by our Lord and Creator God.

The only problem here is that we have confused the present world with the eternal world yet to come. Notice again the verse in 1 John 5. 19, and Rev. 13. 7, which mentions that the beast mentioned in Revelation 13 has been granted a time when he overcomes the saints. Jesus spoke many times, of "the world to come", Mark 8, Luke 18. 30. The idea that truth and justice finally win over evil and death, **is true**, but it is a spiritual victory, not in a 'time zone' which means the present world system. As a matter of fact, just the opposite is true, Jesus said, in this world you will have tribulation, but be of good cheer, I have overcome the world! The scripture also states that all who will live Godly in Christ Jesus, will suffer persecution. People in America, spiritually lost and the saved, have continued to believe that simply believing in goodness, and following the 'rules' they have been taught, will eventually bring about good results. These altruistic notions are only true in limited context. The increase of wickedness mentioned in Matt. 24. 12, tells us that even the love of many who held the biblical views and truths will grow 'cold' and therefore abandon their earlier faith, this is confirmed in 1st Tim. 4, and 2 Peter 3. 14-18, ("…lest you be led away with the error of the wicked and fall from your own steadfastness;" K.J.V.).

This dilemma about good overcoming evil, if taken just at any whim or in the world of events, may bring the churches in America to frustration and many believers will give up the idea that no matter what evil comes upon a nation or a church, it shall finally be overcome, simply because the good finally overpowers evil. Such beliefs are not easily held In context, and this can weaken the faith of many. What we really need to understand today in the world of 'terrorism' and in face of the fact that there is a hatred held by the Islamic religion—of Jews and Christians, is the fact that we cannot expect to fight the present evil in the world on the political, social and economic scene, using the rules of America and other Western nations. This is why terrorism will not be defeated, or even controlled in this present world. When a runner contends with other footmen in a track meet, as we know it, (Jer. 12. 5), he must be a good competitor, but when he contends (competes) with horses, (can you imagine a horse jockey running on foot in a horse race) that runner will need the God of heaven, to speed him on his way. This is what the Lord must have meant, when he told Jeremiah, in chapter 12, something like-" you ain't seen nothing yet…" Our God will fight for us, but it is for our souls safety, and the purpose is to bring 'many sons' into glory. We cannot afford in this country to think that good will always prevail, and that evil will always be defeated. It depends on which kingdom you refer to, and it depends on which world, (this one or the one to come), you are talking about. Today, we contend (compete) with horses, we are as Christians in a race that we cannot in our own strength win, but our God is able to do all things that men find impossible. Our God is also willing to see His followers face even suffering and death as His Son Jesus did, **in order to make a clear distinction between life in the 'fast lane' on the broad path leading to destruction, and the life in the 'right lane'** which leads to everlasting life—(John 17. 2,3). The evil Islamic empire may well be established in this world as a dominate kingdom. But the kingdoms of this world will at some time become the kingdoms of our God and His Christ, (Rev. 18, 19—Rev. 11. 15).

Another issue, which will be of great importance in these last days, will be the issue of Church and State. If Christians in America cling to the alliance with a nation, however great it may be, and continue to tie the soul to the society, and the spiritual, and eternal things of God to the physical and temporary places of this present world, nothing but disaster can result. This subject is addressed in other pages and in other articles, it is sufficient for now to simply say, that God is not the author of confusion, and if there is **confusion in the minds of Christians about their connection to present world orders**, this confusion has come from another source, not from the word of God.

7

Death by Association

✦

Rom.8. 6-8

"…to be mindful of the flesh (or the glory of this world's desires) is death…"
Intent and purpose have much to do with one's perspective!

When the highly trained, professional advertiser wants to show his clients how to present an advertisement for a product, you can see the psychology of his approach. He directs his attention to the emotional appeal that must be made to the audience. When any product is advertised on TV or in print, the product is surrounded (literally) with material that carries a high concentration of all the emotions that will gain the attention of the audience. If the product is an automobile, a food product, a vacation site, new house etc.etc. the audience will see pretty girls, (sexual appeal) a relaxing moment, (self-fulfillment) happy family time, or a myriad of other scenes, before the product or item to be advertised is even introduced.

This is an obvious effort (and successful one) to turn the attention of the viewer or reader, to emotions and feelings that are consistent with happiness, satisfaction, self adulation, self fulfillment and concepts that will gain an approval, and a positive response. Then the product is introduced, and marketed with the **association it is given** with these emotional concepts. This fact does not really need a lot of explanation. Human nature and our understanding of some measure—of how it works, teaches us that an appeal must be made that will gain acceptance by an audience, if an advertisement of a product is to be received with favor and gain a customer.

If we want to sell something, we need to *first sell a feeling, a positive emotion or a desired relationship* with what is already commonly accepted, and attach the product we are selling to the 'already' desirable emotion within our mind. To sell a product that is not universally or obviously desirable to all people of all ages, the advertiser must be sure to make it look like buying the product will assure a purchaser that it will be to his credit, or to his pleasure to have it. A better car, a better house, a better wardrobe, etc. all of these items can be sold by first selling the idea and the emotion, that is already accepted by the proposed customer.

First the advertiser must sell fun, sex, comfort, or some other desirable emotion, and then it won't matter what he tacks on to that concept or emotion, it is already accepted as something desirable or pleasant because of the feeling the product or item has been attached to. People think that they are buying the power of prestige, or the feeling of happiness and fulfillment when they spend their money for the product or item that is being advertised. This seems to be a lengthy discussion of the unnecessary, to prove the obvious. But perhaps the connection I want to make is not so obvious.

When the American public (which just happens to include a large body of Bible believing, church attending citizens) becomes the knowing or even unwary victim of super sales and highly perfected sales methods, there is a tragic truth to be learned. This truth is that we are all influenced by some powers in the present world (Gal.1.4) and the influence to which I have referred in the preceding statements is influence from sources other than the Bible and the Spirit of God. When we realize that something can be pawned off on a person just by the association it has with feelings and emotions that are part of humanness, we should begin to awaken to the serious nature and the potentially tragic consequences of this fact.

If we consider the evidences which support the theory that simple association with the world around us in the present modern, affluent society in which we find ourselves, has made the modern day Christian weaker and even impotent as a witness for Christ to lost people, it might become scary or even alarming to some of us. Consider the following observations; Even try it as a true and false test.

1. The common notion that prosperity and success in the present world (in America) is equal to or synonymous with spiritual maturity.

2. The commonly accepted idea that a great amount of education and attainment of college degrees is considered of great value for Christian ministers, clergy and church leaders.

3. The commonly and usually endorsed idea that America needs more ministers and more churches, and that more money should be spent toward this goal while the 10,000 unreached people groups in the world go without the Gospel which we could well carry to them with these funds we use on buildings and per-

sonnel for our own congregations, (approx. 1.6 Billion souls wait for the Gospel we all enjoy).

If you agreed to any of the above or answered them as true, you are in serious danger of being an example of spiritually 'dying by association.' The above statements all contradict scriptures in the following texts: 1 Tim. 6:17-21, Acts 4.13, Acts 5.1-11). Many Church leaders and Pastors are leading people to believe that the American 'Christian life style' includes a Biblically accepted affluence, prosperity, and extravagance with no association at all with suffering, (as many of our persecuted body of believers around the world endure). And they do not preach messages on Isa. 58, (use the word worship for fasting, it is a term Biblically correct), and other scriptures which show that warnings of extravagant spending on self and personal worldly gain at the expense of reaching the unreached of the world. Check it out! Read Lk. 12.15-21, 12:31-,33. Read on in Luke 12, about the faithful and wise steward, remember the word faithful, which is the same word as commanded of all believers (Rev.2.10, Matt.25.21, 23, Eph.1.1,Col.1.2, 2Tim.2.13, (and many, many others). American Christians have associated wealth and prosperity with great strides in Christian service. However in most all other countries of the world, the Christian family suffers pain and the marks of the Lord Jesus, borne in their bodies, and such is not even recognized by those fellow members in America. Is there something wrong with this picture? The word suffering is somehow divined in American pulpits to mean some kind of mushy "they spoke unkindly to me at work" kind of endurance while death and beatings accompany that word in other parts of the world. Which Christian do you think is the stronger in his/her faith, the one who is beaten for trusting in Christ, in Pakistan, or the Christian in America who is railed upon for carrying his/her Bible to work?

The Christian in America has a great amount of association with the American society, in politics, interest in Government affairs, concerns about the political and financial security of the country, while in most countries around the world, his fellow believers do not have any association with the local governments, and there are not two flags flying in the church house or place of prayer where the churches gather for praise and worship. Seeing this unconnected association or this difference between the foreign land churches, and the American church should make us wonder at least a bit, about the family resemblance, in the total picture of the church. Give it some thought, and then some prayer. See for yourself if we have a relationship problem here and if we are too closely associated with the land we live in, and thereby in danger of contracting a malignant spiritual cancer because of this unholy association.

In the materials printed and circulated by churches, we are reading about the challenge to start new churches, hire more ministers, build bigger and better buildings etc. However, those **who express such needs** as viable, do not have evening preaching service, yet they ask for more churches to be built, they hire more ministers,. but they do not have any one-week long revival, only 3 days for revival, and a missions conference at the church does not even merit three days of missions emphasis but maybe one Sunday for the whole year. This is true with many churches, certainly not all, but it indicates that this talk of how much more we need to spend on ourselves in America for churches and staff, and buildings, *cannot be a result of hunger for the Word of God,* since so many churches, large and small in number, have whittled down the number of services they have, and the number *of days for revivals over the years, and still there is talk that we need so much more* spiritual food, when **in reality we hold less** *time and opportunity for hearing the Gospel. This is inconsistent* at best, and it is hypocritical at worst. All the crying around about needing more preaching, teaching and expansion in America, while cutting down the very tree that bears the fruit.

Some say, "we just can't get anyone to attend evening services…" or "…*people just won't come to a revival for one week* anymore…" but the preachers and churches across the land keep trying to build more buildings and hire more staff. *Which is* it? Do we need more emphasis and exposure to the Gospel in America or not? Are we just looking for a way to appear as if we had good reason to concentrate efforts on preaching to the already saved people? We have bought into the idea that we need more churches, but in reality we are message rich…(Rev. 3.14-22) we are rich and full and have need of nothing, but in spiritual terms, and in deeds of service to a lost world, we are sadly lacking, our missionaries in north Africa are outnumbered 2 million to one, in America there are churches in every town, so preachers in America are more like a ratio of 1000 people to one minister for population here.

Has the enemy made church ministers in America feel that they are **doing great service where they are** so they do not need to move out into harvest fields that are not touched? It seems that any hindrance to world evangelism would come from one who wants to keep the unreached people out of the Kingdom of God. We have in American churches **the good feelings** of salvation, but not *the yearning for saving the lost* that would carry us to the uttermost parts of the world. We have the **warm summer feeling of safety**, so we do not care to share the *cold winter of suffering* of the saints in persecuted countries of the world. The church has been sold a 'bill of goods' by the enemy through the method used by sales gimmicks used on the lost people of the world, "you in America have a mission field too, so why go to other lands, think about how your needs must be met, and do a little mission trip now and then, you will appease your conscience" at least what's left of it.

Just as a person of the world goes out to buy something that has been presented to his feelings and emotions as a real need for himself, the American preacher makes the members of his church feel ok, then tells them a mission field is right at home, so no need to travel to any other place on the earth, (even though America is less than %5 of the world's population). First you buy the feeling, then you take the product, because it was associated with a good feeling. America sells comfort, and security in the present world system, (but this may be changing), and the churches sell 'feelings of mission accomplishment in short term visits,' and so the members of the church and preachers buy the product, which is stay and play, don't go bye-bye and die! No wonder the Bible says that the fear of the Lord is the beginning of wisdom. When a person fears God, he fears nothing else, *but when he does not fear God*, he fears *everything else and everyone else*. **Preachers fear elders, and elders fear members, and members fear the community, and no one seems to fear God.** Any time we as ministers are worried about what the 'people' will think or say about our message, is a time when we have forgotten if the message is from God or from some where else.

Indeed *we have met the enemy and it is us*. But the Bible gives hope of course, it states, "…he who controls his spirit is mightier than he who takes a city by force…" Let us decide whom we will fear. Fear Him who has power to cast body and soul into Hell. (Lk.12.5, Lk 12-14). If the carnal mind, as Romans 8. 6 reveals, destroys or brings death then we should be very concerned about what we accept as 'gospel truth' in the country of America, since by association, the teachings of the American constitution sound so noble and precious. If an American Christian associates his citizenship in the 'land of the free' with the membership he holds in the church, as if the two are of equal importance and of equal value, **this association will be costly.**

The promotion of ideals and ideas such as, "land of opportunity, "…"…let freedom ring…" "home of the brave…"are bold and proud statements that are indeed true. The **American people have shown these traits of worthy and noble character.** But America is today also a land where this same freedom means acceptance of homosexuality as a viable 'lifestyle' and abortion of the young unborn (and even nearly born) as legal and unquestioned in the 'highest courts of the land.' America also allows and provides for support of religions that are not 'from above' and therefore not of God, at least the only true God revealed as Lord in the Holy Bible. So when we wave the American flag, what are we trying to say?

We all make a statement by deeds and words, we shout down the flag burning kooks, and with good reason, but we also go to church, place a sign of a fish on our car, and live in luxury and extravagance. This is not just a problem with inconsistency, it is a problem about truth, obedience to the Living God, and surrender of personal agendas. The whole church seems to be infected with this 'malignant narcissism' to borrow a term from Tammy Bruce's book, "The Death of Right and Wrong." Christian ministers, sing songs and preach sermons about Biblical issues, then give no word about the condition of 1.6 Billion on the face of the earth who have never heard of the Bible, sin, forgiveness, heaven, hell, redemption or HOPE ETERNAL. How precious are the souls well within our reach? Are they given a crumb while we eat their loaf of bread? Are the unevangelized of the world left again this year, with no message of Salvation, while we hire another 'pastor' to counsel our poor underfed, weak excuse of a church member? Would we look to regions beyond, like the Apostles of our Lord, and like the early persecuted saints who died to carry the message beyond their little corner of the earth? There are other just as important questions to be asked, but perhaps we should leave those for another time, another place, perhaps even until the Master of the House returns…!

8

Family Worship or—Worship of Family!

✦

Matt. 10. 32-39, Lk. 14. 24-26
Lk. 9. 60-62 Gen. 22.
Mk. 1. 21-38, Mk. 3. 1-35

The matter of 'the place of the family' in the teachings of Jesus, is well addressed and fully clarified. Jesus is known as 'the Prince of Peace' yet He has himself said—He came to bring division among men, even to the separation of family members as a result of people choosing to follow Him. I have been personally acquainted with the power of the Gospel in the lives of people, as they made the choice to follow Jesus even when it meant forsaking the religion and tradition of the family.

Jesus does bring peace to the soul, but many times He also brings division to the family, because He separates good from evil, light from darkness and salvation from eternal destruction. **In Johannesburg,** South Africa in 1962, a young Chinese family asked me to come from my home and area of ministry in Kimberley S.A., to help begin a house church for them, a church that is only a New Testament church. In making the arrangement to conduct bible teachings in the home of this Chinese family, I began to travel from Kimberley to Johannesburg each week. One young Chinese man, 20years of age, decided to obey the Lord.

When he did, his father who embraced the **Confucius religion** opposed the young man (Gordon Yun), and forbade Gordon to accept the 'new teaching' o f Christianity. I accompanied Gordon to his home when his father began to make death threats to him and to me, for bringing this Jesus teaching' to the Chinese

44

community in Johannesburg. The mother and sister begged me to tell Gordon not to make this decision to leave the teaching of the 'family' and embrace the Gospel of Christ and the way of the Lord Jesus.

When I refused to dissuade Gordon, but rather encouraged him to follow through, on our way out of the house (Gordon with his belongings in hand), the father of the household tried to threaten the rest of the family with death (he had a gun and several knives in the house), so the entire family was in fear and trepidation as we departed. Gordon and I met with other believers in the small house church that same night, and witnessed Gordon Yun's baptism into Christ. We had reported the incident to the local police station as we went on to the place for baptism. Gordon's father did not become more violent nor did he achieve his goal or carry out his threats to turn young Gordon Yun from his chosen path. The father of Gordon did print Gordon's name in the local Chinese newspaper the next week, stating that Gordon would no longer be a son of his household and that his name would be given a 'black mark' among the Chinese people. Gordon went on to become a leader in the small house church fellowship the rest of his life.

I believe I understand well, the meaning of the teaching of Jesus about forsaking the family and self (Matt. 19. 27-30), for I have witnessed the power of such a decision in the lives of many who chose Jesus, and in so choosing, suffered the loss of family relationships. Jesus Himself stated that His family, His brother, sister and mother, were those who heard the word of God and obeyed it, Mk. 3. 33-35. Most of Jesus' own physical family, thought He was mad, and the Pharisees and religious leaders of the time, accused Him of being possessed by Beelzebub, prince of the demons (Mk. 3. 22). Jesus at this early time in His ministry, acknowledged that His family—was comprised of those who chose to believe in Him and follow Him. Jesus set the very example of letting the family of the physical and natural world, be set aside, for the sake of Truth, and for the sake of doing the will of the Father.

To honor the father and mother of this earthly and physical realm does not mean to place them above the relationship and role we have in the Kingdom of God through Jesus Christ the Lord. Those who follow Jesus and do His will, shall have no 'clinging vines' in this world, even family (as dear as they may be), nor shall they even let their own well being in this world stand in the way of fulfilling the great commission and the great will of the Father in Heaven. If any man does not even hate his own life in this world, he cannot make it as a disciple of the Lord Jesus. The love of self is the greatest enemy to the love of God, because protecting self and family first, will keep a person from the suffering, sacrifice and even death that discipleship requires.

1. You can with a little study, see that two very important things happened in the early ministry of Jesus, to set the enemies of God in disarray. 1. When the fame of Jesus, due to His miracles and 'this new doctrine' (Mk. 1.27) began to bring many common people to the feet of Jesus, the Pharisees became insanely jealous and fearful at the same time. The people began to believe in Jesus and become His followers, which meant that the teaching of the Pharisees and Sadducees no longer held the people in fear and submission to the Jewish teaching.

2. Secondly, the physical family of Jesus came to Jesus, not just to see Him, but perhaps to 'take charge' of Him or persuade Him to bend to the 'ruling' teaching of the synagogue. And these two things led the Pharisees to accuse Jesus of being 'demon possessed' which accusation would greatly displease family members who were afraid of losing 'face' with the ruling class. Family members thought Jesus was 'Mad' and the religious leaders accused Him of being possessed. It is surely true, a prophet of God is not welcome in His home town.

Now the day has come, when the test of the American church really gets heavy. There is in America and in American churches, the battle of the ages, and the battle rages as each day passes, and few people recognize either the friend or the foe. Mr. Dave Smith, wrote in an article for Christian Standard in the October 2004 issue, p. 10, the following statement. **"There is no Biblical justification for neglecting our wives in the Name of working for God."** This is quite an interesting statement, since the **Bible in Matthew 10. 35-39 teaches just the opposite**. The *flip side of this statement is actually the truth.*

> **"There is no Biblical justification for neglecting
> the work of God in the name of caring for the little
> wife and family." (A. W. Hamilton).**

With such teachings as Mr. Smith advocates, we know that the love of self—as foretold in 2 Tim. 3. 2 has come upon us. It is a hard thing for a 'soft' church, (such as American churches have become), to accept a hard task. This is much like the example referred to in John chapter 6, and verse 60, when the disciples heard words from Jesus about "being the bread of Life" which words they considered to be—" a hard saying" which would be difficult to explain to the world.

When a hard saying comes our way today, we will not likely recognize it because the church in America has been used to 'milk toast' sayings which require no real effort to decipher, since 'food for thought' such as the disciples heard from the lips of the Master go deeper and penetrate the very soul of man. The

Words of the Lord are simple and easy to understand (Isa. 35. 8), a child or a stranger on the road will be able to find the way of the Lord (Matt. 11. 25). But when the hard sayings come, it is not because the saying is difficult to understand, but rather it seems to be **a hard saying because it will be 'hard' to take**!

I believe that it will be hard for most to consider what is written here, as a warning sign on the highway for the upright, but hard saying or not, Christians need to take heed, because these teachings in America in modern times of America's affluence and therefore the extravagance and excess in which the church in this day and time revels, will make it difficult to 'tear away' from the prosperity gospel. There has been so much emphasis on 'family, fun and games', like a church sign I saw advertising the (Halloween) harvest week-end festivities, that it will be seen as a hard saying to hear that the church has a present day attitude of 'worship of the family' instead of a simple plan for family worship.

It is so easy to turn things around to suit our wishes, and gratify the flesh, even with bible verses to support it. When preachers speak of **wealth as a great sign of successful Christian living,** and **education as a mark of excellence for mature followers of Christ**, something in the picture has been distorted. The weird thing about this kind of message is, that it can only be preached in this 'land of the free and home of the brave'. Only in America does the body of Christ founder in the excesses of modern conveniences. **The reason so much emphasis in today's pulpits seems to be placed on 'family' is not because the bible speaks of the family as some kind of 'number one' priority, but because strong families make a strong country.** How many times have you heard the terms 'strong families' connected to country (American life), not simply to the church family or the individual family? Many children have no knowledge of their early years, they were abandoned, and how can they 'Focus On The Family'? **All this focus on the family, is supported by an effort to make the land of America some kind of 'Christian utopia.'** Make it easy to live the Christian life in this world, and you don't have the real **Christian life any more, you have a state-church social club with a religious flavor.** For what other reason would churches have such emphasis?

You don't have to be in any one of the many countries where persecution abounds today, for any length of time, before your eyes are truly opened to the differences between **'them and us.'** One world but two churches! How can this be? The true body of Christ is not divided into the have's and the have not's. You can't look at the church in the persecuted countries of the world, and then look at the church in America and say—behold how they love one another? **The church in America loves itself.** *The church in countries under persecution, loves oth-*

ers. The persecuted church does not even look like the church in America. How can the Lord have one body, and see it looking so differently in China than it is in America? I have worked with the people in Africa who face and have faced persecution, and unless you have been there you would not understand this sad case of un-similar, and unequal conditions and spiritual polarization. In 2 Cor. 8. 1-15 it is apparent that such inequality is not biblical. The strong faith and obedience at all cost is found in countries of the world where the church is an illegal institution. In America, Christians try to change the government so that the Christian life will be easier and the 'rights' of the church will be upheld. This all sounds very noble and certainly it gives the church a chance to be a light unto the world, and be the salt of the earth that the church was intended to be.

But the difference between being a light that—('as the sun') warms and lights the whole earth and being like the **American church, which seems to be more like a laser beam,** focused in one country, (and that could burn a hole in the place it is focused on), is **that many go without any light or warmth**. If you put all the salt in one place, this destroys the purpose of salt and ruins whatever it falls on, if it pours out on one spot only. Light of the world, Jesus said, and salt of the earth, it should not be that so much concentration of light or salt in one place should keep the rest of the world in the dark or cause the rest of the world to go sour.

The reason the church of the 1ˢᵗ century was scattered by persecution, was so that it could render a service and carry the Gospel of Christ into all the world. If the resources are available (and they are) and if the number of believers is sufficient (and it is), then about 2 billion souls could ask the church in America some day, "where in the world were you?"

In many discussions through the years, while recruiting workers for the foreign mission fields, my family and I have heard the old phrase, "if God is calling me, I think He will also call my wife," to the foreign lands. Here is where family and the worship of family becomes the easy way out, and the 'hard saying' that a person must forsake all that he has for the sake of the Gospel, becomes the real 'precious moment.' Jesus said that in accepting His salvation, and His indwelling Spirit, we may even be divided from family members. Now I see no difference between the call to salvation in conversion, and the call to fulfill the commission. If we really believe that we are called, to serve, and saved to tell others, how can one distinguish between having salvation and sharing that salvation with those who do not know Jesus? What about the little chorus, **'we are saved to tell others'?** Being brought into the light out of darkness means that we become servants of the Light,—which light is—Jesus.

The family emphasis which we see in churches today, is not what we are given by examples such as we find in Matthew 8. 21, Luke 9. 59,60—**This is the record of one of Jesus' disciples saying, "Lord, suffer me first to go and bury my father..." and Jesus said unto him, "let the dead bury the dead but you come and follow me."** Nor is there such an idea of 'family first' in any of the teachings of Jesus when He sent out the disciples. The context (and some of our translators say—context is everything), in **1ˢᵗ Tim. 5. 8,** happens to be in regard to asking the church **to care for people who could be cared for by their own family members, so that the church could look after those who were 'widows indeed.'** This verse has nothing to do with the evangelist going into all the world to preach the Gospel, and putting that calling above his personal needs and cares. In 1ˢᵗ Cor. 9. 5, Paul states that he (and other evangelists), had the right to take with them (lead about) a believing wife as they went on their missionary work. The believing wife is a helper to an evangelist not one who holds the evangelist back from the work of the Lord. Would we dare admit today, that many men are afraid to go into mission work overseas because they know that the 'little woman' would never 'go for it' and she will even use the children and herself as a 'lever' to persuade the husband that they can do 'just as much' for God in America?

The lives of David Livingstone and of William Carey are the best examples, and most well known for the sacrifice and commitment, which best explains my point. If Dr. Livingstone and Carey, had not understood the words of Jesus in Matthew 10.37-42, and if those words had not given direction and meaning for their lives, perhaps thousands of villages in Africa, or India, would never have heard the Gospel. In the biography of these men of God (David Livingstone, and of Carey) is the true story of the power that Matt. 28. 18-2 had upon their lives and therefore their service to God and humanity. They, I am sure would have made no such statement as the one referred to in the beginning of this writing. The writer of the article in the "Christian Standard"—Dave Smith, needs to read the accounts of Dr. David Livingstone & Carey, missionaries to Africa and India, whose lives and commitment to the Lord and His commission to go into all the world, is unquestioned. These men not only neglected wife, and the children to finish the work and calling from God they endangered their own lives. Matt. 10. 35-ff have some meaning to these men and those who like them, found that focus on the Lord and his command to go into all the world, is number one, not self, family or any other connection. For someone to make such a statement, that 'there is no biblical justification for neglect of (wife) or family, is just plain biblical ignorance, and historically untrue.

The history of all men and women of God, who have suffered the loss of loved ones, and the pain of paying the price for putting God first, makes the modern family worshiper look ridiculous and even spiritually weak—to the likes of those in Hebrews ll who died without hesitation because they put God first. The words of Jesus in Matt. 10, would never have been spoken if there was never a 'justification' for neglect of other duties or other relationships. This is only proof of the weak approach the modern Christian preacher wants to take in order to find a nice welcome among the 'soft saints' of the modern American church. When will the real servants of God stand up and be counted? Or we might ask, where have all the faithful gone? Gone long time ago.

In Genesis 22, the record of Abraham's offering of his only son Isaac, stands as the prime example of true faith and true worship of God. **There is no emphasis such as we have today, that some kind of family responsibility must come before the responsibility of God's servants to obey His command, even if it means giving up what God has in His grace,** given us! (Job made this clear), the Lord has given and the Lord has taken away, blessed be the Name of the Lord. If Abraham lived today and was asked or commanded to offer his son Isaac on an alter, **the family lovers would go crazy trying to throw Bible verses around, to show that no such sacrifice was Biblical.** This idea of killing your only son, (or any child), would be seen by the present day church leaders and bible scholars, as needing further interpretation.—Duh...**The leaders of today would question God and condemn Abraham!**

Talk about neglect of the family, or wife. What do you call this, child abuse perhaps or some other social dysfunction? What would the 'family worship emphasis' preachers of today say about this? God can command anything He wants to...Abraham did not know that he would not be required to kill his son, it was at the last minute that God's angel stayed his hand. Then God said to Abraham, "now I know you fear God". This test would not have been passed by anyone today in the circle of 'focus on the family' you can be sure of that!

The reason we have fewer missionaries today than needed to reach the (12,000)unreached people groups, is probably greatly due to the emphasis on pleasing the little family, or seeking the comfort of wife and kids, so that no service to Christ that requires a man of God to go into these unreached people groups, and leave any family at home, will ever seem biblical. What a 'cop out' this is, and what a nice soft, comfortable 'calling' from God we must have invented. In reality, we please us, <u>we find ways to make staying away from the hard task seem acceptable to God.</u> This is not just wrong, it is deceiving.

The day of 2Tim. 3. 2 has come upon the church in America. **Lovers of self rather than lovers of God has pinpointed the** fact that these are the last days! Welcome to the real world, but not the real Kingdom. **Visit the persecuted church and you will find the real Kingdom of God people on planet earth today!**

For a wife who sees her commission from God as that of being a helper to her husband, the man of God, there will be no conflict, and no neglect. **Any number of hours the man of God spends in seeking the lost will be seen as a great thing in the eyes of a wife who loves God** more than herself, and her children will also see **that God is number one in the family.** Ask me, I can tell you about how this works, for this is exactly the family God gave me and I have traveled many miles, by God's grace (and I believe by His leading), and spent many days and hours away from the family. But today all 4 of the children at our house are missionaries, and through success and failure, through ill health and good health, they today can answer any of your questions about who is first and who is not. **They do this with joy and exuberance...Therefore I can address this subject with fact as well as with conviction.**

Another man's opinion,

Al Hamilton
Missionary

9

For Our Joy—For His Glory

✦

Let us not get it backwards!
Ps. 115. 1

What is meant for our joy, is still intended for God's glory; John 15. 11, John 16, 17. All things in the Christian life, should bring us joy for many reasons. **Reason 1**, is that we were called out of darkness into His marvelous light, **Reason 2,** we are to be to the praise of His glory, simply because it is God's good pleasure to make us His own Eph. 1.12. The first reason is related to our salvation by God's grace, acquired through our faith and obedience. The second reason is related to our **service or work** in His kingdom, as a result of our **citizenship** in His kingdom. We who follow Christ enter into His joy, to bring Him glory.

It has become increasingly clear, that the church in America, in this generation will be known as the Laodicea church of Revelation chapter 3 and verses 14-22. If these churches in Revelation chapter 3, are periods of church history as well as congregations of believers in their own time, which gives dual meaning to that chapter, then we must face the awful fact that America personifies the Laodicean church. Much of this fact rests in the lack of humility that is obvious in the present modern, American scene. The American philosophy of self-ism, is well described by Dr. Aaron Stern in his book "Me The Narcissistic American" published in 1979, and the books by Dave Hunt, regarding the "Seduction of Christianity" and "Beyond Seduction" tell the same story. The American church (all denominations) presents the picture to the lost people of the world (and should reveal to the church itself), that church history has entered the 'last days' of it's work on earth. The last days of evangelism are described in various places in scripture, such as the accounts of the Gospel writers, Matthew in chapter 24,

Mark in chapter 13, Luke in chapter 21, and in Paul's letters to Timothy, 1Tim. 4, 2 Tim. 3, and in Peter's second letter, 2 Peter chapters 2 and 3.

If the casual observer who knows some scripture, is watching the American church at all, he will notice how the present American church has become extravagant, lazy, self centered, ambitious and self-serving. This picture is very different from, and opposite of, the church we read about in Acts. The average church advertises in the world as if it was seeking members to fill the church seats, by appealing to the interest of men and women (as well as children) of the world, from some standpoint of self-fulfillment **"we have a program for your family…"** Offering the services of God on some platter of personal self-improvement scheme, is not a picture of the church in the time of the Apostles or even in the time of the so called 'dark ages' or age of reformation. The Bible states that the church is to be the body of Christ, founded upon His Divine (Messiah) Lordship, and built upon the Apostles and Prophets (messages), Jesus Christ being the Chief cornerstone, Eph. 2. 20.

If you want to see the real church, the body of Christ that walks in the footsteps of Christ and His Apostles, and the footsteps of the early saints, learn about the persecuted church in the 70 or more countries around the world where people who follow Jesus suffer and die for their faith in Christ. Richard Wurmbrand, author of several books, and a man imprisoned for 14 years by Communist authorities, in Rumania, in his book entitled "little Notes Which Like Each Other" on p. 121, quoted Wycliffe, who wrote "if the priesthood misuses church treasures, they must be taken from it. Otherwise, you neglect your duty." Wurmbrand also quoted Bonnhoffer on the same page, who said, **"The church is a church only when she exists for others. To begin with, she must give away all her property to the needy. Pastors must live only on the free will offerings of believers. If necessary, they must exercise a secular profession".** Does this statement by Bonnhoffer describe any church you have seen In American? This attitude and purpose does exist in other countries where persecution abounds. The concern for others before self, is not uncommon in N. Korea, China, India, Africa and many other lands where freedom of religion does not exist. What does this all mean? **In the land of freedom, we have less of Christ, and more of self,** and in the lands of persecution we have the obvious picture of the suffering Savior, living in His people, just as the Bible teaches.

The modern and present idea of Christianity proclaimed by most churches (especially mega churches) in America, present a picture of self-indulgence, prosperity and extravagance. All of which become promoted as the evidence of a real Christian experience and as evidence of spiritual growth. From whence cometh this message which pretends to lead people into a 'faith walk' but is without a faith power (1Cor. 4.20)? The normal message from American church pulpits deal with making better citizens for the sake of a country which is part of the present world (Gal.2.4), but speak nothing of sacrifice, suffering and giving up life so that others may receive the word of Life. Churches 'hire' staff to enlarge the borders of their membership list, while overlooking the task to send laborers into the harvest fields of the world. What few mission 'projects' are engaged become something that can be easily controlled by the church leadership, without any great risk or expenditure beyond their own well chosen accountability scale.

Duke Vladimir of Kiev became a Christian in order to marry the Byzantine princess Anne. He forced the whole of Russia to become Christian. When Finland was defeated by the Swedes under St. Eric, the people were compelled to embrace Christianity. This is a quote from Richard Wurmbrand's book mentioned above. Few American Christians are aware of the real history of Christianity and the political 'correctness' which was a part of such 'religious' and political connections, that had no resemblance to the true Church of the 1st century. Pope Leo X, who excommunicated Luther, is reported to have said: "What profit has not the fable of Christ brought to us!" Again, this is a quote from the suffering saint and warrior of the Lord in recent history, Pastor Richard Wurmbrand. Pastor Wurmbrand goes on to state In his book mentioned above, **"The Church of England had no place for either Bunyan or Wesley when they were alive, yet today, there are commemorative plates for them in Westminster Abbey, centuries after their death.***

The world has always (since Acts chapter 5) had it's place inside the church body, which is the enemies way of seeking to control and counterfeit the work of God in the earth. Is it any surprise that the modern American church would have the evil influence of 'love of money' and the 'love for self', as it's tentacles of control, to make the tares in the field choke out the wheat? Who in the church assembly has not noticed the modern music, the modern 'world accepted' appeal to human nature's desire for affluence and importance? The high visibility of the American churches in the world makes the 'hidden' church assemblies of other countries wonder if we are the same people of God as they are!

American churches tell the people what they already know, about things they have already learned, in such an academic manner, that none seem to be aware of any problem with this academic approach to Christianity. Who sounds the warning? The Prophets of God and the Apostles of Christ, always had warning messages from God to keep the people of God turned toward God, and away from the idols of the nations. Perhaps herein lies the cause of present day distress!

The church in America has little warning sounded by the speakers in the pulpit, or on the TV. The call to follow the Bible, obey the Lord, these things are commonly heard, but to announce the evil and deception which is prevalent in religious circles is not so common. Richard Wurmbrand states in his book "Little Notes That Like Each Other" on page 122, "Real Christians are also capable of treachery and cruelty. Wicked men have virtues, Saints have sins. The world is not divided into white and black. **It will sometimes be difficult for you to distinguish between the true and the false.**" Men like Leanord Ravenhill, in his book entitled "Why Revival Tarries" and men like Juan Carlos Ortiz in his book "Disciple" written In the 70's, bring out the warnings of apostasy, and the evil of selfishness. On page 119 Richard Wurmbrand states,"learn to distinguish between the true church and institutions which only bear the name."

Clovis, king of the Francs, became a Christian because he loved the Christian princess Clotilde…and his people accepted Christianity because the king ordered it. Do Americans think that the Devil has changed his tactics? If so, think again, **once more, but now in America, the lure of a society which is blessed with many believers in Christianity, has also become a society that the weak believers think they own. My America, and my church, the theme of 'God and country' is evidence of this obvious philosophy of life.**

I have the opinion that much of the problem with American Christians in their belief system, lies rooted in the idea that, the joy of knowing the forgiveness of sin, and the promise of Salvation, has somehow given the believers in this country some feeling of special ness (see Dr. Aaron Stern's book "Me The Narcissistic American") which entitles them as believers in Christ, to a comfortable life style of prosperity and uniqueness. And this specialness has somehow influenced the church member to take the attitude that they, being 'special' in the sight of God, (as they see themselves), makes them worth something in their own minds, to the point of dismissing the concept of humility altogether. Jesus said, that unless we had the humility of a child, we would not even enter the Kingdom of Heaven. You might get in the local church, but there is a big difference in being added to God's chosen and being placed in membership among local church members. In other words, the American Christian has a way of looking at themselves as 'worthy' because God loves them. God is love, this is who He is and this is what He does. This does not mean that we are worthy of His love, because God's love is perfect, and He loves all of His creation. He saves those who believe In Him and obey Him, not because they are worth saving, but because His perfect love extends even to the unlovely, that includes sinful humankind. Thank God for that fact.

The joy that God gives us in Christ which is in the forgiveness extended from the Cross and the empty tomb, is not for the purpose of **making people feel good about themselves, but for the purpose of making people feel good about God.** We see ourselves as sinners saved by grace, not as prisoners who are innocent and worthy of release. Luke 17. 10 gives the words of Jesus Himself to His followers about how they should see themselves. "When you have done all that is (required) commanded of you, you shall say of yourself, **I am an unworthy servant (slave)". This is how we look at ourselves.** The joy we have in Christ, is indeed one of God's great gifts to His faithful followers, but the glory of our salvation is on God's side of the fence, not on man's. **No flesh (human) shall glory in his presence,** (1Cor. 1. 29, 4.7). It is for our JOY, but salvation is for God's glory. **Ps. 115. 1, is the plea of David, "not unto us, Oh Lord, not unto us, but unto thy Name give glory".**

Dr. Aaron Stern in his book, "Me the Narcissistic American" puts this 'special' thing in it's proper perspective. He states, that this unhealthy idea of 'specialness' is a dangerous attitude in the first place.

If everyone is special, of course the term loses it meaning, and no one is special. And <u>specialness always demands privilege</u>. If a child is special, why should he have to perform the menial task, for example, of taking out the trash? If specialness is carried to its logical end, then it has no valuable meaning. It can only create a pride that will ultimately destroy the person who clings to it. Jesus did not call disciples into service who thought they were special, nor did He ever tell them they were in some way special. All prophets of God and Apostles of Christ, felt just the opposite. They all felt unworthy and helpless. God's great power in His called out people, made the difference. God said, for them to go and He would be with them, and He would fight for them. God makes the difference, the battle is the Lord's not man's.

As far as I have been able to determine, only Christians in America have this proud attitude about their relationship to God. **Humility is so seldom seen, it can hardly be often taught in the American church.** Look at the way the TV evangelists are 'decked' out, and tell me this is humility! Most of them look like Hollywood stars on a Sunday morning fashion parade.

I once noticed a poster on the wall in a Sunday school class room for third graders. It was a pretty little bunny rabbit with long floppy ears and a sweet countenance, and the caption under the picture stated, "**God loves me, so that makes me special". What a joke,** what a <u>misrepresentation and misinterpretation of God's Word</u>. God loves me, that is true, but **that makes God special, He's the one doing the loving,** that **does not make us special, it simply means that**

God is so great, and so good that He loves even me, *though I am not special*! If we can't teach the children in Sunday School properly (to understand the love of God), how in the world can we teach the lost people in the world?

In a church in Colorado, I spoke to a large youth gathering. On the wall in their youth center of the church building, were photos of the activities of the youth which presented the years events. All of the photos were of the youth themselves, i.e. the captions under the photos were something like this—"**this is us getting on the bus, this is us**, getting **off the bus, this is us** at the youth picnic, **this is us** in 'six flags' **this is us**"........nothing but **this is us** stuff...no photos of starving and dying African children, or persecuted Christians as prayer partners. So in my presentation I brought attention to this narcissistic portrayal of their love of self. You could have heard a pin drop. I told them they need to re-write some of the hymns they sing, just to be honest, for example they could sing—"I **am mine** oh Lord I have heard **my** voice, and it told **my love to me, but I long to rise in self esteem, and be closer drawn to me**"!

Most of the churches where I share this message are not to happy with my words of warning either. But a prophet was not welcome in his own home town either. And it is not about me, or our message or acceptance or rejection, the real scary part of these experiences is that **it is common to find in American churches, that the churches narcissism is only exceeded by the pride in the pulpit. The form of Godliness is** there, but the **power of Godliness** has been denied. A call to repentance is long overdue.—awh. *(Richard Wurmbrand in his books.)

10

For Men Only

✦

The American Churches and The Prophecy of Isaiah
Isa. 3. 1-26, 5. 11-30

Woe unto the wicked, and **as for my people, children are their oppressors, and women rule over them**. The Lord stands to judge the people,...because their tongue and their doings are against the Lord, to provoke the eyes of His glory. Say to the righteous, that it shall be well with him: for they shall eat the fruit of their doings (deeds).

The verses of the New Testament which state; by their fruits you will know them, and whatsoever a man sows, that shall he also reap, can be grim reminders of the judgment of God upon disobedient people. When the Lord stands to judge His people, (Isa. 3. 13) we can be sure that His judgment is not going to change just because the years have passed, and a new generation has come. We need to understand the judgments of God and His word about truth, righteousness and their counterparts, wickedness and falsehood will be consistent. Wicked ways will be rewarded in any generation and how God sees the world and sees His people is revealed through the Holy scriptures, of the prophets and the Apostles of Christ.

On the program "60 Minutes" on TV, Sunday eve. Oct. 10th, 2004, was a segment that dealt with the surge in America of women and their role in American society, and the increase of women in the country as judges, corporate heads and positions of exceedingly important social significance. It is a good time to also notice that the status of the children's place in American society has changed as well as that of the place of women, over the last 40 years. In Isa. 3. 4-5, the prophet of God stated to a disobedient Israel, that children would be princes, and youth (babes) would take the role of leadership in the nation of Israel as a punishment for their wicked departure from the purpose and plan of God. In America we can see this parallel, and discover **that when a people displease God, they come under the rule of those 'unqualified' to rule, and the children begin to 'behave proudly' against the adults (ancients).**

The age of oppression in this world has a headquarters right here in America. The church has not warned the nation against this condition, and therefore the church may be held responsible for such failure. Notice that the messengers of God Ezekiel—18, 34 (about unfaithful shepherds)—were set, like Ezekiel 3. 17, as watchmen over the house of God's people. This means that even the nations that the people of God live among should be warned of the coming judgment of God upon sin and wickedness. **The very presence of the Christians in persecuted lands, is a threat to those governments of ungodly rulers, ie. Communist countries.** In America the churches experience great freedom, and can therefore warn the rulers of the nation and the people of the land, that the Lord God in heaven will bring judgment upon wickedness. Isaiah the prophet said, **"woe to those who call evil good and good evil, who put bitter for sweet and sweet for bitter..." (Isa. 520,21). The churches in America have protested and warned against the evil practice of 'abortion' homosexuality and other disgraces and sins.** American churches have tried to present the Bible to the nation and have been rejected and outvoted and out voiced by the liberal media. But the battle still rages, and the government opposition to Christianity is just beginning to become apparent, as the voice of Christians is raised against the evil practices in the land of America, (land of opportunity).

What is needed today is a continued effort, and a louder cry(from those who fear God, and honor His word), about America's sin. The duty of the watchman, (which is the position of the true Church of Christ in America today), is to warn nations, and all peoples of the world, of the coming judgment of God upon wickedness in the world. We can see in the word of God, how those who disobeyed Him, (even His own people) received punishment for their wicked departure from His truth. One punishment upon Israel, recorded in **chapters 3 and 5 of Isaiah,** is that women would be put in charge of the nation (of Israel) and children would be princes over the men. This was an embarrassing thing to any Jewish man, simply because the nation knew that the women would have to leave the home and the children to run the political machinery. Sounds very chauvinistic today to speak of women today as needing to return to the care of husband, children and home, in this great movement toward 'women's desire to be liberated'. America is not the only picture of the departure from God's plan in society for leadership and rule. The church has swallowed this bait as well. Churches, cried out against the 'legalized abortion' against homosexual activity, and against other evils in the land. **But the church backed down on the role and ministry of women in the home, with children—(See 1st Tim. 2, 3—1st Peter 3.7).**

Now we shall reap the harvest in the churches in America and in the land for this departure.

We can see the fruits of the departure of men from their role as spiritual leaders in the home, in crimes that are rampant in the domestic murders of wives and children. The increase in killings, abuse of all kinds and other hideous expressions of hate are the result of leaving the plan of God, and seeking a carnal lust for selfish fulfillment of earthly desires. There is no plan for 'focus on the family' that can successfully solve this problem, only a return to God in repentance and a pledge to obey Him will bring hope again to this American waste land of greed and narcissism.

<u>As I have stated in other articles, the cause of the dilemma for country and church in America, is quite simple and very obvious.</u>

1. **When men became weak, women became strong.**

2. **When women became strong, children became confused.**

As you have multitudes of men who took no leadership role in spiritual realms at home, and who 'caved in' to the devil's trick of pulling the 'liberation' of women movement on the American public, we could see a problem developing. Men had first to become weak, and when they did, which is obvious in churches today, women felt compelled to leave the consistent role of child care and creating the atmosphere of love and devotion for the home, to take a burden and responsibility that was not their nature to be able to manage. Children became confused about the role of man and the role of woman, when the father became abusive, and soft in spiritual development. When a leader falls, the followers will run right over him and look to each other, and in so doing there will be only confusion and error.

Churches are not filled with men who can make spiritual decisions, not today, many 'run home to mama' and then come back with a decision which was no doubt shared with the wife, but not only shared, but arrived at with the wishes of the wife, even if it was a very spiritual decision. It is no wonder that spiritually lost nations of the world, do not seek the democracy of America or the churches of America as their ideal. **The Arab nations (including Iraq) do not want democracy, because American democracy brings with it, the churches which have liberal views of family life. Even though the Arab, Muslim and other**

nations do not show respect for women in most cases, they also do not want to be dominated by their women. Even Israel, the first people of God, prior to the establishment of God's Kingdom people of believers on earth (Acts 2), were told how the relationship of man woman and child, and family was to be established and understood, (1 Cor. 11.7), (1Pet. 3.7).

When a society loses the proper design for manhood, it loses also the design for womanhood, which causes the loss of childhood. When churches lose the pattern which God designed for manhood, then you also have the loss of biblical design for womanhood and then the loss of pattern for childhood. As you read the Bible, it becomes obvious that man is the head of the house, as Christ is the head of man.

Both man and woman show children the pattern of God for childhood. Any real woman of God would follow a real man of God. When men are obviously led by the design of God and word of God, there is no Godly woman who would not feel good about being under that man's leadership. When men become weak in their relationship with God and with other men, those men cannot lead a home, or be trusted with the establishment of a home. It will not work. How then could such weak men lead a nation of people? The Bible made no mistake, God is the Author, there is no need to find some way around the greatest plan ever given for the home, and the family relationship. A Godly woman will be a helper to a Godly man.

Today in American society, children seem to be unmanageable, which the churches in America seem to condone, by catering to the little whims and desires of children by putting basketball courts (at great expense) in church buildings, hire more ministerial staff for teaching Bible to children, and trying to appeal to the interest of children, who for the most part, are under no real authority at home anyway.

<u>**Changes in the churches, are not unlike the changes in the American society. Perhaps the two were so closely intertwined that these changes became slowly absorbed by both country and church**</u>. **The protestant denominations of America cried out, "there is no such thing as—separation of church and State" when the cry should have been, "there never was meant to be a joining of the two"**. You don't have to separate what was never joined in the first place. How did the church in America become so politically tuned in on things which are temporary, when the eternal home and behavior as foreigners, strangers and aliens, is the description of and hope for Christians which God gave His people? The song says, "this world is not my home" but the actions of church members say otherwise. Save the country, give us back our country, give us back

prayer in school...etc. etc. thus cry the churches in America. No tune like this is heard from the persecuted church around the world.

There is really something wrong with this picture and it is not with the people in other lands who follow Christ, the real problem in the world, for the followers of Christ today, lies at the foot of the American church, which so much loves the land, that it abides in, that it can hardly set it's affection on the things above it.

Watchman, what of the night? If you fail to warn the wicked, they may die in their wickedness, but their blood will I require at the watchman's hands. Better read this and the words of the other prophets often today my preacher friend, and leave the 'land of the free' at the foot of the throne of God in prayer, your time and money can be better spent, and your message better aimed at the people of God who need to be about our Father's business. That is winning souls around the world, in case you have forgotten.

Awh.

For students only

It all started in the beginning. That's a good place for good things to start. Always try to start at the beginning. It is so much easier to understand things which start at the beginning. When God finished His creation work, the Bible states,"…and God saw that it was good…" Gen. 1. 12. But this was just the beginning of the story. This is where the story, with all of it's parts, the good, the bad and the ugly, began. This is where we have to go as well, if we are to gain an understanding of creation, of mankind's existence and the place of mankind in history.

It was not only 'good things' that were started in the beginning. Something else, that was not good, also started in the beginning of mans history. The Bible begins, with the great words, which could not have been the imaginative words of a writer of any human intelligence on his own. The powerful and great statement, **"In the beginning, God…"** leaves us saying, "wow," what a beginning. A beginning with God right there, this means that science and all the study of man in this generation and generations past, cannot beat this as an explanation of how we got here. This simple statement as the very first words of the Bible, carry enough meaning and explanation as an affirmation of how 'it all started', to give mankind a lifetime of facts to absorb (or to wrestle with, if he does not choose to simply accept these simple words as the final authority on the beginning of life and all creation).

Early in the life of Adam and Eve, or actually in the very beginning of the recorded history of mankind, is the start of a problem that humanity would live with for ever, or at least until the end of time and things as we know them to be. **This problem that came upon the earth**, was the problem of Sin, caused by the entrance of Evil, into the experience of humankind. Sin, or the disobedience of Eve and Adam, brought upon God's perfect creation, a problem which only God would be able to solve.

This is the same problem that becomes the leaven which permeates the entire 'lump' of human existence. The time when Satan, in the form of a serpent, brought before the human race, an idea that God's command and God's purpose should be questioned, is the seed planted that reaped the 'lie' of the ages. **The problem**, or the lie itself, was first introduced, and camouflaged, as a question, before it is uncovered and later discovered to be the 'trick' that the enemy of God (who is also the enemy of all mankind), used to turn God's created children away from the Creator, and win some evil victory over God. Satan could not be cast out from his domain, without a fight, and without trying to make it appear that all humans, who are given the chance to make a choice for good or for evil, will choose evil. If Satan could gain the victory over the creatures whom God created in His own image, then Satan, even knowing his certain destiny, would in this way, take down with him, as many as he could.

So this is where it all started. Every diversion from truth, and every wicked plan that comes into the heart of human beings, has its beginning with this fall, or this desire to be—one's own god. When Satan through his disguised form, succeeded in the Garden of Eden, to turn man and woman from God's command, the 'game was afoot' and the battle lines were drawn. Man's disobedience to God, became the sword used in the hands of Satan to fight a battle that Satan could not win, and that man's involvement in, could only mean the loss of many disobedient and rebellious souls. Perhaps Satan thought that God would not engage him, but God was willing that man's spirit be given to Him willingly, not by force or by coercion. So the test of human will, and the temptation to be 'gods' on our own, which is to choose carnal desires of the 'wide path' or to know God in love and truth, was underway.

This problem which started in the beginning of mankind's existence, was the problem of man's natural desire and narcissistic tendency to be his own god. **The temptation had two parts**: When Satan brought the command of God to the first humans, into the arena of questionable plausibility, we have part one. **Part two** is when the tempter offers a better deal through his interpretation of God's words. First Satan asks the woman, "…has God said…?" which raises the question of interpretation. How do you see this command, Satan asks, what does it mean to you? This sounds so much like the question and answer period one might have in an office of a psychiatrist, or a psychologist. They love to ask, "how do **you** perceive **your problem?**"

Satan suggested to the woman, that perhaps God has not told them the whole story, since the fruit from the tree that they were forbidden to eat, would make them wise, and they would (for themselves be able to decide) know good from evil, why would this great adventure into knowledge be so terrible, how could this be a bad thing. Perhaps God was not really being fair with Adam and Eve, and perhaps the man and woman should decide for themselves what is right or wrong, good or bad. This part of the temptation was too much for the woman to resist, she thought that they as the new additions to creation, could possibly know as much as the Creator Himself, and this thought must have overwhelmed the ego, and the woman 'caved in' and bought into the 'self as god' idea. Every human sin, and act of disobedience stems from this root, of 'I'll decide for myself what is right or wrong, why not be independent, think for ourselves, etc. Today,

this mind set, could be carried into the 'ballpark' of American dreamland thinking, making it very easy to understand why Adam and Eve fell so quickly and so
completely into the grand 'lie' of the ages, which is, 'you will be as god.' Ooops,
easy mistake, but not an easy consequence.

The personal desire for knowledge and God—like characteristics is present
when man is confronted with a decision about the future. Satan said to the
woman—"**you shall be** as gods, knowing good and evil." This is the first time in
recorded history that we get a picture of the lure of narcissism. **You shall be as
gods**, it would be hard to turn that offer down. Here we have the temptation that
the worship of knowledge, brings to town. To make our own decisions about
right and wrong, and thus to have superior knowledge, is a lot of power for people to have and to hold. Sounds like a wedding commitment, and this is what it
was, mankind was tempted by the Serpent, to see two things brought together in
their own lives as one, the ability to know good and evil, and to thus have a position to be as gods. They had seen the great power of the Creator, God. Now, they
can 'smell' the possibility of knowing enough to make obedience to God, seem
unnecessary. The joining of **superior knowledge** and the **independence** to
decide for one's self, what is right or wrong, is a marriage made on earth, not in
heaven. If it was initiated, it would only be the greatest advancement known to
them. Who can decide what is right or wrong, except a 'god.' So to be able to
make one's own decision about this matter is a real 'booster rocket' to the human
ego.

Today in this present evil world, the big lie, is still alive and active, to know
(love and worship of knowledge) and to decide what is right or wrong, makes up
the components which have become permanent bed fellows, and cannot be separated without repentance toward God and acceptance of truth. Mankind's desire
for these two things, **knowledge** and **power to decide**, became the center of
human nature. We do not speak of **knowledge** only in the sense that it applies to
knowing the will of God. Nor do we speak of the **power to decide** as if it was
alone to be used as the way to obedience to God, to maintain the right relationship with God. But this is what these qualities were intended to provide for mankind. Obviously both knowledge and decision making, (limited knowledge and
limited power to make decisions) are essential to human existence. It is the **worship of knowledge**, and **the worship of independent thinking**, that can destroy
the very essence of spiritual development. To be given the ability to think and to
process information is a gift from the Lord our Creator. It is not intended to be a
problem, it should be a blessing, however it is rather the intense and extreme (a
popular word today) **love for these two things** that turn men and women into

creatures of self—destruction. You cannot serve two masters, said Jesus, and we cannot worship any other God than the God revealed in the Bible. The desire to be omniscient, and to be so independent in thought, that God is not needed, is in itself a ticket to doom.

When the serpent convinced Eve that the command of God was something to be taken as an option, or that disobedience was not catastrophic, it all started to take a turn for the worse. The beginning of man and woman's hunger for more knowledge, outside of the loving fellowship and approval of God, was now a risk that they would take, just to see what new experiences would come to them. For whatever reason, Eve and then Adam, would not find the way back to God paved with this newly found knowledge of good and evil, nor would they become as God or equal to God, even though the Serpent strongly promoted the idea that their new food would make that happen. **A lie believed, is a lie to be lived with.**

In this present age, churches have fallen prey to the big lie that started in the Garden of Eden. When religious groups think that being full of knowledge, or wisdom of the world is some great thing to be grasped, and sought after, (apart from the knowledge of God's will) they should be reminded that 1st Cor. 1. 18-31, clearly states, as does 1st Cor. 2. 1-16, that only the wisdom of God can safely direct and determine the destiny of man.

The present hunger for college degrees and educational excellence is completely out of proportion to the emphasis placed upon it by early Christian reformers. The very word of God itself, gives more credit to disciples of Christ who were not formally educated, than it does to those who were of marked intellectual skills. This is why such emphasis today that is placed upon the value of academic skills in the American circle of religious life, is contradictory to Biblical example and command. Those who must translate the scriptures into other languages are the only people who actually need such academic skill and acumen. The preachers for the churches, should not be required by churches, to have some special advanced academic training. If we used more 'lay persons' in the pulpits, then more of the preachers with special training could move on out into the harvest fields of nations and tongues with needs which match the demand for communication to those people groups who have never heard the Gospel of Christ. If the well educated churches of America do not have leadership that is smart enough to figure out who needs whom, and what is the best use of the Christian leadership personnel, then how in the world can the task of world evangelization ever take place? Using the old 'discover your gift,' ploy, or the old well worn excuse of 'I am seeking the leading of the Lord in where I should serve', is not going to bring us closer to reaching all those people of the world who have not heard the Gospel. There must be a common sense approach as well as clear understanding of the 'Great Commission of the Lord' if we shall see any serious change in the number of volunteers who 'feel called' to find the lost sheep.

Who needs to feel 'called' to simply obey a command of God? When we know and understand the command of the Lord, and the will of the Lord for all people of the world, then we know that—verses which tell us those two things, are in themselves, God's call to service, (2nd Peter 3. 9, Eph. 5. 17). Read Acts 16. 9, and Acts 13. 44-49, these are examples of how the Apostles understood the leading of the Lord. They first understood the purpose of the Lord, which was to reach all the earth (Matt. 28-18-20), then they saw open opportunities to find those who were without a knowledge of the word of the Lord, and they were wise enough to leave alone, those who decided not to serve the Lord. In America, few understand either of these principles. The book of Acts is not just a book revealing the Doctrines of the Lord's church, but also the methods of world evangelism. An example is wasted when it falls on deaf ears. Let us be up and doing, so that when Jesus comes again for His people, we will not be found sleeping at the helm.

We must refuse the lie of the enemy that man is able to decide for himself what the will of God is. We must refuse this lie that knowledge is the tool that makes us a 'god' in our own right, and we can therefore choose our own path, when in reality we have died to the world, that we might live unto God. 2nd Cor. 5. 14-20 means that we no longer have any rights to a life that has been given to the Lord for His use. His will now is the only will that counts. Shall we gather at the Bible, as well as gather at the river?

11

From Here to Eternity

✦

Eph. 6, 10-20—Rom. 12-14

If you have lived more than 40 years, you have seen the last 20 years become in America—a mad rush to excellence. But the motive for this excellency in all things, did not necessarily come from the Bible. In a conversation with a B. C. president the statement was made, and later was printed in his college paper, that…"academic excellence is not inconsistent with spirituality". This sounds ok, and sounds true…but the other side of the statement is this….".nor is it any guarantee of the same…" **where in the Bible has academic excellence ever been even equated with Spirituality**???????? Not in Acts 4.13 for sure!

In recent years we have seen the church in America take the persona of an American corporation…where big means better, and better means bigger. But we too in the church in America may have created our own "Enron" scandal. A look at tv ministries, which shows more like a Hollywood play than a New Testament picture of saved people, makes this clear. This has been especially apparent to me after spending 5 months in Sudan with some of those who are part of the world-wide persecuted church.

SAD to say…there is a difference in the church round the world and the American churches in this present time.

Ie. Here you can see names like…"family fellowship center," "Tabernacle of Praise," "Christian fellowship center," etc.

What you emphasize is what you promote. *Focus on the family* has not been a verse found in the bible…as a matter of fact the Bible says that because of Jesus families will be divided not united…a man must forsake all he has to be a disciple of Jesus.

Actually Jesus was saying, not to focus on family.

We can only focus on one thing—that which is needed—Lk.10. 42.

This family theme is taken by American Christians to promote values that will help the country be a better place…wrong motive, because any country and the church anywhere cannot be joined as one—even the church and America.

Acts4.13,14.

American Christians—have followed the pattern of the pioneers and settlers of the usa, moving forward and going into new territory that would bring expansion and development of more land for the new country. Likewise the church in America began to build larger buildings, hire more ministerial staff (especially since the 'fifties'), and call this an advantage for evangelism, **now we can look at the last 20 years, as the 'great church growth' era.** But in reality the church looked like a big corporation with a board of directors, dictating what methods must be used to 'get bigger' and find more customers. This similarity is too close to ignore and it is a picture of an expanding 'religion' just like a company in America would expand and become financially stronger, and therefore socially more acceptable. There is a big difference between the church that Jesus built and the country man built, (even though the founding fathers called upon the Lord to help in the establishment of the new country). On the side of the American churches, you can look back through the years and see the philosophy of great American ideals, such as progress, development, expansion (called growth), which are not found in the scriptures. In Acts and other New Testament letters, the obvious small meetings, in houses and the spreading of the Word of the Lord by the members of the Lord's body, is simply stated. There is not an encouragement from the Apostles to become so visible, and so entwined with the local government and political process, as we have seen in America in the last 50 years.

Here, below is a picture of the progress of all development in America in modern times when making a better country becomes the focus of interest and development rather than spiritual life, which should be the focus of the churches. For example, if the churches in America begin to pay attention to the development of 'self improvement' plans, and tack a Bible verse on them to make it look like there are spiritual goals involved, but in reality there is the fostering of 'better life' teachings for the sake of building a better country, it is still wrong. Notice the human philosophy clearly presented and instilled in the following:

Direction of the American expansion 'dream'.

1. From struggle for survival…to search for convenience

2. from convenience to comfort

3. from comfort to excess

4. from excess to extreme selfishness,

5. from self-love to self-worship. and the extremism means going to the limit in seeking a self-fulfilling life, and a self-satisfying goal.

Now the country and the church in America are in **a battle to have more and keep more for their own selfish greed, at the expense of about 2 billion souls in the world who have no churches, and no Bible. This is not a time for the Church to be weak!** Eph. 6.10, Because of weakness of the church, Islam has entered in. Those who want this present world as their kingdom, and seek revenge for the past history of lost battles against Jews and Christians—(centuries earlier), the Islamic leaders, want revenge and the destruction of all non-Muslim religions.

The church in America is side-stepping the Bible teachings about sacrificial service to God for God's glory, and trying to use the Bible as a means to gain man-made glory for present, world centered acceptance among other nations. It is not God's purpose or the purpose of the Bible to get people to become followers of Christ, in order that they may **feel better about themselves, but to feel better about the Lord. Self-esteem programs and emphasis in psychology or other fields, which deal with trying to create in people an ability to feel better about themselves, are all carnal in nature, not finding any Biblical basis.** The Scriptures clarify the fact that all of mankind are sinners, lost from God's grace, who need repentance and forgiveness from God. **To emphasize some kind of 'feel good' about yourself' philosophy, and leave out this fact of man's sinfulness is incorrect and will lead to pride.**

The reason to find Jesus as the Lord, which is who He is, is not so we can become improved people, but the motive is so that we can glorify the Lord as the Savior of mankind. We are God's creation and we need to see ourselves as having the purpose in life of bringing glory to God, and finding grace in His sight. We are not here for us, but for God. How God uses His servants is up to Him, it is up to us to be sure that God will find us available to serve Him. If a man's motive in coming to Christ, is only to feel better about himself, and to find things for himself that only God can give, this motive is short of the **real' reason for the season'.** Man must seek God because God is the true God, and this God is willing to receive all who come unto HIM to be saved. To become God's person, and bring glory to the Lord of Heaven, is the sole purpose for our existence, and in this motive alone can one find true joy and true purpose in pleasing God. It is not to please us.

This is not a hunger and thirst after righteousness, it is a **hunger and thirst for success, popularity and growth.**

The enemy, (the other religion in this battle)-the Muslims, finds the church in America with it's high, global visibility, and has become afraid that their people will be attracted to Jesus.

The attention of the enemy is now on the Christians and the Muslim religion will do battle with the people of the 'land of the free'. Muslims of course, seek to overthrow the Christian and Jewish religions...This is the reason the Terrorists (Muslim leaders), have struck at the heart of the American economic and political centers. The Muslims see the church in America as a threat to the Islamic effort to place all people under their wing. The Muslims also fear the propagation of the Gospel of Christ into all the world. What stronger (financially speaking) center or base of operation would the Christians have, than the American sources of per-sonnel and money, which when used fully by the Christians, could reach out into the whole Muslim world.

You might be aware of the fact that in the last 10 years, there has been a great increase of Christian workers—choosing to go into the Muslim coun-tries, with the Gospel of Christ. Why else would this 'all of a sudden' attack on America become a strategy of the "Allah" pushers of the world?

The Muslim world does surely not need the American dollars, since the Arab countries are 'rolling' in Oil money. What the Arab nations, and Arab religions (Sunni and Shiite) want, the Churches of Christ do not even value, that is the present evil world-Gal. 1. 4. But in the churches weak approach to world evange-lism, we who follow Christ are hurting ourselves, by crying for someone to save the country (America), and this love for country, saps much of the energy and funds for world evangelism. If we get blindsided by this illusion of American church growth, the enemy will have no problem in restricting the efforts of the Christians in America to go into all the world, as the Lord commanded. But a strike against the United States by Arab nations, is like a strike against Israel as well. We are in a religious war world wide and this includes America of course. Issues are of a spiritual nature, and the church has been caught up in a confusion and dilemma resulting from this connection with the country—which was started on a basis of some biblical goals.

When American Christians became entangled with the affairs of this life, (which thing Paul warned against in 2 Tim. 2. 4), this entanglement became a tool of the enemy. The full power of the Lord's Spirit in His people, in recent years could have given the church in America great strides in fulfilling the 'Great Commission'. But in these recent years, there has been a sad regression into self, and what is more appropriately called, a condition of becoming 'ingrown' but it was given the name of 'church growth'. As many large congregations in American became more excited by their own size, than they did about unreached people groups, and this quenching of the Spirit led to lessons, tapes, books, seminars, conventions, training programs and who knows what else, on how to 'grow the church' in America, individual members lost sight of our persecuted brethren.

Christians simply cannot give full attention to the work of the Lord, with half hearted interest in world evangelism. We cannot serve two masters, and we cannot be found making friends with the world, which is to become an enemy of God. The real church of the Lord in the countries where persecution abounds, must be praying hard that the church in America does not become completely taken down the road, in the extravagance, affluence and deception that permeates the body in this country at this time, See 1 John 3.16-17, 1 John 2. 15, James 4. 4. Repentance is our way back to the Lord, obedience without compromise is the path to faithfulness. Let us be swift to call upon Jesus for mercy, the task He has given us is still undone—Luke 11. 42. Justice is for all, including the unreached people of the world.

The work and ministry of the Lord's people who live in this land of the free—is indeed a work that will stretch from here to all parts of the world, if there is faithful use of the resources that are found in this country. But if the church becomes enamored with it's own growth and expansion, and fails to see 'the regions beyond' there will be a price to pay. A price we cannot afford. Our lives and our focus must be placed upon the people of the world, who have not heard the Gospel. We must not fail them, or we will fail the Lord. We must go from here to there, for the Lord, if we expect the Lord to come from there (where He is in heaven) to here for us. He will return, but we decide if we go with Him or remain for destruction with the unbelieving.

To borrow an old movie title—"*From here to eternity*" is a way to see the path of our lives for God—used for His glory.

12

Grace Trumps—Hedge

✦

Job 1. 10. 2 Cor. 12. 9

Intro. Playing the 'paper, rock, scissors' game, as I recall the rock would be the best, unless paper was chosen, and paper covers rock. In any case, each choice has its advantage or disadvantage. But in **real** life, take a look at the **real** advantage, which covers all of the disadvantages. In the case of Job, the servant of God whom the Lord found faithful to Him, as an upright man who feared the Lord and shunned evil, the Lord God allowed a contest of unparalleled significance to be recorded in the Holy Scriptures. A contest to see if a servant of God was only faithful to the Lord because of the great blessings received from God, or because of reverence, trust and respect for God and believing the fact that God in heaven is the only true God and loving creator of mankind. The outcome—*Grace covers hedge.*

It has been a puzzle to me ever since I heard someone in church offer a prayer request that a 'hedge of protection' be placed around someone why anyone would seek a hedge to be placed around a Christian, when we have all that grace around us already. It should be noted that this 'hedge' as the Devil put it, which was around Job, is actually Satan's perception of God's care for Job. Other than Job chapter 3, and Isaiah 5. where the word hedge is used, (in Isa. 5, the Lord Himself speaks of moving a hedge from his people), there appears no use of the term as something God prefers as a sign of His protection for His people.

Throughout the Scripture, God speaks of being the one who cares for His people, and being the one who delivers His people, but the idea of asking God to place a hedge around His people, seems a bit presumptuous, at least, and like taking a step backward at worst. In Daniel, the three faithful servants of God who were cast into the furnace of fire because they refused to bow to an idol set up by the king, said, "whether the Lord delivers us or not, we shall not bow down to your stupid idol." That might be a bit of a paraphrase, but it is clear in meaning, that those who served the Lord were not about to turn from God even in the face of death. To ask for the Lord to put a hedge around us, is in my opinion not as wise as asking for His grace to be with us and enable us to suffer the loss of all things and depend upon the plan of God in life and in death. For the Christian today, to ask for protection from the enemy is a normal request, but in the model prayer, Jesus said for us to pray that we not be led into temptation, and that we be delivered from evil. A hedge seems to be asking that we never have anything go wrong, or never have a bad hair day. *We seem to be asking the same question over and over, even after it has been* <u>**answered**</u>. Job is the answer for the question about how God can use disaster for bringing glory to His Name. When a servant of God suffers for the sake of Christ (1 Pet. 4. 16), the enemy, Satan and any of his forces can see the power that God has in the life of a believer. Satan's whole argument falls flat when people of faith chose the fear of God and the love of God in place of selfish and carnal desires. If no illness or tragedy came to the followers of Christ, these great moments of triumphant faith would not be there to exemplify the power of Godliness in the world.

We have no need to keep asking questions like, "" *why do terrible things happen to people of faith*?" Is this not answered and well covered in the example of Job? When questions are answered, it is foolish to keep asking them, as if we were not satisfied with the answer. And when God answers a question, it is very adequately answered, there is no other answer and there is no need for further explanation. One thing for sure, we don' t need books on this question like '**why do bad things happen to good people'**—this is answered by the Lord in this book of Job. So we should not even be asking the question. It is obvious that Job's life and experiences prove that those who believe in the Lord, are not overcome by bad circumstances, pain, loss etc. that is why weird things happen to <u>unweird people.</u> It is like the rod of Moses when he went before Pharaoh. The serpent of Moses devoured the serpents of the magicians, **so the good that comes from God has more power than the evil that comes from Satan**. If the magicians had not been allowed by the Lord God to turn their rods into serpents, look what we would have lost in the account. But to see the rod of Moses, overpower uneven odds, we can now understand that Good conquers evil, and we don't have to ask that question again about why it happened. Clue?

When the lawyer in Luke 10 asked Jesus who his neighbor was, Jesus answered that question with an illustration of the Samaritan on the road to Damascus. Now that we know the answer to that question, which is, anyone in need of our assistance is our neighbor, so we do not have to ask the same question over and over. We need to apply the answer. In the same way, once we see the power of God in the life of Job, we know that God delivers and blesses His servants who, if they are like Job, living in the fear of God, and shunning evil and living an upright life, will be in their final days given much more than they lost in the days of trail. This is a picture of this life and the one to come. The first part of Job's life is—us in this world,—the second chapter in Job's life is a picture of the blessings of our future in eternity.

The account of Job's life tells us that in this world (Job's first experiences before the testing of his faith) there can be great blessings. But in the time of loss (as a natural order of life, the rain falls on the just and the unjust), even when we have no hedge about us, and we suffer the loss of all things, there is another chapter to our lives, this is illustrated in God's blessing on Job in a greater way after Job's faithfulness to God was proven. Our lesson in this message of Job's life (1 Cor. 10. 6, 11) which is written for our admonition, is that reward from God will come, (Jn. 16. 33-Phil. 1. 29 1 Cor. 15.19, Acts 14. 22) in its appointed time.

Job is a picture for us of God's power to provide, restore and give greater blessings when the testing and (even the present life) trials of life have passed. We now go through the trials of this present life, and if we are dead to the world and alive to God, crucified with Christ and He lives in us, we shall see the 'end' (last acts) of the Lord that He is good. Therefore our interest should not be placed in a request that we have a hedge about us to keep anything from going 'wrong' as we may see it, *but rather we should pray that God would be glorified in our trials which show the enemy that we serve God, not because we have a hedge about us, but because we have His Spirit and love within us.* (1 Cor. 2. 1-5, Phil. 1. 29,

It is time that the believers in Christ, the real ecclesia, called out people of God in American churches, begin to live up to the example already set by the 'persecuted' church, in other countries of the world. We should not need, all the fancy buildings, multi-staff, seminar pudding, extras, as some milk toast fed, literature stuffed, church members of this country, seem to need. **It is in the context of this American church that members ask to have a hedge of protection granted. Why would such a materially rich church, ask for a hedge** to be put around them, **what do they think they have now?** The American church does not need to ask for more hedge, the American churches need to ask for more sense! Our brothers and sisters and their children, in over 70 other countries of the world face the roaring lion which seeks to devour (1 Pet. 5. 8) them physically and spiritually on a daily basis. They who suffer daily for their faith in Christ, had no hedge in the first place, **they have the power of the risen Savior, the pres-**

ence of the Holy Spirit the hope of the eternal Gospel and they, having died to this world, already live unto God, and will in life and death glorify the Lord of Glory, (2 Cor. 12. 9) May we be as bold!

In Philippians 2. 17-30, it is recorded that Paul spoke of one of his co-workers who had become ill, and in vs. 27 the record states that this man, Epaphroditus, a brother in the Lord had been sick enough to die, but God had mercy upon him. For the work of Christ Epaphroditus was near death, not regarding his own life, so that he may supply a service to Paul, that the church in Philippi had not provided. This is only one account of illness which seemed to be accepted as a normal turn of events in the journeys of Paul and his companions. **No record here of someone being told to 'rebuke' the illness** or being made to feel 'less holy' because of the illness. Even in the Old Testament in 2 Kings 13, Elisha the prophet of God fell ill of the sickness whereof he died. Who is going to say that among God's faithful prophets Elisha was not at the top of the list? Yet Elisha, even in his illness encouraged the king Jehoash, that there will be victory in Israel in Jehoash's reign. Illness, not to be feared nor fought, has never been looked upon in the Bible as something to feel guilty about unless God announced it as a condition brought on by sin.

Now if you can be reminded of all these things, and if some still whine around about needing a hedge, perhaps they need more Sunday school lessons than can be taught, and more sermons than can be preached, because the faith that saves is the same faith that keeps and it is built not on *hedges around us* but on *grace that is all sufficient in us*. Job proved that he did not need the hedge, he did not blame God nor did he curse the Devil, he said, "the Lord gives and the Lord takes away, blessed be the Name of the Lord." God did not explain Himself to Job, about the trial Job was put through, He let Job (Job 42.11) believe that all the evil that God allowed to come upon him was from the Lord and was nothing compared to the great blessings Job received later, and the lessons that Job learned were nothing compared to *the lesson that Satan learned* when he saw the power of God in the heart of one faithful servant of the Lord.

Check out Romans, 11. 33,; 8. 31-39 and let this message be our source of encouragement. Why go back and seek a hedge, when we have a grace that is greater than a hedge, from Him who is glorified in our trials and weakness because His strength is perfected in our weakness in us, not in His hedge about us. Be careful when you pray, **the prayer you say if answered as you wish, may retard the blessing that you seek.** *Let God determine the course, just be sure you are on the team. As for me and my* house, I'll choose grace any time because hedge makes sissies, grace makes heroes, and God is not ashamed to be called their God

(Heb. 11. 16). Want to win this game of reality, then remember—Grace covers hedge, Once the question is answered, don't keep asking the question again, just live by the answer. Remember the time a missionary convention chose the theme "Who Is My Neighbor?" Duh…That question was already answered, so a strong church does not keep asking questions that have already been answered, and *the strong church does not live on the wrong* <u>side of a good example</u>. The great lesson from Job is the lesson that he did *not have to have a hedge about Him, when he knew the Lord above him.* Job did not accuse God foolishly for the events in his life that brought sorrow, he rejoiced in the fact that he knew in whom he believed and that he would at last stand before that God of heaven on that day, he knew that his redeemer lived. Hedges don't reveal what truth as well as trials and grace reveal. Never pray for what you don't need, pray rather to know HIM who does know what we need (Jn. 17. 3). Why pray for something the Bible shows us we don't have to have? If it is not the hedge, but the Grace of God we need and it is the answer that solves the problem, don't keep wrestling with questions which are already answered but keep applying the answer *so you don't have to ask the question again*. And don't look for a hedge *from* God when what you need is the grace *of* God! Grace and peace be unto you!

Al Hamilton
Missionary

13

Is it Nothing to You—All You Who Pass by? Step in and Contribute—Or Strike Out

✦

Lam. 1. 12

It was the theme of Luke 10, in the account of the "good Samaritan," to pass by on the road, and meet a need without passing on by unconcerned. But as Juan Carlos Ortiz had said, we should call him the 'normal' Samaritan, because the only reason we call him good is because we are so lousy, it makes him look good. (The book, Call to Discipleship, by Juan Carlos Ortiz, & Jamie Buckingham, pub. By Logos Intl.) In reality the Samaritan did that which is the normal thing. The Samaritan saw a man in need and cared, and did something about it. The guts of the Christian life, are in this simple formula, found in Luke 10. *Be informed,* (learn of needs and opportunities*), care* (have compassion) and thirdly **do** something about it, (act*). It's the one, two, three steps and you're* **IN, method of service.**

The reason we as Christians were reminded to care for those of our own house, and to meet needs at our doorstep, was because the heavy emphasis and major interest was in taking the Gospel to others. This is why the Scripture states that we must *also care for our own flesh and blood,* because it was obvious that the church as it spread throughout the whole world would be giving attention to the great commission of the Lord. This was a given, so the reminder to care for our own was needed. You have no need to be reminded of what you do daily and with consistence. When a person whose life has been changed by the power of the

78

Gospel, and by giving full surrender to Christ as Lord of all, then part of that change is to go from self, to others, from narcissistic living to unselfish living. We go From taking to giving, from being no. 1 in all things, to becoming number '0' as Paul said 'though I myself be nothing'(l Cor. 1. 29; 1 Cor. 3. 7, 2 Cor. 5. 15, 2 Cor. 3. 5,; 2 Cor.12. 11). Now that the believers care more for others than they do for their own well-being and safety, they are giving evidence to the fact that others now come first because of this life changing message of Christ. You don't have to remind someone who is self-centered and lost in sin's power, to think of himself and his own family, *all he cares about is himself* and his own things and his own family, this kind of selfishness is also a sign of the last days (2 Tim. 3. 2). Today in the churches, it is all turned around, people have to be reminded to "go into all the world and preach the Gospel to every creature…" because the average Christian is only busy with his own things (Phil. 2. 3, 2.4, 2. 21; 1 Cor. 10. 24), it is now just the opposite of what it was like when the early Church became spread all over the earth (in a figure of speech). They had to be reminded to care for their own, we have to be reminded to care about others. There is something very wrong about this reversal of conditions.

It is only when Christ takes control of our lives that we begin to see the needs of others, and how we can meet those needs as Christ would. Today the church of the local family and me fellowship, inc. has turned back and started to get on some road called the *MY Way—HIGHWAY.* It is a road where we just follow our nose to our own pocket, (but even a dog or cat can chase its tail), the circle of self esteem, can only get smaller. The only way out of this vicious circle, is to seek the will of God first, which will lead us to **concern for others**.

The rule of the Godly life of service is the one that Jesus taught and commanded Ifor His followers, what I have called the one, two, three steps and you're in. *Know, care and act.* It can also be **called, information, obligation and operation. Learn** where lost people are in the world, **care** about them and their needs and have the compassion that breaks the heart because of the need others have for salvation, then **do something** about their condition. Much of our churches time today, the total body of believers, is spent in a mode of three strikes and you're out of the picture of missions, **strike one** against us in America, is the continual swinging at gnats and shadows, things hard to hit. We hold sessions about how to **better ourselves**, how to improve our batting average, without getting into the game. We have team parties, team lessons, team practice, tons of coaching but we never leave the home field. The only information we have is how big the other teams are growing, and how to copy their style. *Strike two*, we swing at curve balls, but we don't hit anything, there is no zeal for evangelism, no heart burning for lost souls, no burden that breaks our own hearts. Compassion has passed us by, and we were waiting for someone to throw us some easy, slow pitch that we can hit that will not require sacrifice, or embarrassment.

I remember a young preacher had invited my son's good friend, to come and minister in Florida with him, after his recent graduation from Bible College. The **young preacher said** the reason was, '**he was in a church with a senior minister who was elderly and soon the elderly minister would need to retire, and then the young youth minister could likely become the senior pastor.** The young minister also said, that he was receiving a 'good' salary and had a nice parsonage, with a two-car garage, and his work was comfortable and easy. I think the young youth minister's words were "I really have a good deal down here." Doesn't sound like a Hudson Taylor or William Carey, does it? **Now do you think my words are too hard? Is this Also-a hard saying?** (John 6. 60).

And strike three—without good information, and without deep **compassion** and **concern**, we will do nothing, since we know nothing that needs to be done beyond our Sunday service. Who can care or act? What's the use to look unto the harvest fields, the big league, where championships are played, where heroes are made? We don't intend to get past the locker room of the practice field, we didn't know about all those major leagues, we didn't take time to get ready for real competition, we were busy looking at each other and discussing our uniforms, and our game plan, and practiced on each other until it became the reason for our existence. What harvest fields? We never heard about unreached people, at our church or distant shores, except for a few autographs we collected from those who passed our way from the majors! Anyway, **we can't all** be on the first team, **we can't all** be star players, we can't all leave home and travel the dusty roads that would take us to games away from the home field advantage. This is what we sound like today! What kind of motivation for winning the contest is this? Those who love the game, don't make excuses about why they cannot try out for the team. Those who love God and love others don't make excuses for not being on the field at game time on God's team either. The real 'Called out People of God' hear the Shepherds voice and they follow,they accepted the challenge when it was offered, (Jn. 1. 12) and they shall be on the team to stay, and they will be the called and faithful....

The reason players take care of their health is to be able to play the game better for the sake of the whole team. And for the sake of our being able to reach all the earth with the Gospel, and be the example of love we must be, it was commanded that Saints remember to care for their own as they went on out to do the work of the Lord, in seeking the lost to bring them to Jesus. Even a baseball player has to be reminded to care for the family since he is gone a lot. But they still play the game, we don't just exercise, and eat right, but we get in on the game. Even so in like manner, we don't just go to the meetings, read the rule book, and visit with the coaches and team members, we step up and get in the game. We also send some money home to the fam.

No excuses are needed by *those who love the game*, and the same attitude goes for those who love the Lord they too *do not find some way out, they find some way in—(Phil.2. 5-8)* a way to be involved, because of compassion, and duty, but also because they have the right Spirit, they have a strong unquenchable desire to please God. Step up and Step In, don't come up with the old mega—negative words…we can't all go, we can't all……etc. and arrive at the conclusion—since we can't all win, or all play extremely well, why play at all, it's only a game, right? (Ps. 19. 5; Isa. 40. 31, Jer. 12. 5, 1Cor. 9. 24, Gal. 2. 2, 5. 7, Heb. 12. 1)*, or is it?*

14

Lessons from the Garden

✦

The Other—B.C. (Before Commentaries)
First the Interpreter than the commentary
Gen.3. 1-7

It is interesting to consider the fact, that the first commentary on the Words of God, were these words from the serpent in the Garden of Eden. I believe therefore we can safely say that the first Bible interpreter was someone in the Garden of Eden, the one who thought he could make Adam and Even think, that he knew more about what God really meant, than the Lord God Himself. The idea of making a comment about what God had said, and making it appear different from what God meant, is indeed not a new thought. The Words of God had hardly been spoken to the man and woman when the Serpent decided to interject a new idea, as if the Word and command of the Lord God, was flawed and needed some redefining.

An interpretation is to show one's own understanding of the meaning of something, or to construe. It can also mean to give one's own conception (as in art or music) of a certain expression previously designed. In this case what we have in the definition of interpret, as **to give one's own understanding *of the meaning of something***, as well as to construe. Satan, in the form of the serpent, brought before Adam and Eve, the matter of God's command to them, (to refrain from eating of the fruit from the tree of knowledge of good and evil) with the intent to 'add to' God's plan or God's purpose, or to use the words of God against the real purpose of God. God had simply said, "...of the tree of the knowledge of good and evil, you shall not eat of it, for in the day that you eat thereof you shall surely die," Gen. 2. 17. Here God gave the first man and woman a command and told them the truth about the consequences of disobedience to that command. **Satan's interpretation of God's words to Adam and Eve, was about to become the first commentary on God's word, that we have any record of.**

The serpent (as the form that Satan chose to take), became the great interpreter of Biblical teachings we could say, but with a purpose to construe and twist the words of The Lord, to mean that God was really trying to hold something back from Adam and Eve. In this way the serpent could bring in an objection to God's intent for the two. As the enemy of God and therefore of man, the serpent gave to Eve, a different impression of God's purpose in giving this command about what to eat. What the Serpent did say to Eve, in form of a question, was, "is this what God really said?." Now this statement,(question) about what God had said, brought into question (in the mind of Eve) God's real motive for giving such a command, and in so doing, the serpent could make it look like God did not tell the man and woman all there was to know about God's reason for this restriction. In this way, the serpent could raise a question about the purpose of God in giving such a command, and the serpent could also add some insight to the power of that forbidden fruit. The serpent could make the fruit of the tree look very harmless, as a matter of fact, the serpent said that God was wrong, ("...you will not surely die..."). So we have the question raised, then we have another comment made, that comment was, God knows that in the eating of the fruit the two would have their eyes opened and would be as God, to know good and evil. The idea of being 'as god' must have stuck in Eve's mind, above all the things that the serpent had said. This is a very extensive commentary on God's few words, and His simple command.

Bible commentators today try to bring different verses of Scripture to light on other scriptures, and they **mean to help people** see more clearly what is being said. But this in itself is an interesting process. This is an especially interesting phenomenon since we know now, that in many parts of the world where comments on the Bible and interpretations of the word of the Lord are not available, people still come to Christ and become His followers. People are saved from sin, establish churches, and evangelize others in their 'people group' without the modern tools of the scholar who is known to many in the modern world as a Bible expositor, or author of a commentary on the Bible.

When people around the world come to Christ and become His servants and followers without anything except the Holy Scriptures, it does make one wonder how important all of this commentary on scriptures really is. If you look more closely you will see that where there is great amount of commentary on the Bible and what it teaches,(in America) you will find the most confusion among believers and a multitude of denominations, each with scholars who cannot, for the life of them, agree on many teachings of the Bible. Yet we go on year after year, generation after generation, without any question as to how valuable this great amount of discussion and commentary, **about what the Bible says,** really is.

There is no way to stop all the comments and interpretations about the Bible, and what the Bible states, but we need to be aware of the fact that not all comments on the Bible are from the Bible or from the Holy Spirit. What the serpent in the Garden of Eden said to Eve, and what Satan said to Jesus years later on the mount of temptation was a portion of some of the words of God, but they were used for a purpose other than God's purpose, and they were not in context as God had given them. Jesus did not say in Matthew 4, that what Satan quoted was not really from the mouth of the Lord, Jesus simply said, "…It is written…" in this way Jesus was putting the words of God in the place where God meant for them to be.

Bible commentators today, do not mean to misuse the words of the Lord, I am sure, nor do they intend any misrepresentation of the Lord's intended use of His words. But what we can learn from Genesis 3, is that *even Satan can take Holy Words and use them for an unholy purpose*. What we learn from the Garden of Eden, is, that there was an enemy who wanted to deceive and to destroy the plan of God in the lives of mankind. One way to deceive and to destroy is to misrepresent, misinterpret and misjudge the purpose of God and the words of God, so that men and women will not be able to discern what it is that the Lord God was saying to them.

There was no doubt that Satan used the words from God in His temptation of the Lord Jesus, to make it appear as if God might mean something other than what was obvious. But Jesus, using the words of the Father in the way they were intended to be used destroys any other possible intention and any other possible interpretation of His Father's words. Since the scriptures state **in 2 Cor. 11,** that Satan himself disguises himself as a messenger of light, we can be prepared for false teachings, to be the result of misuse of the words of God. And since there is so much division and confusion among church leaders in so many denominations, we know that what Satan started in the Garden of Eden was just the 'get go' and there has **been poor understanding of the will of God because of poor understanding of the word of God.**

There may be no evil intent in the minds of those who bring us a commentary on the word of God, perhaps to some extent, this is what we all do when we discuss the scriptures to gain greater understanding. But the commentary about the meaning of the scripture, and the interpretations of Bible verses has become so common that people do not turn to pages in the Bible for answers to their questions, they often seek out other sources for their answers. If today there was a burning of the commentaries, there would be no harm done to the scriptures at all. Again I say, we know this because we know that many Christians around the world do not have any of this added comment, and they only have what God Himself through His writers and translators have provided, if they are blessed enough to have the scripture in their own language at all.

Perhaps a return to the old paths may be what we need, and a return to the old methods of New Testament evangelism (Jer. 6. 16). Just tell someone about the will and the Word of God, maybe the Holy Spirit will direct the words you speak into good soil, it has happened before. My opinion of what has happened in America, is that too much concentration on one country in the world (the USA) made people keep on teaching the same people, over and over, since few wanted to leave their land, to go out into regions beyond,—and this created a condition wherein the church pours all the salt on one spot, and we keep shinning our light in each others eyes until we are seeing more poorly and tasting less surely, the things of God. It is much like my definition of two terms very important to the American social structure. **Political freedom** has come to mean,' something where **no one has to agree with anyone** at any time', and **religious freedom** has come to mean 'something where **everyone disagrees with someone else** all of the time'. **I believe it was the worship of freedom which gave both political and religious freedom this wrong identity,** when the enemy of all that is good, put evil ideas for selfish intent, in the minds of good people. **Sometimes poor understanding of the Bible teachings,** raises it's ugly head in very subtle ways.

One of which is most recent: In an article of the missionary magazine, entitled 'Horizons' on page 11 in the November issue, is a statement by a very good, young friend of mine, who has been submitting missionary insights to this magazine for some time now. Here is the quote, "One of the things that we are seeing **change** in the role of women in missions is their growing role in planning and implementing the vision of mission projects. Oftentimes in the past, the missionary wife was **simply** (my emphasis) seen as dutifully following her husband to the field and carrying out "assignments" or work that he assigned to her."

Now, perhaps it is the generation gap (which is an invented term for use by those who have little appreciation for, or no idea about, the biblical value placed upon the passing of information from generation to generation), and then again it may simply be a slip of the biblical perspective, that makes someone make a statement like this. As one example, among many, my wife happened to see her calling from God, as that of helping to make me able to fulfill my calling from

God. This meant 'being a keeper at home' caring for the children and needs of the family, (Titus 2.), and fulfilling the scriptures as (a wife to an elder), required. In this way, my wife, (as the weaker vessel—1 Pet. 3. 7, a Biblical perception of the woman, and accepting her position in Christ with honor and joy), has not been in the 'spot light' of church brotherhood events, and at all conventions, etc., but we have four children, all of whom are missionaries, with spirit and attitude worthy to be examples to any youth today. The children God put in the house of my wife and myself, have learned how to love others, handle failures in life with God's help, by learning how to trust God's mercy as much as trusting God's power, they learned to overcome peer pressure, (since they did not depend on a college degree to earn their acceptance among brethren), and how to win people to Christ, start house churches in several countries, lead teams of younger missionaries and do what God has given them the calling and strength to do, as His servants.

Now you don't learn these things simply from books, classes and much study. You learn it as Paul stated (**2 Tim. 2. 1-4**) from those who were your family, those who brought you to Jesus, (**2 Tim. 1. 5**) and mentors. If this is a sample of what the author meant by the wife—**simply** being one who carried out duties given by the husband,(which is very biblical), then I don't think I would recommend this change in role, the author speaks of for future missionaries. My recommendation is, to go back to the Bible principles and examples, as well as the bible teachings, and avoid these coming changes in the role of the wife, that the author speaks of in this article.

If the coming changes mean that **Mrs. Missionary** is now doing the work the men should be doing, then perhaps my statement some years ago at the men's clinic in Michigan, (Northmen) is right on target. I had stated that many of the problems in church and country, are due to some changes I had seen coming for many years. Which is—**men becoming weak, women becoming strong (women's lib movement), and children becoming confused.** You will notice that each of these problems causes the resulting follow up problem. When men became weak spiritual leaders or just weak and soft men, then women became strong (in authority, responsibility and position etc.) and children naturally became confused. Children need to know what a man is like and what a real woman is like. If the role is switched, it creates confusion.

I won't take time to give examples of each of these causes, and their results, (though I know of many and would provide this information upon request). But you can very well notice them in the next news broadcast or news paper when you observe some of the critical conditions of our time. In the churches, there are examples of this departure from Biblical principles. You also know that when God called Moses in the desert, He did not run to the wife of Moses **to get her permission** to give the call at the 'burning bush' to this great shepherd. Nor will you find men of God afraid to tell their wives, that God has called them to a task for Him. Check out the lives of men like William Carey, David Livingstone, and many more. **We also see God calling women like Gladys Aylward, Amy Charmichael, Corrie ten Boom and others.**

The point is not that God has not, and will not continue to **use men and women** in His great plan to give the Gospel to the whole world, the point is that each person must follow the path that God designed for them, as they were told in the Scriptures. **Wives have ministry at home with family,** so that their husbands can do their work in the kingdom of God, so states the word of the Lord in **Titus 2. 1-15.** It is not—**a simply** dutiful wife, <u>it is a biblical, God fearing woman, serving as the help-meet to the man of God,that called messengers of God were meant to be.</u> As for me and my house, I will take the dutiful wife, you other guys can have the **new 'role' model,** and may the 'book on new methods for missions', be with you!

A second illustration of how the enemy works the system, and the minds of men, who are somewhat anxious to please the Christian populous, can be found in 1 Kings 13. In this example, a young prophet (man of God) is talked into disobeying a command of God, by an older prophet who was used by the Lord to test the spirit and commitment of the younger prophet. It is an example of the seriousness of God about His own Words. It did not matter that the young prophet was lied to by another prophet, the young man failed to obey the strict command of the Lord, and his life was taken from him for that disobedience. In 1 Cor. 10. 11, the Scriptures state that things in the records like this one in Kings, happen to help us understand the way of the Lord. The things written in earlier times, were written for our admonition and for our benefit, that we may learn from these events and teachings and therefore avoid the mistakes of others and be reminded of the serious consequences of disobedience to the Word of God, and therefore the will of our God. In Acts 5, the death of Ananias and his wife Sapphira give evidence of the same thing, that God is serious about His words to mankind. Notice in 1 Kings 22. 22, when a lying spirit was put into the mouth of false prophets, and the Lord used this to get rid of a wicked king. A king was persuaded to go against the will of God, which will of God had been given clearly to him by the prophet Micaiah, earlier in the account of 1 Kings 22. The heart of the wicked king Ahab, had already decided not to accept the word that displeased his own purpose, so he fell prey to the lies of false prophets.

When commentators begin to take liberties and give themselves 'wide birth' with their explanations of bible verses, they do not often realize that they tread on 'holy ground.' The subject of baptism is a noted and obvious example of how bible commentators, or scholars, become bible 'terminators' they wipe out true meaning to please the Christian population. I have a letter written by a Bible Translator (for a Bible translation ministry), from a file that was given to me by men (Dan Piatt and associate) who had begun a service sometime around 1974 called, 'Final Advance of Scripture Translation' (FAST). The letter states that the young translator decided to translate the word baptize, as "go down to the river and splash water on yourself", because a church in that tribe (or people group) already established was practicing sprinkling as a 'form' of baptism. So, instead of translating the word as (he may have wanted to for accuracy) it should have been translated from the original Greek, **he used some** term which would allow the 'practiced' form to be made 'the acceptable' form. Do we not all realize this is not uncommon? Often men teach doctrines of their own by the comments they make in a book called a 'commentary' on the Bible!

We do not have Christians in other lands, begging us to send them scholars to create commentaries on the Bible, we have them asking for Bibles in their language. Some churches who have been taught that special Christian education material is helpful to their Christian life, do ask for these added aids, but we do not have time to waste bringing people materials they don't have to have, when there are millions of people still waiting for their first words of Holy Scripture. If we can't do both, then lets at least get some help to those who are in greatest need of the most important words they will ever here, words whereby they may be saved, (Acts 10.,& 11. 14). If we have to put **all of our efforts** into reaching the unreached people**, then let it be so,** and **if someone must be without the desert**, so that others may have at least the bread of life, let it be so. It does not take a really wise man to see the difference between desert and bread. Be not unwise, but understanding what the will of the Lord is Eph. 5. 17. If we don't know the word of God we will not know the will of God.

From some of the Bible commentators we learn some very interesting facts. Fact one is that many of them like to add an opinion to a doctrine or teaching. In the New Analytical Bible and dictionary of the Bible, KJV, printed by John A. Dickson Pub. Co. Chicago, on page 1341, under the section entitled, "The sufficiency of Christ," paragraph 2, we find the following statement, and I quote, "The reason why we are free from the law is because of the sufficiency of Christ. **If we were under the necessity of doing something, or something to observe, as a saving measure,** then we would be under law, a debtor to the law, and not under grace. "For the law was given by Moses, says John, but grace and truth came by Jesus Christ. (Jo. 1. 17)" End of quote.

Now what we have here (above) is a shining example of what I call, '**comments that are carriers of man made doctrine**'. The commentator has added opinion to scripture, and in that comment he has added a teaching of his own (which is an opinion held by himself and many others). You will notice **the subtle interjection of an opinion to create a doctrine**. The pre-conceived idea of the commentator is that 'there is nothing man can do to receive the free grace of Christ. This can be worded in various ways and fashions, but you can easily tell that this is the point of the writer of this commentary on verses about the law of Moses and mankind's duty to obey the Lord. If you examine the above quote closely, here is what you see happening.

The commentator says, "we are free from the law because of the sufficiency of Christ." But he fails to state that he is speaking here in context, of the law given to Moses, from God, to the Israelites. Then he adds words that have nothing to do with the subject of the law given to Moses. He simply makes an unconnected statement—"**if we were under the necessity of doing something,** or (under the necessity of) something to **observe as a saving measure, then we would be under law**". **This** statement has no connection to this subject he is discussing. But now what law is he referring to? Is he speaking of the law of Moses given to the Jews? Because if he is, this is different than the law we have in Christ, which is …"that we love God and love one another," (1ˢᵗ John 2. 8, 9—1ˢᵗ John 2, Rev. 12. 17).

Secondly, why does he interject an entirely different thought about "doing something, or observing something of a saving measure?" You know that he is trying to teach you some new thing, which is, that man can do nothing, himself, for salvation, or mankind would be under law. Now what law is he talking about? Because to leave this without clarity, is wrong, since **we who follow Christ are indeed under law,** the law of Christ our Lord, again refer to Rev. 12. 17. And **that law is,** as stated by the Apostle John (and remember we who are Christ's are commanded to continue in the Apostle's doctrine, Acts 2. 42,) to love the Lord and love one another. **So we are under law,** ("…on this law, hangs all the law and the prophets…" Luke 10. 25-28). The friendly commentator, however is saying that "**if we are under the necessity of doing** something, or under the necessity of observing something as a saving measure, we would then be under law." **What law?** Well, **we are** under law, but not the law given to Moses for the Israelites, but under the law of Christ, to love (and obey the Lord Jesus, as our Master and Savior), and love one another, (John 15. 12). If we are obligated to obey a commandment (or commandments), we are indeed under the Law that the giver of the commandment has established. And it is without a doubt 'doing something,' because Jesus said to the lawyer in Luke 10, "…you have answered correctly…**this do and you shall live…." This is observing something as a saving measure.**

My question is, why does the wise commentator not explain, that there is a difference between the law of Moses for the Israelites, and the New commandment (Mk. 12. 31, Rev. 12. 17), that we love God, and love one another. On these two commandments, hang all the law and the prophets. And man is commanded **to observe and do** those commandments. So then, there is something we must do, if we are to be obedient to the will of God, in His Son, Jesus Christ. This means the commentator is wrong, and to believe his opinion about this matter, would be to miss the truth revealed by the Lord and His Apostles.

If there is nothing we can do, according to the commentator, and nothing to observe (as a saving measure), **then why this teaching of Jesus, and His Apostles, about** what we must do, when the people on Pentecost were told …'what they must do' in answer to their question **"…what must we do?"** And furthermore why did Jesus on the road to Damascus say to the Apostle Paul, who was then just known as Saul of Tarsus, "…go into the city and you **will be told what you must do…"**

The commentator in the above example, has not been careful enough, to clarify that the law of Moses, for the children of Israel, was fulfilled in Christ, and now the law of grace is that law which Christ the Lord and His Apostles have given to His followers.

For the man to say that there is nothing that we are under necessity to do, or to observe is not at all correct. The commentator can emphasize the fact that man, on his own could not earn a way into God's grace. This can be said and understood without jumping into a 'quick sand' of inaccuracies, to prove some point about his personal opinions on salvation. **The use of key words like 'sufficiency of Christ'** and other terms to try and tie the law of Moses into the new age of grace is really an awkward way of writing his own commentary on salvation, but to do it, he is guilty of the misuse of simple verses and of overlooking basic Bible doctrine, which is, "…He has given His Spirit to all who obey Him…" Acts 5. 32. Try obeying God without doing anything! Sorry commentator, you missed not only the bull's eye, but the whole target. If Baptism is done in obedience to a command, and if obedience is necessarily required of a person to be saved, (since the disobedient—those who do not obey will be condemned), than baptism is necessary for salvation. Only those who obey receive the Holy

Spirit (Acts 5.32), and no one is saved who does not have the Holy Spirit, so we can know how important Baptism is, and all commands of the Lord and His Apostles, if we can add 2 + 2 and get 4. Jesus said, "man shall not live (or receive life) by bread alone, but by every word that proceeds from the mouth of God." Matt. 4. 4.

Is it now becoming clear what we mean by commentators who turn scripture that is clear into doctrines of men that are clearly wrong? Perhaps the lessons from the Garden, in Genesis, did not get across to the man who made the comments I have quoted from in the "New Analytical Bible." Can you see how subtle is the purpose and plan to make a doctrine of man's design, (that is so commonly expressed), by using words like "...there is nothing you can do for salvation, since it was all done by Jesus on the cross."? So many people jump on this 'band wagon' and say Yeah' yeah', (like the old movie cartoon of the 40's, where the crow on the scarecrow's shoulder just simply agreed with everything the scarecrow said, by saying-"yeah yeah').

Notice what is happening in the development of a 'man made doctrine' by this example. A person (usually a preacher) takes an accepted statement, such as 'man cannot do anything to save himself,' which is a statement that can only stand when you consider it with the added statement such as, 'man cannot do anything to save himself—without the fact of God sending His Son to die for the sins of mankind, (for man cannot forgive himself for the sins he commits against the Holy God of all creation). And he takes this accepted statement of man's inability to save himself without Christ, and brings into it, a command of the Lord, such as 'to be baptized (immersed into Christ)', and makes the command of baptism seem powerless to have any part in man's response to the Lord's call to salvation. And yet Baptism is a command of the Lord. And in the book of Acts the Apostle Peter said—"save yourselves from this crooked generation."

But many commentators do not want to give such lengthy explanations for sake of being biblically correct, many of them want to use the Bible to make a point for their own belief system. This just happened to be what the first commentator on the Words of God, had in mind in the Garden of Eden. I know as you do, that not all comments of the Bible commentators are incorrect, or meant to twist the meaning of the speaker in the Bible record. But what we do need to learn is that all commentators on the Bible are not sent by the Lord either, just as many prophets of the Old Testament record were not sent by the Lord. Test the spirits, said the Apostle John, for there are false brethren (2nd Cor. 11. 26), **and many false spirits in the world,** some of them are called, Bible scholars. Oops, easy mistake. (1 John 4. 1, 2John 7,8).

15

The Gnat and The Camel

✦

Matt. 23. 24

In countries all around the world, there is not a sign of people out shopping for the cosmetics, the nice clothes, the new cars and new houses, nor do people wait for the results of the stock market reports. There is no rush to buy tickets for the ball games, or long lines at the rides at Disney Land or Six Flags, no choices about how to spend the pay check, or how to apply for a new job.

The things that are different about the church in America and the Christians in other lands, are so obvious. It's the things that are missing. ***It is what does not happen in most of the world, not what does happen***. In a recent article by Lou Dobbs, in U.S. News and World Report (Oct. 13, 2003), Mr. Dobbs wrote an article entitled America the Unloved. He spoke of the Billions of dollars that are received in aid all around the World. A 1998 study of U.N. votes found 7 4% (seventy four) of foreign aid recipients voted against the United States the majority of the time. India, for example which received $143 Million in U.S. aid voted 80% of the time against the United States. Egypt, which received more than 2 Billion dollars voted against the U.S. 66 percent of the time. Mr. Fouad Ajami says that most Americans are asking the wrong question about this problem. They ask "why are we so involved with these nations, what's wrong with the United States?" They should be asking, we are so involved with these nations, ***what's wrong with them?*** This is a most distressing dilemma for most Americans, and trying to decide which is the right question to ask, certainly is perplexing. Yes, other nations should be grateful to America but that's the world for you, it is all dirt, you can't sweep the planet off and clean things up. It goes clear to the bone (in this case to the core).

As Alvin Toffler in his book, "Third Wave" wrote some years ago, it is far better and far more important to ask the right question, than it is to get the right answer to the wrong question. If the question is wrong, it won't matter what the answer is, the answer is irrelevant. You can't get the right answer, if you are asking the wrong question. For Christian people we have a similar dilemma, they too ask the wrong question. They always approach those of us in foreign missions, with the old question "…what will happen to all the people who die without hearing the Gospel of Christ.?" That is not the right question, the right question is "'… what will happen to the believers who do not take the Gospel to the multitudes who have not heard (Rom. 10. 14)? That is the question that should concern the saved people. (Matt. 24. 14., Rev. 7. 9,10) states that *the Gospel will reach all nations*, the question is not, 'will the game be played, but rather the question for us is, *are we going to be on the team, not-'will there be a game.'*

We know the Gospel will reach the ends of the earth before Jesus comes, so the question for us is not what happens to other people who die without the Gospel, that matter is in God's hand. The question that concerns the church is, what will happen to us when we face Jesus and have nothing to say when we give an account of our failure to get in on the task as stewards of the Gospel (1 Cor. 4. 1), to carry out the great commission in our years of opportunity? (1 Pet. 4. 17).

To answer the question about America's involvement with nations around the world who show no gratitude, is simple. The nations of the world are run by people who do not understand the values of America, truth, justice and democracy. At least that is how Americans and most other nations, see America. So to change things in the world where war and suffering exist, America will always need the oil, and resources to carry out the American goals of being a major military power to help establish and maintain justice for all. The resources of the whole world, are vital in trying to bring some measure of harmony into the united world scene, for the purpose of promoting and sustaining the values that America holds dear, which values many nations accept as equally important to world peace.

When we compare the country and the church we see some parallels with purpose and goals. The church in America looks so modern, plush, rich, and prosperous with the nice buildings, the multi-staff churches, the seminaries, the extravagant even elegant show of unparalleled wealth, that Christians around the world, wonder how all of this wealth can be accumulated and remain in the hands of such a small minority of the total body of Christ, while the rest of the world languishes, some without a knowledge of the Gospel (in spiritual draught) and some, though saved, yet left by their brothers and sisters in Christ in America, to suffer alone.

The country of the United States is very similar in its appearance to the rest of the world on a social plane. Here is a small percent of the world absorbing such a large and unbalanced percent of the world's goods. It doesn't matter how it was obtained, with centuries of work, planning, courage, effort etc. etc. and all with freedom of worship which brought the favor and blessing of the Lord God of Heaven. What matters to the world now, is why they see such prosperity, no matter why or how it came about, and their question is why can they not have the same standard of living, under their own government (which is perhaps not democratic or a republic nor free), They may not realize that the path to prosperity is paved with freedom that is both spiritual and social.

Since, however, these nations which used to envy America, now begin to hate America, a whole new picture has been drawn. Since the U.S.A. could not help everyone, and since not every nation wanted to follow in its' footsteps, we now find the envy turning into jealousy and the jealousy into hatred. Much of the world today, seems to be saying, since we cannot equal America, and since we cannot defeat America, we will oppose it, in the media, in the world courts and in all areas open to us in world wide communication until we make others the enemy of America and we build an embattlement of distrust that will bring America to its knees before a bitter and enraged world, we will call this effort the "***court of world opinion.:*** In this arena, the enemies in the world think America can be defeated.

The church in these 'perilous' times should be setting an example. We too, like the country are seen by others around the world, even other ***Christians as living in extravagance and luxury.*** Instead of looking like the country it lives in, the church should stretch out it's hands with a giving that is sacrificial, (not just 10% with bragging) and that is determined to find these who are listed as 'unreached' and put aside selfish involvement in further embellishments that would embarrass the Apostles and Prophets of God of years gone by. It is obvious that the government of America is not going to change the world by making every other country accept its persona. But the church in America, with it's wealth and extravagance could well get it's job done, as the Lord commanded, because many souls around the world can become followers of Christ right under the terrible conditions of their social Hell they have to endure. Jesus plainly said, "***in this world you will have tribulation,*** but be of good cheer, I have overcome the world." The suffering that people endure for the Name of Christ, only shows that faith is more powerful than politics, love and Hope are more powerful than fear of tyranny, dictatorship and deprivation. So this Jesus who first suffered and died for others, leads an army of followers who are ready to do the same, which simply proves their oneness and sincerity and their faith in the Holy God of heaven. These who suffer today in Christ, for Christ are the people who will be found faithful upon the return of Christ. *The people who need to be concerned in America are the unconcerned church members who bear little resemblance to Saints of days gone by.*

Is the church in America gagging at a gnat while swallowing the camel? Check out your own congregation, what message do you hear every Sunday? Is it a *fix everything in America first message* (or mush-age) America is *also a mission field, we have to take care of our own,* we can't all go to the regions beyond, *wait until we solve all the drug problems in everyone's life, all the marriages are fixed, all the crime is stopped, everyone in the country attends church* (the right one of course) with regularity, and all the kids in school love one another? If that is your goal in your life or your church, you are in deep troubled waters my friend. Jesus finds as faithful those whom he (Matt. 24:42-51) finds *GIVING FOOD AT THE PROPER TIME TO THOSE IN THE HOUSEHOLD.* Most of the feeding and funding done by American churches, is going to the American church…Check it out for yourself. If any part of the world is left out, any part of the household was not given equal opportunity, to have the Bread of Life, someone is going to pay, (see 2 Cor. 8.) The field is the world, the seed is the Word of God (Word of Life) and the sower is the one who proclaims that Word (Rom. 10. 14-21). The Lord of the Harvest will make the seed grow, when it finds good soil, God will give the increase in other words, but the task of the body of Christ is to keep moving, keep sowing, until the whole world knows. What the hearer does with it, will (as in America or any country) be up to the heart of the recipient. WE must be about our Father's business.

In the Churches across the land, there are small and unimportant diversions, which occupy the time and attention of this rich and affluent church age. (see Matt. 23. 24). *There are matters of concern which do not compare* to the terrible atrocities that face our brothers and sisters in Christ where persecution abounds and continues. *The gnats* which Christians in America seem to 'gag' at are so numerous and ridiculous that it could hardly be necessary to innumerate. *Worried about prayer being outlawed in public schools are we?* Concerned that the wrong politician may be voted into a seat in the Senate or some other high level government position are we? This is the talk you hear about, in churches even when over 5,000 Christians die around the world, every two weeks, for their commitment to Christ. America has a church attendance list of over 85 %, of its' entire citizenry. Over 80% of Americans claim they have a 'born again' relationship with Christ. When we look at the definition of a 'reached people group' as presented by the most reliable sources of missionary and Christian resource authorities, as being any group with 20% of its society being adherents to Christianity, and an unreached people group being those where less than 20% are Christian, you can imagine how out of balance this equation is and yet we hear that American preachers (pastors they call them) think the country needs more churches, more ministers, and more buildings. This means that the concern of the believers in America for the people who suffer without the Gospel (and that is real suffering too) is so diminished, that every Bible congregation in America should be embarrassed to sing, "Onward Christian Soldiers," (although many have quit singing hymns anyway) *Today we look more like the Israel of EZ. 18. 48-50,* when God told Ezekiel that His people were like their sister Sodom, wow, what a smack in the chops…God said, '**this was the sin of your sister Sodom**, <u>abundance of idleness, fullness of bread and they did not care for the poor and needy.</u>

When I was in Sudan, as a volunteer for Voice of the Martyrs, we were distributing clothes and 'life packs' to the people, and in one village an elderly couple, were in the crowd un able to move to the huge pile of clothing to find something, so I watched them to see what they really wanted, and then I caught the gaze of the woman who must have been in her 80's. She was noticing a dress which was brightly colored, and I moved to the front of the anxious crowd of people and took that dress to her, for she had only old and worn out pieces of garment,barely enough to cover her tall frame. She received it with both hands, which is the custom, and in tears she stated in her own 'dinka' language, "this is the greatest day of my life." Now for someone 80 years old, that is saying a lot. The donor of that dress has no idea how this made her feel. I felt that I had seen the face of Jesus who said, "…you have done it unto me…" (Matt. 25). This is why failing in our duty to care for the poor and needy is a sin. This *sin was what led to their debauchery in the days of Ezekiel.* Sexual perversion was not the sin, *it was the result of the sin.* They had *idle time* (maybe Idol time), *affluence,* and did not *look after other people* in need. This is a sin in any generation by any people. America has the same problem, it has sinned, so has the church in America, we have become affluent, idle (Disney land time etc. entertainment conscious, basketball courts in church buildings etc.) and leaving out of our lives the poor and needy of the land and of the world), so now like America, (abortion, compliance with homosexual conduct etc) reaps the results of it's sin, and the church looks too much like the country and it too may find judgment unfriendly.

My point is clear, let's get ***real,*** so we can decide how to get ***right*** with God. We do not face the reality that God is expecting the people who call themselves by His name, to also care about others who have no chance to help themselves. We do not seem to realize that the God of Heaven who sent His Son from heaven to earth because He so loved the whole world, expects His followers to also love the whole world and not just plow one small (5%) part of the world, but sow the seed over all the earth. The necessary data on where the unreached people of earth can be found and who they are is already on hand. Does your preacher tell you about this? Does he announce anything about the number and names of people who died last week for their faith in Christ? These people, my friend are your brothers and sisters and mine. I think we should know when a family member needs someone to stand up for them and with them in this period of "last days" events. All the talk about when Jesus will return is not going to 're-set God's time piece, but if we want to deal with the real question that concerns us, we better ask ourselves at Sunday school and church, when will we be told how to be about our Father's business instead of how to vote for the right politician. *Matt. 24. 14 is a clue however about the timing of the Lord's return!*

You can't get to the right place by taking the wrong road, and we cannot walk in the fear of God while we are so afraid that we might offend the community or the country or any other creature. No wonder the Lord said, You shall love the Lord your God with **All your heart, all your soul and all your strength. This** is so we won't have any room left to while away the hours on lesser things. This camel might come back to bite us when the books are opened.

Al Hamilton
Missionary

16

Mixed Messages

✦

Or/Mush-age, the age of the mixed up church
1 Samuel 3. 19

The Lord was with Samuel, and let not of his words fall to the ground.

What happened long ago, when Jesus was tempted by the 'Old serpent' the Devil (Matt. 4), who had tempted Adam and Eve in the Garden, (Gen.3) was a trick of the Enemy that has not changed. It is the plan of taking verses of Scripture which are the Word of God to His creation, and making them appear as if they could be used for our human nature, or for personal opinion to be substantiated. This is the common ploy of the Tempter. The Devil quoted a Scripture or some words from the Word of God, which are true words of God, but Satan uses them to mean something out of context or to support a purpose that is different from the real design and intent of the words when spoken by the LORD within His intended purpose. In 1Cor. 5. 9,10, the Apostle Paul explained the true and real context of his words, when he said, "I wrote to you in a letter, not to company with fornicators (sexually immoral), yet not altogether with the immoral of this world, or with covetous, or extortionists, or with idolaters; for then must ye needs go out of the world." In this example words are given within a context that deserved explanation. This teaches us that the Word of the Lord must be taken within its context and intended purpose, a very common and general rule of communication. If explanation is needed it will be given, as in this case in 1 Cor. 5.

Yesterday in an e-mail I received a word meant for encouragement from a dear Christian friend. Nothing could have been a more clear and exact example of the very point to be made in this article. The following is a portion of that E-mail message:

"May this encourage you always:" was the title, the following is an excerpt from the message.

> Don't spend major time with minor people. If there are
> People in your life that continually disappoint you, break
> Promises, stomp on your dreams, too judgmental, have
> Different values and don't have your back during difficult
> Times...that is not a friend....Surround yourself with
> People who reflect values, goals, interests and lifestyle.
> (of your own I presume).

The author of the above message, did express her personal faith in God, and gave thanks for family and friends, she went on to say, "Remember what your elders used to say, "Birds of a feather flock together. **If you are an eagle, don't hang around chickens**: Chickens can't fly." Then the author spoke of Phil.4. 13, and agreed that she was nothing without the Lord, but with Him she could do all things...That is very real. I agree.

But let me explain what is mixed up on this message. A person, will see the parts they want to see, and be encouraged, if they are looking for some theme that exalts their ego. Especially if the part that suits their agenda about success, and about being positive and progressive, can be supported in a way that makes it appear he will receive God's blessings. As I just stated however, if you don't think past the words that say, "If you are an eagle, don't hang around chickens because chickens can't fly," you will miss the error of this very encouraging (to some) message. **I suggest** that even though eagles fly, they don't provide you with eggs and meat for nourishment either.

When you are hungry, go kill an eagle and eat it. Not me, I will be happy to be around the place where chickens hang out. I can get eggs and meat from a chicken, and I will at least have food, and you eagle lovers can just stand and watch your dinner fly overhead, happy hunting my friend.

Soar all you want, when you land don't come to me and ask for eggs for breakfast, I'll send the person who values self-esteem to the nearest zoo, maybe they will let him hunt their eagles or even sit in the cage with them, so you can observe their greatness up close! Now, would you like to examine the encouraging message (mush) further? Take a look at part one. "Don't **spend your major time with minor people**." Now that would go over good with Jesus and His Apostles, for thing one, *__there __are __no __minor __people__ .* So now (if you follow this advice), where will you spend your time? Perhaps in your little den of other important eagle like souls such as yourself. Jesus chose followers and Disciples who were finally called the scum of the earth (a title that they gave themselves). So if you learn that Jesus, the Son of God, the Lord and Creator of all the universe and of all things therein, including mankind, chose simple men, and the poor and the outcast, the rejects of humanity, why **would you seek** to avoid the very people that Jesus collected? But wait, here is the clincher, the writer of the wonderful encouraging message of mush says a lot that is true. She acknowledges the fact that we are nothing without Christ the Lord, and in Him we can do all things. Why is this such a conflicting word or Mush of message? Notice how **two thoughts are run together as if they are equal**, but **yet they are opposites**. Point being—when Paul wrote these words in Philippians, the context-(Ah-there's the rub) is about being able to abound (or have plenty) or to do without, (have little or nothing). It is a context of being able to be content with whatever supplies and necessities are available to him. "I can do all things through Christ who strengthens me." This is stated in the context of, being content with much or with little of this earth's goods. Now you can use this out of context if you like, to mean all things at all times for any reason, since it is a verse that looks good when covered with any coating of choice, and it is hard to argue against it when it stands alone.

But you have no verse of scripture which supports the idea that you should avoid the people whom you consider minor persons, because the book of James states that it is a sin to show prejudice against the poor and those in low economic status (James 1, and 2). Let the brother of low degree rejoice in the fact that he is exalted (In Christ) and the Rich should rejoice in that he as the flower of the field will soon pass away and be gone from his position and his prominence. Then there is the verse that states, is it not the rich who oppress you and bring you into court? (James ch. 2).

Now I wanted to use this little example of mixing scripture with poor philosophy, as an illustration of man's error in trying to be a Christian in order to be successful, rich and well liked by all, even by the unsaved souls of the land. It helps to explain the dilemma we have today in the church. Today the church wants the 'ear tickling' message of prosperity, this little message related herein is only a small sample of **this hunger for success, freedom and yet for acceptance by the Lord of Heaven.** But this is not a hunger and thirst for righteousness, it is a yearning or hunger for acceptance and affluence in a wealthy society, couched in the frame work of Bible verses so **a Christian can base his worldly attitude on heavenly teachings.** The very lives of many Christians today are themselves a message that is mixed. ***When   you   mix   the   message*** you may find that you ***have   lost   the   meaning*** which you supposed was hidden therein. I believe a mixed message is no message with heavenly power or Biblical hope. When you run a Bible verse through a concept or phrase that is from the world or that is carnal in scope and purpose, you will find that the verse will not carry the Holy Spirit power, for it has been corrupted and misused, therefore it is not under the divine pronouncement of God and it does not have to be somehow magically applied to the false and fleshly intent of the speaker or the writer. The Devil used many verses to turn Jesus from His intended purpose in the ministry of the Lord's redemption plan, but Jesus used verses or words from God His Father within their intended context and purpose, which made His words more powerful against the enemy than the words spoken by God that were used by Satan for intended selfish ends. Much ***like   the   time   when   Moses   threw   down   his rod   in   front   of   the   Pharaoh   and   the   magicians   did   likewise, but the   serpent   of   Moses   overpowered   and devoured   the   serpents   of the   false   gods   of   Pharaoh.*** Both used the same miracle, one was from the man of God, the other from the Ruler of darkness. Here is an answer to those who ask, why bad things happen to good people. It is so we can know how powerful the Lord God is over the evil in the world or in our lives, ***His miracle eats the Devil's trick for breakfast!***

Today, we face a time and a message that has come into the churches around the land, which message is being flown like a kite in the wind, for all to see and admire, but the string is held by the religious, self-esteem promoting, narcissistic religious leaders who have more interest in a temporal, visible reward of wealth, health and fun life style, far removed from the true and real holy life that our brothers and sisters around the world in persecuted conditions experience. Again I must return to the example of those who will live without ever owning a motorhome, or nice clothes, ranch-style house etc. yet with hearts full and spirits soaring above the skies where eagles fly, having only Christ and His redeeming love, knowing that such is all they need, because it was all they wanted.

Jesus said, in the world you will have tribulation (troubles galore) but be of good cheer, I have overcome the world. This means to me that His power is so great that we who follow Him, do not need to depend upon the modern, American dream, nor the statue of Liberty, or the stock market, or the right political agenda, we do not need the safe little social elite group to surround us with accolades of 'good ole boy' acceptance, or a church (denominational) membership which is a farce and empty of power (form of godliness but denying the power thereof). What we who follow Jesus do need, ***is   a   mind   that   thinks*** past the selfishness,and we need a **_heart_** that can only be filled with the humility that comes from serving the hungry souls of the world the beautiful words of Jesus, we need to be **_a body_** that can move through the crowds of affluence and entertainment and travel to the ends of the earth to hold out a hand of brotherhood that has been extended because we have one Father who loves us all equally. This horrid search for religious brotherhood of all men, without the true and real Fatherhood of God is like a smoke in the air, no substance no endurance, much like the mixed message, a little word from the world and a borrowed word from the Bible, void of power and useless for life. Give me Jesus, that's all, and that's enough! His word used in His way for His purpose and His glory have power to save and to preserve, and all who obey it will endure forever. The continual effort by religious leaders of America, to make the Gospel appear as a nice cloak of pleasure and spice for alluring members to their choice congregation is simply a way of giving humankind a voice in the decision making process of God's requirements for salvation. Speaking of soaring with eagles, we should remember that we are the ones carried on the wings of the eagle in God's illustration of this very example in Deut. 32:11, we are the helpless, God is the Eagle in that illustration.

In Isa. 40,31 we shall mount up with wings as eagles, run and not be weary, walk and not faint, true, and in the previous verses, 28,29 He (the Lord) gives this kind of strength and power to the faint, and they that have no might, to them He increases strength. I would say that God comes to the aid of the weak, and those about to faint, it is a verse that encourages one to wait upon the Lord and not depend upon human strength nor to give up in times of weakness. This too is for the suffering church, those who endure pain for the Name of Jesus, and for affluent American Christians to assume that the strength supplied here by the Lord for suffering servants, can be used to promote a continued supply of 'goodies' in a land of plenty, seems to me to be stretching the intended point of such great and Spirit filled words, which were intended to aid the fallen, the helpless, the hurting souls of men, women and children who have no refuge in this life but the loving promises of the Great Savior of men. The Savior who first suffered and died, calling all (as Dietrich Bonhoeffer said) to come and die, in real discipleship and show the world and the enemy that death in this world is nothing compared to bringing honor to the Name of the Holy God of heaven by faithful suffering in this present world.

When Christian writers and speakers in America pump their followers full of verses that are intended for those who really suffer for Jesus, such as the persecuted Christians around the world, and invent applications of Holy Scriptures which can only really be felt fully in the intended context, there will be no place to turn to when real suffering comes to America. For example, when an American Christian feels persecuted by some rejection of his witness at a work place, what would he do when the real persecution comes, such as imprisonment, beatings and even death for the sake of the Name? Notice Jer. 12:5, God said to Jeremiah who was feeling sorry for himself, *"... if you have run with footmen (as in a track meet) and they have worn you out, how will you contend with horses?" And if in the land of peace wherein you trusted, they weary you, how then will you do in the swelling of the Jordan?"* I believe in like manner, if the affluent church in America is feeling so burdened with troubles, and feels persecuted with simple little trials and mole hill size tribulations, how then will the American Christian fair in the days of real tribulation? Will we have used up all of our 'big' helper verses, with small little problems, and be broken and choked by the weeds growing up around us when real persecution more serious comes upon the land? Mark 10. 28-31 states in part, the promise of receiving in this time, the houses, lands, family we leave behind for the sake of the Gospel, *with persecution*, and in the world to come, eternal life. Notice this promise deals with family, (a larger spiritual family, I believe, and houses, and lands to occupy which are related to the total family of God, anywhere in the world—a place to call home). The missionaries of years past and many in this present time, share the love of people from many nations, and languages which they can call the new family, replacing the loved ones they left in order to go into all the world and carry the Gospel.

May the church cease to rob itself of verses and meanings that God has intended His Word to have for serious adversity, by forcing an application of these lovely and powerful words of hope and encouragement into a context of affluence, plenty, extravagance and waste. Shame on us, when we take up the verses of the Word of God and mix those intended meanings with applications that are not meant by the original setting. Is this not handling the word of God deceitfully? (2Cor. 4. 1-5). Anytime a person takes a word from the Holy Scripture and uses it as a means to make his own agenda seem covered by the Lord, the power of God will not be in that word, for it has now become his own tool for a purpose that is foreign and it can only fall to the ground (1 Sam. 3. 19). Misuse of God's intended words and His power brought pain and suffering (Acts 19. 15,16) to those who tried to use the Name of Jesus and His Words for their own profit.

The purpose of the encouragement in ISAIAH chapter 40 and verses 28-31 are to give encouragement to the weak and faint of heart. And all of us need that word at some time, "...they that wait upon the Lord shall renew their strength, they shall mount up with wings as eagles, they shall run and not be weary, and they shall walk and not faint." And the eagle is a great example of God's care for His people (see Deut.32. 11). The context is not for seeking more wealth, more prosperity and comfort or ease. The Lord is the mother eagle in this context in Deuteronomy, and the encouragement in Isa. 40, for all of us when we need added support and reminder of God's care for the times of our weakness. But the idea of 'hanging out' with people who are eagles, as compared with people who are 'chickens' is not in the context or intent of the words in these scriptures. This is when the Word of the Lord is used to make a point for man's ego or for carnal ends. With a message of man's ego and God's Word, that becomes Mush-age, what we see is exactly what takes place daily in American churches and in the media, in Christian literature, seminars etc. etc. It is a mixing of God's word with the intent of a selfish or human end in mind which brings confusion and misunderstanding among American Christians. The Lord says, "…the poor have the Gospel preached unto them…" so are we to assume they are the chickens? Who are the eagles? Did Jesus not die for the sake of all lost people? How do you win a poor person to Christ, in some different way than you do a rich one? Not if you have love for all men like Jesus and the Apostles had. Perhaps the unreached people of the world are Chickens? *That little poetic injustice about eagles and chickens sounds more like a business seminar for sales persons, than an encouragement to suffering, saints of God in a dying world.* Try the Spirits, the Apostle John says!

In a recent news letter (Nov. 2003) from one of the campus ministries, there appeared a great example of **what we mean by mixed messages.** In this case, (since I work with students) it caught my attention and should be a wake-up call to all campus ministries. There are students who come to the Lord, and bring with them, concepts that are not yet corrected or may never be corrected in the campus ministry environment. In a personal testimony on page three of the campus news, of a certain campus ministry, was the testimony of two young ladies who were baptized at their campus retreat, they were roommates, and they gave their testimony as follows:

"…we share a suite at _____(name of University). Then in the testimony they shared as follows, "Of course baptism is not some magical thing that saves people, but for us it (their baptism) was an awesome way to publicly profess our faith in Jesus Christ, and we were excited to do it together."

Now the example here is common. A statement is made that is obviously correct, (because the word magical has no place in a command of God), "**baptism is not some magical thing…**" that part of the testimony is true. Then you add to that true statement a following and connected statement that is not true ie—"…baptism is not something **that saves you**.", It is the word 'magical' in the sentence that is **connected to the command of baptism—which is a subtle way of making the command of God in baptism appear as if it was standing alone. As far as not being some magical thing, we agree. But as a command that does not save you, I disagree. I agree that baptism is not some magical thing, but I do not agree that it does not save you.** As a command of the Lord and when obeyed it does save you, just as belief, repentance and confession of faith in Christ saves. Read Acts 11. 14, (words whereby you and your household shall be saved) (Acts 10. 47)—they were baptized. **Baptism which now saves you** are the exact words used in 1 st Peter 3. 21. And this harmonizes with Acts 22. 16. When you read the statement by the young college students you have the tendency to accept the whole statement as true. But unfortunately it is not. The Bible states, in 1 Peter 3. 21, and in Acts 4. 12, and Acts 19. 5, that Baptism saves, and that some who had not been baptized into the Name of Jesus, were so baptized, since Acts 4. 12 **states that salvation is only in the Name of Jesus.** Baptism is a command of Jesus, and it is His words that save people from sin, when His words and commands are obeyed. Notice also, the biblical fact that Jesus said, 'he who keeps my commandments, is the one who loves me,' (John 15. 9, 10, John 14. 21) John 6:63 for example states—His words are life, and He is life, and in John 14. 6, Jesus states, "…I am the way….and life" so **you cannot separate Jesus' saving grace from His own words** and their saving grace.

The Words of Jesus are life, and He is life, so which saves us, **Jesus or His words?** The answer—***Both.*** People like to separate Jesus and a relationship with Him, from the very Words that Jesus commands of those who will belong to Him. As I have stated in other pages, this is like saying "my boss hired me, not the application which I had to fill out by his order…" Now which is most important for receiving a position, the application which the boss requires, or the boss's words? Both are necessary, because the boss is the one who required that the application be filled out. Notice the unintended fallacy here, the sincere young college students start out with **the assumption (as so many do), that their baptism into Christ, has no saving power or grace.** A false assumption to begin with, and it is connected to a statement in one sentence, with an obviously acceptable premise, that baptism is not magical. But when you tie the accepted part of the statement, to a statement to follow which is not biblically acceptable, you end up believing what is false. That is, if you accept the conclusion of the testimony made by the young girls in this case. It is amazing how Christians can find a way to decide for God, how important His words are to Him. To make a statement that "baptism (immersion) into Christ does not save us, it to decide for God, who is the one who gives the command, what it does and what it does not do. Duh...To put an opinion of our own into the meaning of a Bible verse that nullifies the meaning is not cool. **Whenever a meaning is taken away** from a message, the **power of that message** or word of God, goes with it. **Subtract meaning = subtract the power** it has. The Word says, "...the **Gospel is the power of God** unto salvation, to all who will believe." Rom. 1. 16. There are many powerless messages floating in America today, because someone has tampered with the meaning of Bible verses like this.

Mixed messages are messages with man's intentions or purpose but words that come from the Holy Bible. If the motive is for human and selfish purpose, or if the motive is to carry on some misguided concept or teaching, (Matt. 16. 23) and is intended to present a position chosen by people that is not true to scripture and not of God, the word of God will be made of none affect Mk.7. 13. **You cannot put man's intentions and goals and carnal, selfish plans or ideas, into a verse of Scripture and have the power of God behind it. And we cannot put Scripture into a man made purpose and expect to have a God designed result**. If our words fall to the ground, then they did not come from a sincere heart, or from God by His Spirit, 1Sam. 3.19. Anyone can speak a verse of Scripture, but only God in His power can bring His will to pass, and fulfill His promise in the lives of people. Get real and you can get right, get selfish and you can get lost. Mix the message of God with the purpose of carnal man and you miss the power of God. *Mix it, you miss it, mean it for God's purpose and you can make it. A mixed message has lost meaning, and when you lose meaning you lose the power behind the meaning.*

Al Hamilton,
Missionary

17

No Government Acceptance—Can be Acceptable

The recent news from Voice of the Martyrs, to those of us who are volunteer reps., on Jan. 13, 2004, provided the evidence for my statements regarding—the Christian's responsibility to the government authorities.

In the VOM news, quoting, Compass Direct, the weekly prayer request cited the following incident in China. "Nanjing, China, Jan.5, 2004, Registration (of churches and Christian meetings) is still a hot issue for China's long-suffering house churches. The Government insists on registration as the only means of legal existence for Protestant and Catholic churches."

Some time ago, in one of my pages (from articles entitled "The Assembly Line of Faith"), I had mentioned the verses in Matt. 24. 9, and John 17. 14, 15. 18,19, that it would be expected that nations of the world will hate the church. The church in America has not been surprised that it was more of a friend to the country than an enemy. However, the Churches of the Lord should have seen, at least in recent years, that this close encounter with the country of 'America' is not a spiritual blessing. This relationship seemed to puzzle some, but others in the fellowship of believers, took this friendly relationship as a blessing from God. There needs to be some reassessment of this connection. Especially when you read in the news paper, such as the Dallas News paper that the pastor of the Oak Cliff Bible Fellowship church was quoted as saying that he believes there should be no separation of God and Government, (Dallas new paper Oct. 28, 2003). This is strange since Christian pastors in China believe just the opposite, that there should be no connection between the two. I believe the time will soon come, and even now is, when the United States will, as a government, begin to show even more disdain for 'religious groups' which do not have the tolerance for 'legally accepted' 'life styles' and marriage laws, which the government has embraced. Remember James 4. 4.

There is no doubt that the words of Jesus in these verses (Matt. 24,9 etc.) will come true. Even though the United States as a government, from it's beginning, sought favor in the sight of the God of heaven, this same government did not go far enough, and declare that ONLY the God revealed in the Holy Bible, would be worshiped and served as the only God of this new country. This friendly little 'walk in the park' with the church, that America has had, where each traded favor for favor (i.e. tax exemption) church to country and country to church, was not to last forever. Our present generation, just happens to be right on the verge of a total collapse of this 'little happy hour' romance between church and State. When it all goes down, it will be better for the Church, although the government has profited from the close alliance with the Churches of America.

The announcement of this condition In China, between a 'Communist government' and the total assembly of believers in that country, is only a shadow on the horizon for America. The church in America will be caught off guard for the most part, because of this 200 year 'courtship' carried on by the America government with the Bride of Christ, in America. We as a church have known that peace and freedom in the world is not a normal condition for the followers of Christ. The church vs. Rome, since the days of the churches history in the book of Acts, and even since then, in the so called, 'dark ages' was really the normal existence for Christians in this present evil world (Gal. 1. 4). We who follow Jesus, as His true Bride, for whom He shall return soon, to take unto Himself into His eternal home, must not be led into a loving relationship with the world. That means—not being led to fall in love with any country in the world, and it just so happens that America as a country, has a lot of 'worldly things' to tempt a lover with. We must remember, 1st Jn. 5. 19, James 4. 4, are the words of God.

When we see the believers in China facing 'tough' decisions about their relationship with a communist country, what do you think will be easy about Christians in America facing the dilemma of "God and Country" in Her battle against spiritual adultery? **Notice the following quote from the same VOM prayer letter of Jan. 13, 2004.**

> "…registration in China means subjection to the Communist Party's religious affairs Bureau, and other party organs, all of which are controlled by atheists. In registered churches, evangelism, appointment of pastors, the content of theological training and Sunday sermons are all ultimately managed by the Religious Affairs Bureau…A house church leader in Jilin province, northern China, recently wrote a letter summarizing the arguments for and against registration. Her letter vividly illustrates the dilemma faced by many house church meetings."

"...in 1994, a sister in our village voluntarily opened her home for house church meetings. In recent years, God has saved 40-50 brothers and sisters. At the end of 2002, officials from our county Religious Affairs Bureau and Public Security Bureau, forcibly closed down our church because we had not registered with the government."

Now there is more to the letter quoted above, and you can receive the entire copy from VOM (www.persecution.com), but I am skipping down in this prayer request letter to another paragraph, where the next issue dealt with in this letter from the sister in China, deals with the problem arising from questions about 'obedience to the governing authority' and what the Bible teaches about faith and doctrine. Because the Bible speaks of being subject to the governing powers, there was in the neighboring village, a large registered church. Based on Romans 13, their leaders believe the church should be registered with the government. Because the two viewpoints of these two churches are so different (in this political aspect and the Bible verses in Romans), the leaders have no spiritual fellowship. So we have believers divided on this issue of 'government laws and Christian faith'. All of this problem in China, in a communist country, where religious faith clashes with political control.

To me it would seem obvious, that religious freedom means exactly that, a person's religious freedom to share their faith with others. But in China, the religious faith is not allowed to be shared outside the home of those who embrace that certain faith. So this means the command to go into all the world and preach the Gospel, which came from the Lord Himself, cannot be obeyed in that country where such **religious expression** is strictly forbidden and strictly punished. In a recent message preached by a Pastor in China, when he addressed hundreds of Christian people, the pastor of house churches said, the Church of the Lord, must remain separate from the government. The worst thing that can happen to the churches of the Lord in this world today, is that they would have any alliance with or association, connection or other affiliation with any government regulations, or with any kind of government, political policies. This is the message of the persecuted church around the world. There cannot be any connection in world government policies or cooperation with government that will make the church appear to be a part of this worlds order and political system. This thing that has happened in the churches in America, with involvement in political events, political process and alliance with government policies is not biblical and it is therefore not right. The 'real' churches of the Lord Jesus, around the world, pray for the Christians in America. They pray that the Christians in America will be faithful to the Word of God and not allow themselves to be overcome by the world. Matt. 24. 9, states clearly, that the followers of Christ will be hated by ALL nations of the world. The time is coming when the American government will also hate the churches of America.

When I have been called upon to share the scriptures of Romans 13, and others, which apply to this concern about political legislation and spiritual obedience, I explain it as follows: The reminder and the direction given in Romans 13, deals with civil obedience to laws regarding the well being and safety of all citizens. A Christian is already obedient to these laws as a result of their obedience to the Lord Jesus, to love one another. No law in the government can be as strong as the law of the Lord to love others and 'to look out for' the well being of all people. When the government imposes a law that deals with moral behavior which holds Biblical issues as unlawful, or if that government imposes laws that forbid the obedience to God given commands, then we know that we must (Acts 5. 29) obey God, **RATHER** than man. I pray that the brothers and sisters in China will know, that sacrificing the freedom in Christ, for the bondage of communism, is not a good idea. **In Christ we are commanded to share the Gospel, and no law made by man, against that law is obligatory**, nor should it be considered honorable, nor worth losing the favor of God, in order to make it look like we are obedient to verses in Romans 13. Romans 13 cannot be used as an excuse to escape some punishment that will be imposed by the authorities, who, are not accepting the authority of the Lord Jesus Christ. May the churches in America be wise enough to be ready for this same advice, is also my prayer. **Ist Peter 4. 12-19.**

You can imagine the tough time Christian's in America will have trying to sort out, to whom they will listen, when freedom is already part of the governing principles of this country. I foresee that American Christians will rather try to change the law, and fight it out with social and civil liberties groups as well as oppose the legislators who will (if not already planning it), bring some condition like this one facing the church in China, upon the "home of the brave." This approach too (to fight against them) will not be wise I think. It will be more subtle perhaps, but there is no doubt, that the true church will be hated by ALL nations, (including this one), in this present world, before Jesus comes back to take His Bride home. Christians had simply, best be prepared in heart and mind for what's coming. **We are only beginning to see the onset of this onslaught**. My suggestion to Christians in America is, "wake up brethren, to the fact that, your party is almost over."

18

Places Have Power!

In the article 'Sublimating Strife', copied (by permission) from the Jewish World Review, the famed psychiatrist Carl Jung, had been noted to have put forth the idea that 'places have power.' He wrote in "Civilization In Transition" (1918) "the soil of every country, holds some such mystery...just as there is a relationship between mind to body, so there is a relationship of body to earth."

Think about the time of God's call to Moses, when God said to Moses...'remove your sandals from off your feet, for the place where you stand is holy ground'. And there are other references to the fact that 'places have power' or we might say at least influence on people who inhabit those places. In the article by Rabbi Avi Shafran, director of public affairs for Agudath Israel of America, the influence of place called Pumbeditha, which is today Fallujah, has been one of violence and tribal emotions, having a long history, he states, of bloodshed.

Perhaps on the other hand, America and its relationship to the 'church' which is the dominate religion in the country, should be given some attention. When the country was strongly favoring the things of spiritual concern, in the early years of its beginning, the ideals of righteousness and justice had a very honored place.

As years went by, and the call of 'freedom' from the shores of the new America, brought in nations of peoples with religious views and beliefs that were contradictory and not compatible with Christian teaching or Jewish heritage, and gods of a different kind became acceptable and lawful. The land of the free began to wear a different 'hat' and perhaps this strong influence has made the land of America a different place than it used to be. I strongly believe that the churches of America have been influenced in a negative or anti-Christian way by the land, while American Christians still try to hold on to the country and their faith in such as way as to make it impossible to put the two in one package. God instructed the Israelites in the Old Testament record, to destroy the evil that was in Canaan, when they crossed over into that new land 'flowing with milk and honey' so that the new 'worship of one God, the true God only' would be possible.

It is worth considering as a phenomenon of today, that America is a land where sin and gods of other nations have been given 'equal time' and equal privileges, in a land that was once dedicated to the service of the true and living God of heaven. So perhaps we should ask ourselves, if our allegiance to the land, has been influenced by the land or by the dictates of our Christian heritage. If the land has influenced the church more in recent years than the church has influenced the land (laws and government), perhaps it is time to part company, **and join the ranks of the 'body of believers' around the world, known as the 'persecuted church' whose only claim to a country is cited in** Hebrews 11, "...<u>**the world was not worthy of them...and they acknowledged that they were aliens and strangers on the earth...**</u>" They desire a better country (vs. 16), that is a heavenly one.

If Carl Jung was right, (at least about this theory) we should waken from sleep and awake unto righteousness, so that we do not align ourselves with the temporary, at the cost of losing what is eternal! Let the American Christian remember, not to repeat the mistake of those of whom it is recorded in John 19. 15, when the Jews cried out "...we have no king but Caesar." Sooner or later, a choice must be made..."choose you this day whom you will serve..."Joshua 24.15.

19

AMC
Pick One
vol.1 doc. 1
The Purpose Driven Life—or
Holy Spirit Led Life

2 Cor. 5. 14—The love of Christ compels us:

Motivation—is a very great principle, not just a statement of fact that was discovered by athletes and those who are involved in activities that require dedication, commitment and concentration for physical self-improvement. This idea that a person must be highly motivated to have success in this present life, is a readily accepted fact. Great Price = Great reward-(Matt. 13. 44, Mk8. 34-38), it will cost your life to follow Jesus and receive from Him such rewards as only the Lord can give! We should have watched the persecuted church around the world, instead of setting our eyes on the popular preachers of the mega churches. 'Oops, that was an easy mistake! Anyone in the USA could have made it! That is, anyone who valued the material, carnal, and visible, over **the invisible and the eternal**. I guess the 'purpose driven' crowd would say the suffering saints of God in China, North Korea and 70 other countries are all 'purpose driven'. But they say about themselves, they are humble servants of Jesus. That term of being 'purpose driven' is never used to describe the death of William Tyndall, John Wycliffe, Polycarp, or others listed in the record of Foxe's Book of Martyrs. Why not? **If purpose is so great and motivating, where is it in those records**? We know there is more to living such a sacrificial life, than just announcing our purpose (Rom. 12.1). These saints of God had more than purpose, just check with the writings of Richard Wurmbrand. He speaks of the love of the Lord Jesus constraining him not just purpose. I believe that any **motive that <u>can</u> be of the flesh, usually <u>is</u> of the flesh.**

Having a purpose is not necessarily a divine attribute. Only men and women with the Spirit of God can understand the things of God.

But being purpose driven, can be understood and even used by, the world of lost, success motivated, corporate salespersons, who may not even know Jesus as Lord of their lives. The Apostles and Prophets were men looked upon by the world and the ungodly people of their time, as abnormal, different, strange, aliens, or crazy people, as those who did not belong here, **Acts. 26. 24, 1 Cor. 4. 9,10, 1 Cor. 1. 26-31, 1 Cor. 4. 13. But the Christians of America, in life style, look much like the lost who seek the goods of this** present evil world. (Gal. 1. 4).

Look at it straight on ie.—any purpose I can choose to have is under my control, if I am driven by purpose, whatever the purpose or however good it is, such purpose is still under my control. **But if the love of Christ compels us, this is something God has done, initiated by Him, and we are stewards of His grace** and presence in us, and this power of the love of Christ over our hearts, and in our lives, leads us to follow him. **This is more than just being purpose driven.** Is your marriage for example, purpose driven? Is it just the purpose of being faithful to the marriage vows which makes you remain faithful to your spouse? If someone asks you, why you care for your wife and children the way you do, **would you say it is because you are purpose driven?** Would that explain it? Purpose indeed may be present in our relationship with our loved ones, but that would leave a lot to be explained. Purpose should not be called the driving force behind our love for spouse and children, it would sound like we are more concerned about fulfilling a goal, a purpose, and concentrating on that, so that all the right moves and decisions were from self, rather than the simple fact that our love for them leads us on, making love the power, not our purpose.

What if John 3. 16 read like this—"...For God was so purpose driven that He gave His only begotten Son, that whosoever was purpose driven to believe in Him, should not perish, but have a purpose driven, everlasting life."

We must give up all dependence upon motives, goals and human qualities or traits, which any human being could have, that might appear to motivate us instead of just the presence of Christ. Perhaps we should be willing to pay the price, of fancy ideals, in order to receive simple commands. Perhaps we need to give up our American, promotional themes, our sales gimmicks, and great motivational, material reasons (lust for things)—for living a holy life, and let it be simply the result of God's grace and love that leads us on. Instead of trying to gain the approval of the population, and build a 'church' that people would come to, perhaps we should seek the approval of God, who shows no favoritism. Jesus stated that the Kingdom of heaven is like a man finding a pearl of great price, or like a man finding a treasure hidden in a field, when he finds this great treasure, he sells all he has in order to have enough money to buy that field, or that pearl, Matt. 13.

If we don't repent of this materialism in the church, our intentions, and present emphasis on 'happy hour' family fun, could be construed to overshadow our dependence upon the grace of God. Notice the advertisement bulletins that the mega church uses to call in members. If we are purpose driven, what happens when the purpose changes? Is it our purpose to make the church look like a 'Disney World' experience? As Bonhoeffer said, "Jesus bids us come and die" in His call to discipleship. What is the American church calling people to do, come and enjoy family, fellowship and games? Is this play time or war time? For the church in America it seems to be 'feel good about self-time! **There is no more powerful motivating force, than the desire to know Him and the power of His resurrection, and the fellowship of His suffering.** Even if it is my purpose to serve Him, it is still **His presence not my purpose** that empowers my new life in Christ. To emphasize purpose is just to get close, and this life is no game of horseshoes. It is just hard for me to imagine (after working in countries where persecution 'goes with the territory') **that saints of God** in **lands where there is no government freedom lending it's assistance to the holy life, will have to 'hunt'** for some reason to be faithful to God, beyond the sacrifice of Christ the Lord. If today you said to 'house churches' in N. Korea or China, they need to have a purpose driven life, they would look at you like you were 'a few bricks shy of a load'. Why would it not be sufficient just to use the terminology of the Bible, when we speak of Bible things?

THE MODERN DILEMMA, A FULFILLED PURPOSE IN LIFE BUT AN UNFINISHED TASK IN THE WORLD—HOW CAN THIS BE?

If we are so spiritual, in the present time, and with the amount of resources and wealth that American Christians have, and if we are so 'purpose driven', why is the work of the Lord in reaching all the lost peoples of the world, still the same size task it was 10 years ago? Is this goal and fulfillment of this command, not in our 'driving purpose'? We know that Large and so called, 'mega' churches with many souls in membership can simply receive an offering on any given Sunday morning to collect enough money to reach an entire tribe of 'unreached' people, with at least a visit to understand their plight more fully. Small, rural churches, and small congregations who have been in ministry many years, can mortgage their buildings and use the money for the mission of reaching someone among the unreached souls, right away, to investigate and learn what is needed or what will be the cost, to get the Word of the Lord into their hands. And if we like '**purpose**' so much and have **the right purpose**, which is to please God and obey Him, why have we not already reached people groups of the world who have no Bibles and no knowledge of the Lord?

Perhaps our '**driving purpose**' is not the right purpose, or it has limits or boundaries or nothing driving it besides our own fleshly wisdom and worldly mindedness! Sometimes the prize, the treasure we want to find in the kingdom of God, must be found at the cost of putting away any trust in great moral or human qualities or characteristics. **The concept of having a great purpose, sounds so noble, and finds itself enthroned in the castle of high moral ethics,** which makes such an honorable trait easily mistaken for a 'fruit of the Spirit', but if you look more closely you will see that 'great purpose' is not in that list. **Purpose may drive you,** but only the **Shepherd can lead you.** Better to cut off the hand (or in this case some great ethical characteristic that is dear to your collection of mentally gained and emotionally charged traits), than to have yourself tossed out, because of trusting in the arm of flesh instead of the grace of God. **Isn't it amazing that one of those who preaches so much on grace as the only way to salvation, and proclaims that a person can't do anything to save himself, is the source of this platform for 'purpose driven life'? I thought he said a person could do nothing to receive God's grace, If you only have to believe to be saved, then why all this fuss about a purpose driven life? Isn't just being saved enough for anyone?......duh! This is really hard to excuse.**

In the Bible, no great thing was done or great, unusual deed accomplished, without an equally great price being paid: To get the Gospel message into all the world, the American churches must sacrifice and be willing, at great cost to themselves, to illustrate that the purpose driven life, (which should be directed toward the benefit of others—the unreached people in foreign lands), **will be a holy work, not a selfish goal.** We need only the purpose of God that Jesus gave His followers, to go into all the world and preach the Gospel to every creature. Jesus told His followers to have the purpose of losing their lives in order to find life in Him. So if you lose your life in Jesus, whose purpose are we talking about? Jesus said nothing about the power of having a 'purpose driven life'—as if that in itself held some spiritual value to be 'labeled' on believers. He simply stated, that if any one will follow Him they must lose their life. This is costly!

Now if God's purpose drives a person, that's very good indeed, but the idea of the purpose is not paramount, and the thought of being driven,—not led—still stuns the humble soul. It is the command of Jesus, which reigns paramount in this context. It is not a purpose that drives us to serve Jesus, it is His command to follow Him, that we respond to, seeking to please our creator. To be driven simply by various purposes which surround the command of the Lord in Matt. 28. 18-20, would not be enough to do the job. Just to be driven by purpose is not the point. If purpose is all that drives you, it is better to surrender that 'precious' ring of purpose (as in the Lord of the Rings) and pay the full price of true discipleship, which is to be compelled only by the love of Christ. Hear the words of that old hymn," nothing in my hands I bring, simply to thy cross I cling." We could also say, nothing I have done—makes me sing, simply to His grace I cling. We should emphasize the command, the main point, **not glorify the idea of having a purpose.** Being purpose driven, can be a motive for any number of goals in life. There needs to be only the leading of God's spirit, that carries us into His service, and this would make us Christ centered**, not purpose centered or purpose driven**. **It is the love of Christ that compels us, not just purpose!**

Moses, led a nation of people out of Egypt, but it cost him his position in the land of the Pharaohs. It was not simply purpose that drove Moses, it was his desire to follow the will of God, that made him who he was. He did not say, "I was purpose driven" *this would have given glory to him as a man of great purpose*. Many prophets of God, lost their comfortable homeland security, their flocks or herds, their family, friends or countrymen. Everyone who does something great, puts aside everything he has in order to accomplish that something. Read again in Foxe's Book of Martyrs the records of the great people of history who had God's leading in their lives, not just a purpose built around Bible verses, but the actual Holy Spirit power leading them to paths they could not have seen as having purpose, yet the path they took led them into some kind of usefulness to God, not to some success in the eyes of others, so that they might hear the words—'wow' what a purpose driven life, 'he is really some great leader'. To say that they were purpose driven, won't cover the bases that only Grace bestows.

Churches today, want to carry on some mission work in a few places, and hope this will satisfy God, and the congregation. **Mission programs that are well within the financial giving that is already a current statistic,** is normal procedure, for most churches, but far from a great sacrifice. But who wants to go the second mile, and let go of all the riches and modern conveniences of the American life style for the sake of others in far away lands? **It is much easier to simply call all of this extravagance a blessing from God, and try to feel right**

about what is really wrong, (because it is wrong to ignore the needs of others), (1 John 3. 17), and hope that the world doesn't catch on! To late friends, the world is already aware that most churches are in the "form of godliness stage." Churches and ministers of churches, feel very proud when they count the number of missions they support, or the workers on the field, but they **do not bow in humility and shame over what has not yet been accomplished, nor do very many volunteer to do something about it**. No Pat Tillman's in our church today, sorry, maybe we should try to borrow a few from America the beautiful, at least the American soldier has guts.

Recently, as you know, this young man who was a successful pro-football player for the Arizona Cardinals, with millions of dollars in his future and fame to his credit, left it all and volunteered for military service, because of the impact that the Sept. 9/11 tragedy in America had on him personally. Pat Tillman, left it all and volunteered for service in the Army, because he wanted to do something himself about the terrible attack by terrorists against his beloved country. He finally paid a price that he knew might be required, when he was killed in action in Afghanistan, a country not his own, but for a love of freedom that was his own. **He was purpose driven,** protecting or fighting for the freedoms which should rightfully belong to all of mankind.

But even the world (Lk. 16.8)—recognizes that the extreme measure i.e. going the second mile is what will be required, if one is to reap extreme results. People of this world show more courage in their purpose driven lives, than American Christians show to the world by their, supposedly, Spirit led, lives. Perhaps Christians in America have settled for 'purpose driven lives' a life goal that anyone could have, be they lost or saved. Maybe the purpose is that of 'larger numbers at church meetings' or some other purpose that **makes them feel inwardly great,** but leaves them **outwardly useless** to the task of finding any lost sheep outside of their own little neighborhood. **If the American Christian was willing to make greater sacrifice, perhaps the world around him would believe that God was really in him.** The emphasis on 'The Extreme' is everywhere in America, except in the churches. Unless you apply it to extreme spending on self, and extreme selfishness in the land of plenty. This kind of extreme is not the idea intended by the use of the term, it is extreme dedication and sacrifice made so that one may reach a worthy goal—that is the intended meaning of this term 'Extreme' in today's vernacular.

This, I believe, is the reason that there are still unreached **tribes and languages of people in the world without the Gospel.** Without making an extraordinary effort, there is no extraordinary result. Giving, precedes receiving.

As a man sows, so shall he reap. **There is not one person in history that is remembered for anything great, who did not pay a price that was equally as great**. Let the sacrifice be equal to the accomplishment. From the Cross of Christ and His resurrection, (such as was illustrated in the film "The Passion of The Christ" by Mel Gibson), to every death of soldiers at war, a price is paid for a vision or message that is bigger in the mind of the soldier, (or the Savior of the world) than the cost required to attain it. How about having the purpose of reaching all corners of the globe for Jesus, and making all the necessary sacrifices to do it, in His power, right away? Sending the ministers out, selling the seminary properties, letting the deacons preach, this is only part of a good purpose. **Too bad this kind of purpose doesn't drive us**, if it did, it might even pass for getting us closer to 'the love of Christ constrains me' verse.

Even death is necessary as the price to pay for life. No dying, then there is no living. Great scientists, inventors, artists, and a host of other examples underscore this great truth. The higher the price to be paid, or what it would cost to fulfill the vision or dream, the greater the result or reward. Jesus stated that in this way. "He that forsakes not all that he has, cannot be my disciple." Lk. 14.33. **Can't Christians just be Christians? This would in itself mean that it is the "…Love of Christ that constrains us (compels us)" we would not have to emphasize purpose**, or goals or other related motives.

ANOTHER DILEMMA FOR CHRISTIANS—PURPOSE OR PRESENCE:

In this new millennia—churches and ministers in America, have run head-long into the great marathon race to success, and joined the ever popular theme that somewhere within the right formula of deeds and service lies that ever-so-elusive prize called, 'successful living'. Focus on the family, then focus on the fellowship, focus on bigness, and whatever you call it, the **church in America took the bait,** and made sacrifices alright, the church in America has sacrificed humility, sound doctrine and trust in God, for the **mess of pottage called success**. This is not the kind of sacrifice we need, to give up Bible teachings, and sound doctrine. The sacrifice we need to make is to give up, and get rid of all motives and goals that are not from the Lord. It seems to me that the idea of being purpose driven, is actually depending upon the idea of purpose, **as if the purpose would provide the power to reach the goal**, or some effort of the flesh, could help us to attain a spiritual high! This is not going to happen. <u>You can have a purpose that drives you, if you are a lost sinner or forgiven saint</u>, but sheep in the fold of Jesus **are**

led, not driven, and it is **not JUST purpose, <u>it is a person</u>, the person of the Holy Spirit.**

The worst part of today's picture of the American church is, that the word success was defined, not as it is used in the Bible, exemplified by holy prophets of God and Apostles of Christ, and multitudes who died for their faith in the Lord and for His Name, but instead success was defined by those with popularity in the pulpit, who had exciting results in finding a following among the sheep who didn't look closely to see if the shepherd was a man of God or a man of the world in Christian clothing. The Scripture warns, that **in the last days**, there shall be false prophets 2 Pet. 2.1, 1 Jn.4. 1, and I take this to mean **false ideas, messages of mush, and token religion that passes for Christianity.** Is anyone in the American church awake during these hours of trial that are testing the love, obedience, faith and patience of God's holy people? I am not asking-"where have all the flowers gone" as the hippies did in the 60's, my question is more real, "where have all **the followers** gone"?

In more than 70 countries around the world, people put their lives on the line just for meeting together as the Lord commanded, and for reading a Bible, (if they have one). What a bunch of sissies the American Christians must look like, compared to the warrior saints of God in foreign lands. The scene in the United States, must make the saints of God in other lands feel like they should ask 'what happened to the American church?' In all of this extravagance and spending on multi-media, for a church service to be easily followed, while most of the saints abroad don't even need nor depend upon these expensive items, how can we justify the use of the theme "Purpose Driven" and speak such words without the blush of shame on our faces? **Our examples of purpose**, and goals **should be found in the lives of our brothers and sisters around the world who pay the ultimate price** for their service to God. Where are the Pat Tillman's of the American churches, who will drop the extravagant life style for the sake of fighting the 'good fight' of faith, to bring the word of God to the Bibleless tribes of the world?

We speak of being purpose driven, what a joke, whose purpose? Our own purpose, or God's? Love driven would have been a more appropriate word for the life of a believer, but purpose? Give me a break, this concept gives glory to the idea of purpose, but **Even a baseball team** can be **purpose driven**, the terrorists of 9/11 were purpose driven, the Taliban, and every other disciple of terrorist leaders is purpose driven. Their purpose (success they call it), is to wipe out those who are non-Muslim, infidels in the world. For the church in America to brandish the banner and theme of the nice Baptist man in California, 'purpose driven church' or 'purpose driven life' is not close enough, any theme or program that the world or people of the world could copy, is of the flesh, and comes from human motivation. It is not my purpose I want to glorify, it is the Lord's Name. (Ps. 115.1). The Spirit led life of a saint of God can only spring from within a soul that is dominated and powered by the presence of God's spirit, and the Word of God.

The disciples of Christ were not 'purpose driven' they were Spirit of God filled, and Spirit of God led (Romans 8. 1-14). Sounds like a nice call, to be "purpose driven" but this is not horse shoes, and close won't cut it! It is not a purpose, it is **THE PRESENCE** that we are promised, to take us to the end of the world and the end of the ages. Let's get real, so we can get right! The real fact is, that the love of Christ compels us, and that is something you find only in Christ. Purpose can be found anytime, anywhere, among any people…but the compelling love of Christ which empowers the true believer, because of the indwelling of God's presence, is not for anyone but the elect. You can have your purpose driven life, or your purpose driven assembly, I choose, the 'love of Christ compelled life" which is all **from God, for God and of God**…no human element gets the glory in that kind of life. And no human wisdom can understand it. But I wish you all the luck in the world, because if you are purpose driven, luck is what you will need, since purposes can be many. The love of Christ carries in it a oneness of purpose, but **it is the love not the idea of purpose**, it is the **essence of what love of Christ is, not the reason for it** that motivates the saints of God. That oneness cannot be mistaken for anything else. **Have a good future, friend of purpose,** I am sure you are not far from the Kingdom of God!

A.W. Hamilton, missionary

20

The Reason for the Season

✦

Matt. 19. 17-21 The way to Life.
Mk. 13. 10, The purpose for new life,
Mk. 13. 19-23. ~ Matt. 24. 7-12,
The price to pay for walking this way.

The Private Life of 'Mr. and Mrs. Christian.'

There is an unwritten code in the American church today, that seems to mimic The independence of the country, or the new nation's Declaration of Independence, as if the declaration of Independence was not only for the citizens of America as a nation, but for the church as well. At least the church as a whole in America, adopted the philosophy that the country adopted, independence for all, and all for independence. This is one of the areas where it becomes apparent to even the casual observer, that so many of the 'freedoms' 'rights' and 'privileges' of a new well meaning society began to influence the religious sector, which is basically 'Christianity.' Now it should be clear, that everything in the new social order, the new land of the free, does not necessarily become an adopted code for the body of believers in Christ. However this was not a 'given' it was not taken for granted that whatever the country adopted in congressional session, even in the Continental Congress, was not intended to become a code of ethics or a 'Magna Carta' for the people of the Lord Jesus. It is in these areas that confusion arises, this area of 'no man's land' between the 'Church and State.' At the border between Kenya and Uganda in East Africa, at the Malaba border crossing, is a space of land about 200 yards wide. It is called no man's land because neither country owns it or can claim it. Perhaps today this has changed, but this is what I remember it to be. If there can be such a distance or space between the Church in

America and the Nation of America, then perhaps that is where we have to discover this unbiblical connection between citizenship and church membership. There is a discrepancy that the church has failed to deal with in this 'assumed' union of church and state. For example; if a person's rights as a citizen allow for an abortion of an unborn child, this does not make it an acceptable act for a Christian. Furthermore my allegiance to the country does not mean that I accept the code of ethics that the Supreme Court accepts, or that the government in Washington represents my views on issues which it puts the 'stamp of approval' on in congress or in the house of Representatives. There is no connection between citizenship as an American and membership in a church. But not all church members nor all citizens see this fact or readily accept it. This is understood to be true when you watch the public protests going on in a major city or in Washington, and religious issues become a part of the discussion. It is hard to distinguish between the religious feelings attached to speeches and the political position presented. A candidate for political office is 'marked' as being a representative of 'the religious right' or he/she is considered worthy of the Christian vote, based upon a certain political platform. It is a very difficult subject to address, and just as difficult to conceive. Try to picture in your mind a political candidate who has no religious connection at all, and yet receives the recommendation and support of religious, church people. Here is where the season is revealed. I believe America, citizens and church members are much like the people referred to in Charles Dickens book, "*A Tale of Two Cities.*" As he introduced his story, so it is with us today, we also are in the 'best of times' and the worst of times' at the same time. We too in this country, are in the "winter of our discontent."

The reason for our season of discontent, first of all is that the increase of wickedness in America has brought about many kinds of fear (Lk 21. 26). It is exemplified in the health of people, the economic market, war all around the world, but mostly it is fear of what the future brings. Check out the emphasis on depression, it is now a disease, very common even among college students, where we used to see high levels of confidence, exuberance and hope for the future. Today, even as good times are promoted in every aspect of advertisement, people are showing more signs of emotional and mental stress and signs of uncertainty than in the years before all the modern technology and information was in our grasp. In my opinion the reason for this present condition, at least in America's part of the world is this; ___when men became weak, women became strong and children became confused.___

You can trace most of today's problems in America to the above developments. When men became weak as spiritual leaders, and weak as men, in other words, they began to bend to the wishes of the liberal women of America, (not all women of course but the liberal set) and 'woman's liberation' became woman's domination, and therefore man's subjugation. And the natural result of these two conditions resulted in the third condition, a confused country of children. The children did not know if they wanted to be male or female. Most of your psychologists know this is true, and that the condition I have suggested is true, but for fear of reprisal or other fears from obvious sources, they would not dare voice this. The weakness of men began to appear at the very beginning of the end of the 2nd world war. When women sought public approval and then public support for their so-called liberation (from what~ we can only guess, perhaps liberation from woman-hood) men began to feel guilty and therefore responsible somehow for this condition that the women's lib. movement began to blame men for. I believe that the movement called the women's liberation movement (NOW) Natl. Organization of Women) was so linked to the abortion issue, which was so linked to the hideous worship of freedom in this country, that men saw no recourse but to back up, and back down as men and kneel before the new 'goddess of liberty'.

You can never have such a generation of children who can't tell if they want to be male or female without some cause that is traceable to this change of behavior and philosophy in today's men and women, wives and husbands, fathers and mothers. When you have men who are weak in their basic 'manhood' there is going to be a result (we reap what we sow) in the woman and her behavior and philosophy of life as well. You can't have one without the other, as the old song states, "...love and marriage,...go together like a horse and carriage, I'm a' tellin you brother, you can't have one without the other." Some of us remember what Stan Freeburg did to that song, and it was a great rendition. So it is as well, you can't have failure and breakdown in the spiritual level of man without suffering some kind of deterioration in the relationship between the husband and wife. All the focus on the family you want will not replace the focus on Jesus Christ as Lord. Any focus that is short of focus on the commandments of the Lord of all creation, will not hit the target much less the 'bull's eye.' We have seen an effort on the part of religious men, to return to the manhood of God's design, in the 'Promise Keeps' organization. But what was and is really needed is not an effort to be promise keepers until we have been 'commandment keepers'. The 119th Psalm in the Bible speaks in every verse except one, about the glory and power of the statutes, laws, and commands of the Lord God. God will take care of the promises, since He is the only <u>real</u> promise keeper, mankind needs to occupy himself with keeping the laws of the New Covenant, to love God and love his neighbor, (there are other commands, but they will easily follow when these two are obeyed fully). Jesus said, if you love me, keep my commandments (Jn. 14. 15, 23). He did not say keep your promises, He said, Keep my commandments. Too bad the promise keepers didn't start at the beginning of the page, maybe we would still be hearing about them.

One speaker at a NOW gathering in Washington D.C. said, "…what we want as women of America is Aquality, Aquality, Aquality." She didn't even know how to pronounce the word, and I doubt if many in her organization could understand the meaning either. It is not equality the NOW women want, it is superiority, domination. For the most part what I believe they want is to be men instead of women. Some in our American, free, society have tried to change their sex. Their mind had already gone out of balance, so now they sought to change their body. Try as they might, people like this can only be one or the other, male or female, so far they have not achieved being neutral humans. They can't keep the sun from shinning either, but they can always close their eyes and play like it is not there.

So what we have today is men trying hard to be promise keepers (when what we need is commandment keepers) and women trying hard to not be women (at a time when we need wives and mothers). No wonder children are confused and some are on medication for depression before they reach High School. I believe that the reason for this kind of season in our history, is that men in America, fearing each other, or the power of women, or fearing their children (that they might loose their love if they disciplined them), and just plain walking in fear of everything and everyone around them, forgot to fear God and keep His commandments. You should choose your fears carefully, because they will run your life for you, I choose to fear God, one fear is enough for anyone, and that is the only fear we were told by the Lord to have. With the fear of God you can survive the attack of your enemies, the hatred of your pretended friends, and the darkness of world disorder. You can in the fear of God, reach the highest heaven, overcome the strongest foe, fight the hardest battle, walk the longest road, climb the highest mountain, cross the widest sea, pass the hardest test, endure the most severe pain, be the best of men the greatest of women, and when your race is ended, you can bow to the God who made you and say praise Your Name, and thank you for putting me into the race, the human race.

Our churches are so filled with the wimpy, whine of what I call the "private life of Mr. and Mrs. Christian," that it seems any interference with this private

Christian life would cause great distress. Some are saying, they are too busy for church, but they are the members, like the hand is too busy to hold the fork, so we go hungry until the hand on our body thinks it might feel a convenient time for eating. Churches which have good leadership still have to beg for participants in the field of serving one another, and preach 40 sermons on the subject of giving, until someone decides he can let go of what he calls the Lord's money, and then it has to fit his personal agenda. Ministers with skills and training that would make the Disciples of Jesus look uneducated, don't preach like the disciples of Jesus, because today these high-toned highly educated scholars have to appeal to the interest of the members, or they won't get the 'job' as 'pastor' if too many are offended at what they say. The children of the 'Pastor' don't want to go 'into' full time Christian service many times because the example at home was a bit short of the ideals and examples seen in the New Testament. But I can assure you that the children of the persecuted believers in many lands around the world walk in the footsteps of their brave parents. Maybe in our private world for Christian living, we did not have enough Bible lessons, or instruction classes on counseling, or perhaps we missed the seminar that included 'choosing to die for your faith.' And we wonder why Muslim children run out into a crowd and blow themselves up. I am sure *They* have the wrong message and the wrong idea, but there is no lack of courage. I am also sure the Muslim militants want to rule this present world, oops, that is an easy mistake, only one world shy of a good goal, and one religious view shy of being right, because Jesus stated, to the faithful servants of His, "...I will make you ruler over many things..."(Matt.25. 21). Some Christians in America who claim the right message, the right purpose, have little if any courage and do well just to take a little trip to Mexico to visit the orphanage, and that will last some of them for a lifetime.

The big surprise is, there never was really a 'private life' for Mr. and Mrs. Christian, their lives belonged to the whole body of believers. Maybe many of those who like their little private Christian life, missed that Sunday School lesson too. This idea which prevails in America today, that independence and freedom give all people the right to choose all things or anything they wish, as their reason to live, has left a wake of disaster and destruction in the lives of all who choose freedom and rights over 'faith' and conscience. In the Kingdom of God, we do not make the choices about whom to worship, or whom to serve, we do not make individual and independent choices about what is right or wrong. These matters are clearly set before us in the Holy Bible. When a Holy people connect and intertwine so completely with unholy and unbiblical government legislation something has to give. Some people give up their faith, and others give up on accepting social order as a path to hope and internal peace. But everyone makes a choice, because this cake cannot be held and also consumed.

21

Saved to the Uttermost
Used to the Fullest

✦

(Servants of God)

In the life story of John Newton, there are many reminders of the work of the Spirit of God in the lives of those who seek Him. John Newton became a preacher of the Gospel, from humble beginnings, without formal education and **without acceptance among the 'church elite.'** The accepted normal religious primadonnas who linger behind the scenes to judge who is worthy of denominational support or who is not, have influenced churches from ages past, and they have not departed from the scene of our modern 'religious culture' as well. Such 'church elite' do not make the path easy for the servants of God who are raised up to light the way for others.

John Newton, like many of those who paid the price of being associated with 'dissenters' as they were known,(but who were simply Christians who sought their own personal and evangelical approach to serving the Lord), is now known for his unswerving faith in God. Today, those churches which still sing hymns, know John Newton's hymn the best of all…**"Amazing Grace."** When one man whose faith is uncommon, and who measured life in levels of his usefulness to God, as he could best determine that usefulness, is remembered for a hymn as powerful as **'Amazing Grace'** we must take notice and give honor to one—to whom honor is due. A man whose words from his own heart, poured out to God, have spoken the words of millions of hearts, is worthy of double honor. This is not a paper to discuss the spiritual level of a man's acceptance and place in the mind of God, it is a small note to remind Christians today, that the Lord God uses people who are classified and described in 1st Corinthians chapters 1—4, by the beloved Apostle Paul.

It seems that these days again demand such a reminder of the type of people God uses, when much of what we can see in the modern churches, is just a shadow of such servants of God as we have learned and heard of in the years gone by. **It has not changed, this method of the Lord Almighty,** to use the foolish things of the world to confound the wise (1st Cor. 1. 27), and for God to use the weak things of the world to confound the things that are mighty. The Bible states that real servants of God find that their weakness is God's time for revealing His strength. Paul said, 'I glory in my weakness, for when I am weak, than I am strong (2 Cor. 12. 1-12). This kind of description of strength and weakness is not a common sight today in the grand, multi-staff churches of American society. If the theologians of today, rejoice in weakness, why do they become academically so strong, and if they, were to be like Paul and these who walked in Paul's steps, why do these modern theologians look and sound so differently?

Is this a hard saying? Perhaps we need some examples, of that to which I refer. When men like John Newton, David Livingstone, Watchman Nee, and others of their kind, proclaimed the message of God, there seemed to be a power that is beyond the average pulpit talk of today. We hear different sounds, when we go to a church today, not the sounds of broken hearts for lost souls, pouring out before the people through tears of repentance. Today we hear on TV and in person at Sunday meetings, 'lessons on how to get more from God, how to know your personal gifts, how to find answers to prayers, etc. We hear, 'come and get your healing, get your better income, get, get, get. What men and women of God in days gone by, proclaimed, is a very different message. They spoke of that life which must die more, give more, and repent more so that **God would be pleased, not that man should be eased**. The easy load we carry for Jesus is an inner and spiritual burden that becomes light because of our joy in Christ. **The soul must be burning with the fire from heaven, before we can ignite the flames of revival in the land. (Jer. 20. 9,** 23. 29).

It was the weakness of God that took down the walls of Jericho, and parted the waters for the children of Israel. It was a simple plan that God called His time of 'foolishness,' easy play time, for God to out—wit the smart players of the world's stage, when He turned water into wine, when He made the plans of Herod to destroy the small Child King, (who would establish an eternal Kingdom from above), fail completely. And these children who died at the hands of the mighty Herod of Palestine, became some of the first martyrs who shall rule a world without end, at the appointed time.

This God whom we serve can take a simple fisherman from Galilee and make him walk on water, can take 12 ordinary men from among the crowd of followers of Jesus and send their words and deeds into centuries, far into the future, and to nations that had not yet become nations. And this same Lord of heaven chooses to use the men and women among His flock, who are the weakest(1st Cor. 1.25), least educated, and often rejected among their own, to put the words of life before kings and princes of the world, with astounding power and grace. These men, called ignorant and uneducated, (Acts 4. 13), the weakness of God, were the ones God chose to confound the scholarly, Jewish religious teachers. So why is today's emphasis in seminaries on high levels of education in the field of academics? If this was only for translating the Word of God for the sake of others, we would understand that emphasis. But if it is only for the glory and personal enjoyment of the scholar, if it is an emphasis for self and not only for the sake of others, then something is wrong with the picture. WE have again met the enemy and again, it is us! There is scripture that speaks of this idea, of becoming ones own worst enemy—(those who oppose themselves…2 Tim. 2. 25).

My question is, why have we seen so many narcissistic clergy, who preach in such extravagant buildings, replace these great spiritual leaders of the past? We have forsaken the 'old paths' of sacrifice and honor to replace them with, a new highway of pleasure, and affluence. We, the church in America have seen popular TV personalities like Oprah Winfrey go to Africa and give 50,000 children in Africa, clothes, medical help, and not to mention care and hope, for Christmas, for about the cost of one large church building in America or one year's budget of a large congregation in America. I think she said it cost 4 million dollars. You know this if you saw the Monday night program of Oprah Winfrey at 6pm cst. On ABC Dec. 22, 2003. **It should be embarrassing for the churches in America to know that the humanitarian services of one TV personality, outshine efforts by the Lord's people at Christmas time**, (of all times) before a nation wide audience.

The church was commanded to go into all the World, and we have in America, people who are doing this, just from their heart of compassion because they see the presence of physical and emotional suffering around the world. Where are we? This is a loaded question, because it is meant both ways, where are we in the spiritual, inner man, in our spiritual walk with God, in His ways, and where are we in the world of human needs?

A friend and co-worker in South Africa asked me a question one time, when we were visiting some people in Johannesburg, in the part of the city that might have been classified as an area where people of a lower income lived. He asked 'Hamilton, where do you find these people?' referring to some of the 'types' of humans I am usually found working with in God's Kingdom, and I replied, **"I**

find them where they live." Isn't this what Jesus did? He found us where we are, where we live. You have to be in the neighborhood, you have to walk in the streets and you will find people there, walk in the country, or in the town, you will find people there. Where we live is where we can be found. Pretty simple, but not only simple, it is also important. If we are not willing to be in the flowing tide of humanity, if we do not want to busy ourselves with the difficult business of survival in lands of desperate souls, we will not likely answer the call that Isaiah the prophet of God answered when he said, **"here am I, send me."** (Isa. 6).

The servants of God who are saved to the uttermost, should expect to also be used by the Lord to the fullest. It was Jesus, Lord and creator of man, who said, "the harvest is great, but the laborers are few, pray therefore the Lord of the harvest to send forth laborers into His harvest." This is one of the few things we are commanded to pray for, and it has to do with soul winning around the world. It was the Apostle Paul, commissioned by the Lord to go out into the world and evangelize the Gentile nations, who said, "how shall they hear without a preacher, and how shall they preach except they be sent?" Though we **are not worthy** of this burden for the lost souls, let us give our 'all' to **at least be faithful to it.** We are commanded to live a life worthy of the calling we have been given, (Eph. 4. 1). We are not just called 'out of darkness into His marvelous light,' we are called into service, to be the salt of the earth, to be the light of the world.

It appears very strange indeed, that in the 21st century, there is such an emphasis on the material and social (graces?) of evangelism and ministry in the churches. **We insist on fine buildings, highly educated pastors**(?)and multi-staff ministries we call them, but you can find none of this kind of emphasis, in the lives and ministries of these earlier men and women of God. There is little connection at all to the past ministries of these whom we call heroes of the faith, (in this assembly line of faith), and the modern churches of America. Does this not concern anyone? It is certainly my concern. **I believe that we have lost sight of our task, while enjoying the study about the message.** The message of salvation, the Gospel of Christ, was given along side the great commission, to go into all the world. Just as you cannot separate the Lord Jesus from His own Words, as the source of our salvation, you cannot separate the great commission from the Gospel of Salvation. Luke 24. 45-50, Jesus opened the understanding of His faithful few, and stated, that **this suffering and resurrection happened that repentance and remission of sins should be preached in His Name among all nations.**

If the Christians (church) of today lose the connection, of the commission to the message, then our failure in this loss, will cost more than all the songs and

Sunday services in America's churches can repay or replace. Will the church in America hear words in the judgment like those in the Revelation,? "I know thy works, that thou art neither hot nor cold...as many as I love, I rebuke and Chasten: be zealous therefore, and repent."

22

"See You At The Top"

✦

(Of What?)

The four spiritual laws of the Bible, as I have found them, which are not in your little 'tract' or booklet on the subject used by most people for soul winning are—**Salvation—Service-Sacrifice-Suffering, these are the real 'four spiritual laws'.** This is the progress of the true Christian pilgrim, those who walk with and in Jesus, who will find that each one of the above spiritual laws, leads to the other. Those other spiritual laws dreamed up by some evangelist, are very nice, but a spiritual law is what Jesus makes, like "you shall love the Lord your God,…and your neighbor as yourself"…not some made up slogan, that speaks of the subject of sin, & salvation after the manner of a denominational view. I have read the **"four spiritual laws"** that many pass around in the form of a nice little tract, but the Bible records the Words of Jesus as stating that the law that saves, hangs on two commandments, 'Love God, and love one another.' Those who love God keep His commandments, and Jesus commands that we who follow Him, Repent of sin (Lk. 13.3), be born of the 'water and the Spirit' (John 3. 3-7), and live in the newness of life which He alone is able to give. (Rom. 6:3-10). **All the laws of Christ the Lord for His people are spiritual laws. And they are all equal in importance and power, (Rom. 1. 16)** and must not be separated from one another by man's ideas of their value and their place in our redemption, whether they are hard sayings or not (John 6. 63).

Where these other spiritual laws came from is the imagination of an evangelist who leaves out about half of the Biblical plan of salvation.

Saved people serve others, this requires sacrifice, and those who really sacrifice are willing to accept suffering as the norm, not the exception. But again, a common philosophy of the world, has entered into the fellowship of the church body, and turned the usefulness that God designed for His people into some kind of business scheme which makes people in the church seek an alliance with the present world system, creating a kind of "see you at the top" philosophy that makes success in the present world into some kind of spiritual prize that men can award to men.

We are saved for a reason, not only to belong to the family of God, in Christ Jesus the Lord, but to become useful and fruitful workers in His harvest. (Lk 10:2). As Jesus did, we also now live for others.

To borrow a theme from the popular book written by "Zig" Zigler, entitled "See You At the Top", we can see the plan for those who follow Christ. There is a top to reach in the service of the Lord, we might say it is the top of spiritual commitment, i.e. Jesus said, they who do the will of God and teach it shall be called great in the kingdom of Heaven. But it is not reflected by the worldly view of success in some standard of financial attainment which impresses the lost as well as unsaved church members. There is a 'top' level of service in the Kingdom of God, if you use the idea of what is most pleasing to The Lord. Heb. 11, speaks of those people of whom, the Lord is not ashamed, when they are called by His Name. These would be the kind of witnesses who find favor in God's sight. **That is the real 'top'.**

In the book that bears this title, by 'Zig' Zigler, a fine Christian business man, it was not clear to me why the author never told those to whom he addressed this material he presented, **just what they would be at the 'top of'** when they reached the top as he called it. **The top 'can' on a garbage heap is still in the garbage dump, so it is important to know what** we are going to be at the top of, when we get to that place. To be at the top, seems very desirable, but if I am only at the top of a group of salespersons, or if I am at the top of the financial ladder, or the top of the company 'ladder' then I want to know what meaning that has in my life. We can easily assume that Mr. Zigler meant that those who worked hard, achieved success and found popularity and prosperity by their faithful compliance with the many 'rules' for development of great salesmanship skills, would reach the 'top' of the 'ladder of success'.

When the importance of a persons position among his peers or the status in social circles becomes the dominate feature in one's life, there is nothing ahead but a spiritual 'dead end' street. There is no way to find the will of God in Jesus the Lord, while trying to become important in the eyes of mankind. John 5, in the New Testament is a clear mandate for the followers of Christ. Be it ever so humble there's no place like home, when that home is death to self, and honor that comes from God, John 5. 41-44.

If God brings a humble soul to a prominent position, or into the view of others, it will make the humble soul embarrassed not proud. He who humbles himself will be exalted, and he who exalts himself will be humbled. This is a very clear and unchanging factor. The top of human success is not the same as the top of the success list in the eyes of God. The Lord counts success as faithful obedience to His Word, and a willingness to place others ahead of one's self. Rom. 12. 3, 10,16, Phil. 2.3. When the view or opinion held by lost people in the world is the same about a certain matter or subject as the Christians view, there is something wrong with the view of the Christian.

When the world measures success (in this world) with the same ruler as the church member uses, you can be sure the standard of measure being used did not come from the Bible. People who did not believe, including the Pharisees, Scribes and the multitudes in Jesus' days on earth, considered Jesus as an imposter and one who was misleading the people, and the reason for this rejection of Jesus and His identity as well as His teaching, was because the religious leaders wanted the praise of men, and they did not like seeing the multitudes follow the Lord Jesus. Luke 18.9, John 5. 16, 18. **Be sure that when you follow some guidelines which are guaranteed to take you to the top, that you ask the all important question, "at the top of what?" You need to know what you are at the top *of,* before** you make an effort to get there. There is so much sales-gimmick, personal satisfaction seeking, propaganda in the churches today in America that you have to have wisdom from above, to decipher the worldly knowledge from beneath.

Being at the top of the world's pinnacle of pride and progress, will not be any guarantee of success with God. It is more likely to put you at the bottom of the list of those who please the Lord. Don't let the world be your guiding light if you want to see the things of the Lord more clearly. That would be like a chicken inviting the fox home for dinner.

There is more selfishness in the church today, in many cases than there is in the world. At least in the world people admit they are serving themselves, people in churches make it appear they are pleasing God while serving themselves and gaining an acceptance among fellow narcissistic members. Check out the kinds of books in Christian book stores that are among the top sellers. It looks like a self-improvement seminary library in most book stores. I recently saw on the cover of Oprah Winfrey's magazine, an article entitled "making yourself get what you want" now it may have been "letting" yourself...(I am going by memory).

This is about what a Christian book in a Christian book store could be entitled. Getting what you want, or becoming who you want to be...a lot of self improvement, self motivating, self everything, and nobody seems to be bothered by this love of self movement in the Christian circles. Whatever happened to the verse in the New Testament which states "…except a man hate even his own life also…he cannot be my disciple"? To love your neighbor as yourself, does not refer to a self-love that becomes exaggerated narcissistic, Pharisaical pride that accompanies today's emphasis on 'getting what you want in life.' To love our neighbor as ourselves has to do with an **unselfish good will to consider our neighbor worthy of our attention, not our worship.** This worship of self is a thing that has come in the last days, (2 Tim. 3. 1-5). I am sure you knew that we are in the last days. If not, then look around and wake up to the facts, the statistics, and the daily news.

You can get to the top of the popularity totem pole, or the top of the financial bracket, or the top of anything in this world, but if you do, then don't expect to substitute this position as 'top can on the garbage heap', as being equal to having your name on God's 'top ten' when it comes to judgment day, because He counts things differently and sees things differently than man. Check out Luke 16. 15, which states, **ye are they which justify yourselves before men; but God knows your hearts: "…for that which is highly esteemed among men, is abomination in the sight of God."**

This continual emphasis on education (PhD's and Master's degrees for the average preacher now, and college degrees for anyone who wants to serve the youth of a church) is not something that came from the Scriptures, but from the mind's of men who sought to have glory for themselves and applause from one another-(Luke chapters 12-14). Jesus taught that the people invited to the great supper, and who refused to attend because they were too busy with their own affairs, would not be allowed to taste of that supper, but those humble souls from the streets, and (places where the homeless of America live) squalors of desperation and hopelessness would instead be welcome in the place of the wealthy (check out the average church parking lot),

Times do change, but the proud and selfish are always the same, they mock the poor and homeless, (James 2. 1-17) and present themselves as the great example of 'prosperity and wisdom' saying that "…the poor people of America should have been more frugal and industrious, then they would also be successful just as they." The proud, and wealthy American church member who justified himself, may be very surprised to find when judgment comes, that he passed Jesus by on the street, and failed to see any resemblance to the Jesus he had heard about from the church pulpit. But wisdom is justified by her children (Matt. 11. 16-19). **A man is known by his fruit** (Matt. 7. 16), not by his degree, popularity with people or any other such measure. We will also be judged by our works, and rewarded accordingly, (Rev. 22. 12), not by the standards of carnal men in prophets clothing. (Matt. 7. 13-21). Is the modern American church ready for the day when, the secrets of men's hearts are made known (Rom. 2. 16, Eph. 6. 6)?

There is room for the wealthy American Christian, (1 time. 6 . 17-19) he is to be rich in good works, if he is rich in this world. Many in this category have sent missionaries overseas, sent evangelists around the world and become fruitful in the labor and work of the Lord. But the example of Acts 2, must not be forgotten in these modern times.

The wealthy land owners sold properties and in this way, met the needs of the poor Christians. This is the real church of Christ, and this attitude and spirit must not change with the times.

It is the extravagance that this modern American church has embraced which embarrasses the saints in other lands who suffer daily persecution and deprivation. It is not wealth in itself, nor 'being rich in this world' as Paul speaks of in 1 Tim. 6:, that is a crime, it is the unwarranted and unnecessary extravagance which makes a body of Christ people (church) look similar to a corporation of the American dream, which must turn the Lord's stomach (Rev. 3. 14-20). It also turns the stomach of the real believers who are growing along side the tares in the present world (Matt. 13. 24-30). This is a vexation similar to that referred to in 2 Pet.2. 6-8, when reference is made of Lot and the vexation of his soul over the sinful behavior of the people of Sodom and Gomorrah. Those who are numbered among the faithful in the Kingdom of God, feel this vexation of spirit when dwelling in the midst of wicked people. The Bible states that God is angry with the wicked every day, Ps. 7. 11. Surely the righteous, (not self-righteous) made righteous in the Lord by faith and obedience, must feel the pain, and taste the soured flavor of a country like America whose churches have become only a form of Godliness, void of Gospel power. Those who are in Christ, have definite signs of salvation. They love the Lord, which is shown by obedience to His every command, and they love others, they also make sacrifices to reach the lost souls of the world who have not heard the Gospel, and they are ready to suffer persecution for the sake of the Lord.

The real spiritual laws are those given by the Lord which makes a believer in Christ grow from the position of 'saved' and added to His Kingdom, to service in His kingdom and on to sacrificial living and giving, willing to mature in Christ and reach the next level—willing to endure Suffering as those around the world who bear the same Name. In a chart form it would look like this as a picture of the dimensions illustrating the progress of the real Christian's pilgrimage.

	Suffering (Persecution)
This is the real 'top'	**Sacrifice**—(Cost of discipleship)
	Service—(Faith expressed by deeds)
Salvation (Where our relationship begins as Christians)	

If we seek a top place in God's kingdom, we need to remember, that Jesus said, "if any man seeks to be first he shall be last." In Christ, those who sought only to please God and do His will, were considered by the Lord as faithful servants. **Lk. 17. 10, states, "when you have done all that is required, you shall say of yourself, 'I am an unprofitable servant'** (slave), like the Apostle stated in his writings, we are 'bond servants' and slave in this case is still a good word. This 'see you at the top' philosophy is an American society, achievement centered and self-adulatory concept, not a biblical one. The Bible places a child as the center of God's attention in His Kingdom, and a humble, child-like spirit or attitude is the most valuable to God. This is why the above chart would place the person willing to die for the Lord, as the one who will reach **the point of expected service in His kingdom**. Americans call it, being at the top, concept perhaps, **but Hebrews 11, calls it the normal Christian life.** Let's just keep Rom. 12. 1-3 in mind and we won't need to concern ourselves with 'top' and 'bottom' idea, because in the Kingdom of God, He alone is at the top, the rest of us are His servants. That should be enough for anyone!

Al Hamilton, Missionary

23

The 4—F Factor

✦

Has Replaced,
<u>*Spiritual Fire Power—Jer. 20. 9, 23.: 29*</u>

In the days when the military draft was imposed and in position, each male in America was required to register for the Draft, at age 16. This obligatory responsibility to serve in the military for a required period of time, was a normal part of every young man's future. If a young man was considered to be physically unfit for military service, he would receive a classification as 4-F on his registration card. If he was considered to be physically fit and eligible for military service he would be classified as 1-A. In the 50's a person could be deferred for some other reasons as well. In the late 50's while I was in college, in Kimberlin Heights, Tennessee, attending Johnson Bible College, some of the neighborhood kids used to taunt the Bible College students, for being draft dodgers.

In the days of the Korean war, (which society, the news media, and Washington, called a police action), often called the Korean Conflict, (however, you are just as dead in a police action, whatever you call it), there was a real animosity on the part of young men who went to war against those who stayed behind, or in some way dodged the draft. In those days, you did not go around burning your draft card. Sometimes, the Bible College students would be 'ambushed' by a bunch of the 'country boys' we called them. In the fights I remember, the Bible college students whipped the attacking foe,—I think the ministerial students would have been good soldiers, and most of them were not in college to 'dodge the draft.' **If we could get some fire power from faithfulness to the word of the Lord, we could overcome this 'power failure' that has resulted from the four factors** which I believe have sapped our energy and distracted the church so thoroughly.

In the Bible, in the book of <u>Numbers, chapter 32 verses 6—11,</u> the great man of God, Moses, had to deal with some men of the children of Israel who wanted to avoid going to war. The two tribes of Gad and Ruben, wanted to stay on the 'comfort zone' of land where they were, when the order was given to go over into the new land and occupy and possess it for the Lord. In these verses, Moses says, "…**Shall you sit here while your brothers go to war**? "Why do you discourage the hearts of your brethren from going over into the land that the Lord has given them?" They were told they could come back after the battle and live in the land they chose, but now it was time for battle. So Moses, persuaded them to go as one people, one army of God, to take out the wicked nations, and settle the land for the people of Israel. So it is today, there is some discouragement prevalent in ministry. When 1 out of 10 trained ministers ever end up in foreign fields, no wonder missionaries are often discouraged. This is exactly what Moses said happens to those who engage the enemy without the support of the larger number of soldiers. Consider the scripture application to wartime conditions in the battle for the souls of men. (2 Tim. 2. 2). It is not smart or feasible **to use 'peace time' strategy in war time conditions**. Therefore the church must be armed with the Word of God, and each member must be in active duty. There are the draft dodgers among the religious elite, who care only for their own comfort, and there are the true soldiers of God who can follow commands and instructions, to go into all parts and countries of the world to bring the 'good News' of salvation, to others who sit in spiritual darkness. Notice the fact in the Bible example, (1st Cor. 10. 11) in Numbers, that Moses stated a very true observation, that it is a serious discouragement to those who go into the battle (fields of harvest world wide), when others (of their comrades), sit by as if the battle did not belong to them. God was saying through His man, Moses, when Israel goes to war, everyone fights, there is no one who should sit by and just 'watch the show.'

What a great lesson for today, the whole body of Christ must feel the urgency to accomplish it's task to 'preach the Gospel to every creature.' And if any part of the task is **not** being accomplished, if there **is one sheep left stranded** out in the desert, then the whole church body, needs to be made aware of this fact, and it is time to regroup and re-evaluate our strategy and our emphasis in this modern, American church setting. When Jesus said, the good shepherd gives His life for the sheep, and when Jesus says, there was a case where the shepherd left the 99 sheep to go out and find one that was lost, **we can do no less.** The four factors I mention here are the major areas of interference to the accomplishment of the God given goal to go into **all the** world and preach the Gospel to **every creature. Wartime conditions require wartime strategy.** And this is war. Satan has owned nations outside the United States, and it is time to reclaim, recover and **bring in the sheaves** that belong to our Lord Jesus. We sing it, we say we believe it, now we must do something about it. Forget this craving for, and allegiance to, the goddess of freedom, and let the church march on like a mighty army, and in the power of the Lord, reach the unreached souls of the world for Christ our Lord and our Captain.

Today, if a man says he was classified by the draft board in the 50's as 4-F, most of us who were in college those days, would know what that meant. There is another four—F classification that I have applied to a religious condition for today. It has much of the same connotation as the term I have just referred to above. But the letter F for failure as well, is often one of the grades given in school for those who fail their test. Enough 'F' s and you do not pass the course or maybe even to the next grade level. In light of this use of the terms I have described, it would be helpful to see what has happened in our church circles in recent years.

I believe we have fallen prey to an experience that limits the evangelistic outreach of the church, and brings most of what Christians become involved in, to extremes that are bringing people into themselves, rather than out to the harvest fields of the world. Keep in mind that the book of Romans, chapter 12 and verse one, in the New Testament, states, "present your bodies as living sacrifices,…acceptable unto God **which is your reasonable service.**" I have outlined these experiences and conditions as follows, after observing them for a number of years, and making comparison to the New Testament church and the emphasis that is obvious in the early history and acts of the ecclesia that Jesus built. What we have today, in America, as I have seen it, is **not a worship service** on Sunday as much as what I would call, '**services that the church worships.**' Use Isaiah chapter 58 as an example. In that chapter, the word Fasting is used, as God corrects His people for seeing themselves as deeply devoted to the Lord in their religious rites. But in Isa. 58, God tells the Prophet Isaiah, to speak to that hypocritical fasting they were engaged in, and tell the people what a true devotion really is. It is not a day, set aside to just 'bow the head' or act in a holy manner, (and our word worship could be used in the place of the word fasting in this context I believe), God says, "…Do you call this a fast?" "…I'll tell you what a fast is, a real fast or time dedicated to the Lord is—'to loose the chains of those in bondage, to care for the poor and needy, feed the hungry etc." All of these things are directed toward the needs of others. Read it and weep', this is how God wants those whom He calls His people to honor Him. With unselfish acts toward others, showing love and compassion, not just some 'praise of praise service, and a worship of worship.

Today in many churches, there is more dancing and singing about the wonders of God's love and grace, but at the same moment, somewhere across the seas, millions of souls lie in spiritual darkness, seeking someone to come and light the way. Is it nothing to us, all we who pass by, (Lam. 1. 12), that such sorrow and suffering exist, while the churches in America sing praises to God, then go home in their fine cars, to their expensive house, and live in their extravagance and luxury, reading verses in the Bible, that state, "how difficult it is for a rich man to enter the Kingdom of Heaven." Conditions that make a person think in such terms, (worship of things or services), develop over a period of time, and we are not aware of the leading causes when they just begin to appear.

Christians in a prosperous land have been made to feel that—since God provides all this prosperity, then they must be really holy people and God is surely proud of the average, Christian American's success, and wise use of this talent that God gave to each 'prosperous saint.' As the famous old nursery rhyme says, **We have put in our thumb** (into the American pie), and pulled out a plumb and said, "What a good boy am I." All the emphasis in recent years on the following terms, which I call, **the 'famous four'**, has led me to believe **that a serious condition,** of a negative sort, has led American Christians into a trap that is best described **in 1st Tim. 4, and 2nd Tim. 3. These conditions** are known as 'events of the last days', meaning the last days, of the work of the Lord's church on earth.

The services or areas of greatest concern and attention are as follows:

1. Worship of Freedom, (resulting from the freedom of worship in USA).

2. Worship of Family, (resulting from trying to rescue the USA).

3. Worship of Finances (resulting from the prosperity 'gospel' of the USA).

4. Worship of Fellowship (which is a result of self-indulgence in the USA).

◆   ◆   ◆

To most people, the use of the word worship in front of these four things, would seem a bit harsh. But I find it unlikely that giving so much money, time, attention and commitment to those 'Famous Four' things, I list above, can be called, anything but **the four major things that receive our deepest devotion,**

in the average American church today. The dictionary describes worship as, reverence and devotion to a deity, and/or **extreme devotion or intense love or admiration of any kind.** The book of John, chapter four, verses 23 and 24, are where it is recorded that Jesus said to the woman at the well, "True worshippers shall worship the Father in Spirit and in Truth, for the Father seeks such to worship Him." In Matthew 4. 10, Jesus stated to the enemy, Satan: "get from here, for it is written, you shall worship the Lord your God and **Him only shall you serve."**

Now, look at the list again; America's love (intense love or admiration) for freedom, is one thing, it is even something to be admired in the citizenry of the nation, but for a Christian, to have such equal, and similar, intense love and admiration for freedom, is a very different matter. As I have said in other pages, a Christian must love the Lord God with ALL of his/her heart, so there is no room left to have equal and similar degree of love for anything else. WE cannot serve two masters, money and God, even so, we cannot serve, freedom's call, (give me liberty or give me death), in this country (even for the churches sake), and serve God fully with our whole heart, mind, soul and strength. **God uses people who are not politically and socially in a country of freedom**, as well as He can use American Christians **with** their political freedom. A Christian lives the same life, whether or not he is politically free to do what a Christian wants to do, or what he is commanded by the Lord to do. Freedom is not an issue.

Christians all around the world today, as in every age since the death of Abel in the Garden of Eden, have suffered and died for the Name of Jesus and faith in Him. So freedom was not the dominate and controlling force or motive in the minds or hearts of the Martyrs. Each one who has died for Christ, (in this year 2003, approximately 166,000) will have died, simply because that person refused to accept Freedom as a substitute for Faith in Christ. So obviously freedom **is not worshipped or revered as the most important feature or gift in life**. However the emphasis that freedom is given in churches in America has led many of us who serve the Lord Jesus, to believe that it is not number 3 or 4, but number one in the American Christian's list. When Jesus spoke these words in Matthew at the time of His own temptation to have worldly things and kingdoms, He secured the victory for those who follow Him, if they who follow Him will make the same choice. The Lord God only, shall you serve.

This means that **nothing else can take the place of Christ**, even a good thing, Jesus alone has been given all authority and power by the Father, in heaven and in earth and, in the Christians life. Today, young Christian, American soldiers, fight for freedom for others, (remember the picture of the young men being baptized In the deserts of Iraq before the war began), and they fight for justice, truth and opportunity for weaker nations. Placing freedom high on the scale of values, in life as an American and as a Christian is Biblically sound doctrine. But to serve freedom, or worship it, **as if we could not live without it**, is wrong. The Bible says, do as much as possible to 'live peaceably with all men,' it also states, in Prov. 24. 11, 12, that it is the duty of the godly person to deliver those who are in danger of death or face destruction at the hand of the wicked. This is not the same as bowing at the feet of a goddess of freedom, as if it was deserving of the same devotion, time, attention and reverence or homage as we give to God.

This is the point, that concerns believers in the Western world, we must ask, the question,—**have the Christians in America become so enamored with the idea and concept of freedom**, that we neglect our duty—to free lost souls around the world from the slavery of sin? It becomes a matter of emphasis placed upon certain responsibilities as believers and as citizens. The efforts of soldiers under the American flag, fighting to secure freedom for innocent souls around the world, enslaved in political bondage, is a task worthy of our attention and involvement, certainly this is needed, and it is Biblical—see (Prov. 24. 11,12). The point for American Christians is, will American Christians, fail to leave this 'land of the free' and 'home of the brave' long enough to carry the Good News of salvation to others, as ambassadors for Christ. Or is our **attachment to our political freedom and it's glorious relatives (opportunity, affluence and success etc.)** holding such a power over us as servants of God, that we cannot see that a hideous 'love for the world' has ensnared us? In the last days, many will forsake the way of the Lord, for the way of the world, 2 Tim. 3. 1-13. Paul the Apostle described this in his own time, as a very real problem, 2 Tim. 4. 10 when he stated, "Demas has forsaken me, having loved this present world." If a nation can worship an idol, (and it can), and if a country, though founded upon good principles and holy ordinances, can fall into the ditch of self-satisfaction, (and it can), then America is as vulnerable to these conditions as any nation in the world. Those who, having once known the will of God, if they forget Him and His way, they too shall be forgotten. When Israel turned it's back on the Lord, and become wicked in their deeds, the nation of Israel was likened unto Sodom, and linked with that wicked city in God's eyes.

In Ez. 16. 48-50, The prophet of the Lord was told to give this picture to the people, saying, "...you are like your sister, Sodom, who because of affluence, abundance of idleness, and losing sight of the needs of the poor and needy people, have became a disgrace to God, and these sins had led to terrible sexual debauchery. America has given evidence of these sins, and deserves the same pronouncement. But the churches in America, with their affluence, abundance of idleness and little concern for the poor and needy of the world, must also take some of the blame. The **worship of freedom is not the same as freedom of worship**. In the American church, the constant emphasis on 'freedom of worship' became an obvious worship of freedom. Freedom was a gift from the country, and the church welcomed it with open doors. How many flags fly in your house of prayer? Jesus said the purpose of His Father's house was to be a house of prayer. "…My house shall be called a house of prayer, and you have made it a den of thieves," Mk. **11. 17**. What had happened to the Jews who were making a market place out of the Temple area referred to in this scripture, was a spiritual departure from the original purpose of the 'house of prayer' for all people. The money changers and those making merchandise of the things that God had established for spiritual purposes, was being used for material and carnal purposes.

Freedom, in it's political and social dimension, as a product of citizenship in America and other 'western' countries, must not be confused with the liberty and spiritual freedom we have in Christ as believers. The believer is free in Christ, but this speaks of an inner and eternal freedom, as to be set loose from the bondage of sin and it's consequences. Freedom in Christ, is liberty to be His servant or bond-slave. These 'four F' factors that I refer to, which begin with the social and political freedom, available to citizens in Western countries, are four major problems that I have noticed came upon the church in America, while it was enjoying a time of ease and comfort. It is my belief that the four things disrupting the world-wide evangelistic outreach of the church have been unnoticed or at least unmet with any effort to make necessary changes in the direction that the church should be taking on the path that leads to being 'used to the fullest.' Each of these four factors, Political Freedom, Family emphasis, Finances and Fellowship, are in some measure to be the tools for servants of God to use in the work of world outreach. But in America, the church has allowed these **four things to become the 'influences' which dictate the direction that the modern church would take in it's path toward** success and growth, which two items are rarely used as descriptive of spiritual maturity in the Bible, when referring to the duty of God's people toward the Lord.

◆　　　◆　　　◆

If we trace the number two influence: 'Family' to the time when it became a strong emphasis in churches, we can see that such terms as 'family worship' began to overrun the common sense, and Biblical approach that was valuable to Christian development. Now we see what can more aptly be described as 'worship of the family.' Notice these two things; Number one, some people who love God, do not have a family to focus upon. The 'Basic Institute in Youth Conflicts' and 'focus on the family', emphasis that has been part of many churches in America, has made the issue of 'family' so important to the recovery of 'American values', that we may have forgotten that Christian obedience to God, is the purpose of the church, not the recovery of a very noble government. The church was not commissioned to go into all the world and establish a good form of government. Our duty to God as followers of His Son, our Savior, is to lead every person to a knowledge of His will.

The concern that Christians in America (who also vote) have for a stronger and more 'Christian' government, has so occupied the mind and even the Bible lessons of church goers, that it was just a short step into 'world service' and service to country. Believers just wanted to carry the two along together. The popular theme, **'God and Country'** became the cry of the Christian as well as the cry of the citizen, but not all citizens are Christians. <u>So in recent years, here is what happened in America.</u>

Family, had to be in tact, in focus (under Christian perception of course), but not much was said if the nice family was completely dedicated to God, of if the desired American family was just going to be nice and accept some Christian values, and hide behind an appearance of some Bible principles in form only, so that the country (USA) would be a better place. This would probably mean, voting against abortion rights, voting against the acceptance of homosexuality as a 'viable' life style and going to some church on some Sundays, hooray, this would make a better America. What a motive for Godly living! …Duh. If the country was going to have citizens who were conscious of God, and would give attention to holy things, churches would also accept this close encounter with God as close enough, to pass as a 'Christian inspection, wow, what an arrangement. American Christians want their country **and** their God, and if they can't have both, they are not sure which of the two they should choose. The heavy emphasis on 'Christian family values' was not just to bring people to the throne of God, it was an emphasis, that had as it's purpose, even if it was a secondary purpose, the tying of Family to country, and both to God. Churches in America wanted to link up the three (family, nation and God), as if that would solve the world's problems, make God happy and give everyone peace and quiet. **No wonder many countries rejected our religion, it was fastened to our nation.**

The emphasis on family and family values as found in the main line churches, became the 'driving force' in the last 20 years or more, behind the unholy union between church and state. I call it an 'unholy union' because there is no biblical principle for such a close walk together, of a single nation of the present world (Gal. 1. 4), and the Saints of God, or the ecclesia. Some people in America who love and serve God, do not enjoy the privilege of a 'family connection.' So what will these people 'focus' on? If the church continually emphasizes the need for 'Christian Family ties' what do you tell the child, or man or woman for that matter, who has no real family connection? People on the streets, those in any socially unusual condition unattached to loved ones, would have no close fellowship with this 'family centered church' that some Americans are privileged to enjoy. **This message of Family, and it's exaggerated importance is a message for only a small percent of the 'American pie' life style.** Jesus said, that His message, when accepted by some, would divide some believers from family, and even make them hated by family members. I have seen this in many countries, including this one called "land of the Free."

It is very good and biblical to call for families to obey the Lord Jesus, but to send a message to the United States Government that having biblical family values will solve all of their problems, is not true. The United States Government would also have to stop sinning, and turn to Christ for forgiveness, if it, as a nation seeks to be at peace with God. There is more to Christian service than just having a happy family. **And as long as the church in America seems to worship this family connection, or be so devoted to it as a premise, that it looks like a worship of family**, then we are still in troubled waters. And if you don't think this family focus has become a number one 'hot item' for believers, just check out' the names of churches and how they have changed, "Family Worship Center", Family Fellowship Tabernacle," replaces the word church, and you can go on with such titles and descriptions of 'places of worship or prayer' as you travel across the land. Everyone is afraid of the term 'church' now, because their **emphasis has changed** to such things as 'fellowship', family and worship services. The family of God, is the extended family that belongs to each believer, because Jesus said, 'He who forsakes all that he has as my disciple, for the kingdom of God's sake, shall in this life have manifold more in this present time, houses, parents, brethren, and in the world to come—life eternal, Luke. 18. 23-30.

◆   ◆   ◆

The number three, 'F' that has influenced the church in America, is finances. There is prevalent in this country among believers, the common notion that some kind of promise of prosperity follows the disciple of Christ. It has been often called, 'the prosperity gospel', though it is not THE Gospel of Christ. Much teaching, many books, tapes and material has been presented to the Christian public, in the USA about how God wants every one 'healthy, wealthy and wise. Although the Scripture states that the servants of Christ, (which is obvious to the persecuted church around the world), shall suffer persecution (all who live Godly in Christ Jesus), and in this world the Saints will have tribulation, etc. and again, 1 Tim. 5. 23, 2nd Tim. 4. 20, and other verses refer to the fact that health and wealth is no sign of spiritual maturity.

Any good, study of the Bible, makes it clear that suffering is part of service, and that rich American Christians are not necessarily the shining example of holiness. Financial gain, has become the theme of many who preach that good stewardship and financial prosperity make for deep spiritual insight and character. But this teaching is not a biblical one.

The influence of the Christian Bible upon the United States is unquestioned, but in like manner, the influence of America upon the church is also an obvious fact. It is hard to walk together and not be accepted by observers as having some agreement in some things. **The world and the church, or at least America (a nation of the world) have been walking hand in hand for 200 years**. It has been such a connection in recent years that many other nations see the country of the USA as synonymous with Christianity. Some have made great gain on the very popular place of religion (Christianity) in America. Books, tapes, seminars, and a multitude of highly paid 'pastors' have made many of the fellow believers in other lands, where persecution is rampant, ask a lot of hard questions.

I have been in enough countries of the world where the church is under serious suffering, to know what the questions are and how the brothers and sisters abroad, view the American church member. Our God provides some prosperity for some of His children, but prosperity is not our God. **Our God created His church to bring us together in fellowship also, but Fellowship is not our God**. WE are given spiritual liberty and freedom in Christ, but freedom is not our God. Many Christians of a strong financial position, look upon the poor believer as if he was some kind of 'other' person, who is not like them, and should have been wise, hard working, and the poor would also become like them, wealthy and wise. But economic conditions are not the conditions which bring someone to faith in Christ and keep him there.

Financial power and popularity, should be a tool for a believer (1st Tim. 6. 5-19) not a ruler by which to measure all other believers. If a Christian's devotion is directed toward how successful he is in finances, and he sees all who are poor as people below his level, that Christian will find walking with Jesus very uncomfortable. And he may also soon fine his walk very lonely, he may look around someday and wonder where everyone went. Wealth makes people independent, but independence like this also makes believers proud and self-centered.

◆   ◆   ◆

The fourth 'F' which lingers in the heart of Christians as a force that can be a good motivator for spiritual development, is Fellowship. It is also a command of the Lord's Apostles, to continue in 'fellowship', breaking of bread (Communion) and prayers. Fellowship is something that many missionaries have spoken of as a missing link in their early days on a foreign field. The importance of fellowship, is a 'given' we cannot overlook its importance in the Christian life. But again, it cannot be looked upon as a major need, to be placed above the command to preach the Gospel. If we are in a place for God, that has little or no Christian witness, therefore little fellowship of other believers, we cannot run away and hide, from our assigned task from God, to sow the seed of the Gospel in hard to reach neighborhoods. Our God provides fellowship of believers, but fellowship is not our God. We cannot worship this particular experience, any more than we can the other 'blessings' that God provides for His people. If someone who seeks to serve the Lord in a foreign society, and has little or no Christian fellowship, this is not a reason to become discouraged and leave the 'hard to reach areas' of the world without a witness for the Gospel. **If the lack of fellowship is the cause of a missionary or missionary family returning to their 'homeland' it is a very weak excuse.** Local people became our source of 'fellowship' in Africa, when we arrived there in 1960. It was many months before believers were added to the Lord and His church. Our limited fellowship with other believers did not become a reason for dropping the entire project. I have seen the time when this lack of Christian fellowship became the reason given for some missionaries to leave the field of service in foreign lands. Today there is a great need for workers in the harvest fields of the world, in difficult places where there will not be a large crowd of fellow Christians on Sunday to fellowship with, and to share with. If a missionary bows to the goddess of liberty, and the hunger for fellowship, there can be little chance to let God's Spirit show the way to enter the hearts of people of another land, and language.

The four 'F's were to be gifts from God, but not gifts to replace God. The present day emphasis by American Churches on these 4 things, political freedom, family, finances and fellowship, do not need to become the major players in our personal service to God. We must not let these tools, become our master, and we must not let the blessings become our God. There is but one God, and his gifts and his blessings cannot be what we worship, we must rather please Him by keeping our priorities in line, and our emphasis on Him, who is the giver of life, not upon the gifts in this life that God provides. This is another lesson we learn from just knowing Him, who is Lord, and it is a lesson (1st Cor. 2. 1-10), we must not fail to observe. We too, walk on holy ground, it is the calling to serve the Lord Jesus only. We must **determine not to know any thing among others, save Jesus Christ and Him crucified. So let it be written, so let it be done!**

Our God provides a family connection for many, but family is not our god.
Our God provides finances for some, but finances is not our god.
Our God provides fellowship, but fellowship is not our god.
Our God provides social freedom for some, but freedom is not our god.

American churches need to remember, that only God is God!

24

The Calling

♦

Phil. 3. 7-14

A friend of mine, when we were discussing the unreached people of the world and the unfinished task of taking the Gospel to all people on the globe, said to me, that he agreed, with my sense of urgency up to a point, yes we need to get the task accomplished, as God leads, but we need to get it done right. I suppose he meant what we would all agree with, that is, in the philosophy that, __*no job half done is well done.*__ My response to this most noble and very popular truism is, *that not being done at all is certainly not being done well either.* My remarks had been written at the close of a letter I had written to my co-worker, I had stated in the close of my letter to him, "lets get it done." When I read his kind reply "yes lets get it done, but lets get it done right," at the closing of his letter, those words stood out like a clown in a church service. These most 'educated' and planning centered words which would comfort the student, the educator, and the average American church member have in them the power to slow us to a grinding halt in our movement toward fulfilling the Great commission of Jesus to His followers. I'll tell you why.

If we are to hear the words of the Master, Jesus, that all of His people and servants hope to hear, ..."well done, thou good and faithful servant, you have been faithful over a few things, I will make your ruler over many things, enter thou into the joy of thy Lord." Matt. 25. 21, then we can agree with the statement I have just made, *no task half done is well done.* We are taught the value of that concept from an early age in most homes, and in most churches and certainly in the "land of the free" and "home of the brave." A very logical response to a 'lets get the job done," is a resounding, yes, but let's get it done right. At the time these two statements were made some years back (in the 70's as I recall), there was a great interest among young Christians in the mission fields of the world. I would have carried the discussion further, which I did in many talks to churches about world missions. We surely cannot be thinking that the job left undone is "well done." And if it (the task we speak of here) is not being done at all (in most corners of the globe) then how can that be called '*doing the job right?* This heavy emphasis on training at the time this discussion came up, is still upon us today.

This is why so many of our young University students who love Jesus, cannot seem to put their career and their calling, where their mouth is. They still feel unqualified, and unprepared. The magic words of 'be prepared' and be sure you are qualified has stunted the eager yearning of young hearts to share the Gospel of Christ with other nations. It sounds so wise and so noble to say, I don't want to go out into the woods with an ax that is dull, I must first take time to sharpen the ax. Oh, how intelligent that sounds, but now what we have after 40 years of sharpening, is a shed full of sharp ax's which are unused, because no one felt quite qualified to go into the woods to work. What does the word 'qualified' mean, or the term 'prepared'? These terms are a way of defining someone's effectiveness by using man's terms to evaluate other men.

Perhaps the scholars of today have forgotten their history, as it relates to the effective proclaiming of the word of the Lord by early martyrs; i.e. Anne Hutchinson, born in 1591, died in 1643.

Anne Hutchinson, mentioned in 'Foxe's Book of Martyrs, p. 277, ff is a good example. Anne had no formal education, and several times had been arrested for speaking out about her Puritan beliefs, she broke with the Church of England, as an avid student of the KJV of the Bible and with high moral life and standards, she opened her home to large classes of women in her farm house, and she taught and believed that true godliness came from the inner presence and working of the Holy Spirit. Soon even the Puritan pastor rejected her continual presentation of simple Bible teachings. In 1637 she was brought to trial for her religious convictions in New Towne, on the Charles River opposite Boston. She was found guilty of sedition and contempt, she was banished to her limited choice of places to reside and in Vredeland, near what is now Pelham Bay in New York, she and her family were killed by hostile Indians. Annes minister of the Puritans in Massachusetts Bay colony drove her out because of her Biblical views, which were different than the accepted and established church. *Her freedom in America for religious views, turned out to be her passage to death* due to the intolerance of the established church. Anne Hutchinsons name is remembered, not because of her education and eloquence, but because of her faith and commitment to her personal relationship with the Lord Jesus. There are many such examples.

The very warning itself, of the educated Christian elite to be well prepared, is in itself the proof that they—who want all this time spent in education and training and preparation (as they call it)-are the ones who have left the great task of going into all the world *half done*. Actually, it is worse, these who love education, training and 'sharpening of ax's have not been getting any of the 'trees felled,' in those parts of the woods where 'unreached' trees are located. *Those who are so particular that everything gets done right,* have evidently decided that since it is so difficult to determine when a task is done *right* they don't even do it at all. So what can be right about leaving this task not done at all? I would rather fumble the ball sometimes than be one who never carries it at all, for fear of not making a touchdown on every carry. When Jesus said in Mark 1. 17, follow me and I will make you fishers of men, this was to let the person following know that they did not have to seek out some method or means of learning how to fish for men, Jesus was clear, He said, I will make you fishers of men. In other words, follow me, and let me worry about how you are going to do the job, that I will give you. Just as the Lord told Abraham, "leave your land you now live in, and go into a land That I will show you, future tense. The present tense in that command was, leave where you are, and go into a land that I (will show you) future tense. So Jesus said, Follow me and I will make you (future tense) fishers of men. There is no word here about some duty on their part to get ready, the get ready was, drop what you are doing, and go where I am leading. In Acts, the Apostles were told to tarry (wait) in Jerusalem *until* they received power from on high, that is very clear as well, an instruction to wait, receive and then go into nearby areas, and finally into all the world. Believers now receive the Holy Spirit upon immersion (called Baptism) into Christ (Acts 2. vs. 38) Very clear instructions, no way to misunderstand that. We do not all have to go to Jerusalem and wait for anything.

Now preachers tell us, go to *your Samaria*, or *your Judea*. We don't have one of our own Samaria or Judea today, this is a mixed message, some words from the book of Acts, then an added interpretation that in someway we each have our own Samaria and Judea. This really makes Christians feel they can stay anywhere and call it **into all the world**. Not so, we are now in the final level of the command, which is "into all the world" this is all that is left of this command for us, because the other areas of the world were just the starting point. Don't try to reinvent the task, just get on with the work. In a relay race, each runner does not have to go back and start at the starting block, he takes the baton from the hands of the previous runner, and proceeds from where he is. We have received the Word of God from others, we don't have to go sit down and rewrite it, or try to start from the age of William Tyndale, or John Wycliffe. We take up the baton, and move on forward. This is part of the reason the job is not getting done In all places of the globe, everyone seems more interested in going back to the starting block and waiting for some special call that will not be given again. Or there is the problem of 'the teaching' that some special man given qualification, or level of education (none of which is mentioned in Holy Scripture) is required before the sower of the seed can go out into the field. I am not against education, I am just in favor of truth, and we seem to fit well into the category spoken of by Paul, we are ever learning, but not able to arrive at the Truth!

It seems that today Christian workers are being told that they must first know all about how the seed is created and they must examine the seed carefully before they sow it. I got an idea, why not just trust God to be able to cause the seed to grow? Now there's a novel idea, found in 1 Cor. 3. 7, maybe that will work, and we won't have to waste time, trying to do God's part, we can just do our part as good stewards of the manifold Grace of God.

You may know that in a town of Potiskum in Nigeria, in 1995 a Christian believer, Azubuike, was stoned and macheted nearly to death by Muslims. Another Christian was beheaded. This man's head was then placed on a stick and carried around the town by a Muslim who shouted, "Allah Akbar!" (Allah is great). This happened when about 5000 Muslims, mostly young students of the Koran, invaded Potiskum with the same shouts. We see these listed in 'Foxe's Book of Martyrs,' p. 352, as heroes of the faith, and they are not remembered for what the studied, they suffer and die around the world, whether or not they have an education. These faithful believers have little or no time to know anything except Christ and Him crucified. Sounds familiar does it not?

I have seen new converts to Christ in Africa, lead their friends and family to Christ, although they have themselves not been able to even read or write their own language well. What made them qualified to preach the Gospel? How do these new,young believers know that they are prepared to go out into the other villages or homes of lost people and tell them of the salvation we have in Christ? But, the most highly educated, the workers most familiar with the Bible, still sit by the fire discussing what they already know, and feeding the full, while starving hungry nations of the world wait upon the educated elite Christian worker to decide he/she is really ***prepared*** to go out into all the world. Lets be sure we do it ***right*** the young man told me. So define ***right***! What does it mean to do this work of God's Kingdom ***right?*** It means whatever we want it to mean.

For some who do not feel the urgency of 1.6 Billion souls waiting to know the Salvation of the Lord, it means wait until they feel led to go into other lands. Of course no one can describe or define this business of **'feeling led'** so few will con-test any definition of the idea of 'the leading of the Lord,' and this is a shame because we already know **the will** of the Lord, He is not willing that any should perish, but that all should come to repentance. Whenever a command of God appears difficult to fulfill or to understand, men who feel confident in further study of theology will run 'home to mama' and try to learn more. Those who feel confident in their **comfort zone of family** and friends will 'run home to their mama' which is filed under the section of **'responsibility'** in the library of safety. Those who feel comfort and confidence in the mind-set of the magic word **'accountability'** will run home to their mama of **failure fear.** You can always tell the heart of the Christian worker who lives in the lake of fear, there are big words or statements that impress others in their camp, floating all over the lake. State-ments like, 'I must look after my children, and my wife, I could not put them in any danger,' of course you don't see statements like that in the biography of Wil-liam Carey, father of modern missions, but this does not stop the fearful little worker whose calling to go into the hard and needy places of service, is about as hallow as a metal baseball bat. This makes me ask, if William Carey is the father of modern missions, where did all of his children run off to? There have been a few good men and women, like Gladys Aylward, Hudson Taylor, and those few in the early years of American History. But try to locate many from your church today. The great names and authors in America today whose names appear often in the spotlight of the American church stage, seem to be among those who have found some measure of 'success?' in the American pulpits, and television pro-grams, with occasional trips abroad and more books on how to help us get closer to God without having to leave town.

I always worry about a minister (or Pastor) who has on his shelf a book enti-tled, "What The Bible Says About God." Can you have a book under that title in a minister's library without his being embarrassed about it? That is like an ant writing a book entitled "the delicate intricacies of the power of electricity." If I want to know what the Bible says about God, would I not just read the Bible?—Duh.

As long as there are Christian professors, psychologists and seminarians giving advice to young people in the churches today, about how qualified and prepared a servant of God must be before he or she steps out in faith to give the Gospel to those who hunger for the Word of God, we are going to have this phenomenon of inadequacy haunting the minds of the 'not far from the Kingdom of God' searchers in the American churches. Many sincere young Christians are turned away in their zealous search for fields of service, where they know that suffering and agony fills the hearts of souls in distress, simply because they are told by scholars that preparation and qualification, (as defined by them of course) is a prerequisite to adequate, useful ministry in foreign lands.

And of course these advisors recommend that the young college age student attend the college where the professor or academician (advisor) happens to be teaching. We have placed the emphasis in the wrong place. We have admired and announced the greatness of Christian Martyrs, but we have not learned from their example. WE need what the Martyrs had, and we don't need what they did not seek or covet. There is _no time_ for filling out plate with things that do not motivate us to reach the lost souls. If we give time and money to study and ego, we will let many perish whom we could have reached who only wanted to know Jesus as Savior and Lord, not how much we know. This is not good!

When the worship of freedom, opportunity and narcissism all converge at the same office in the American church dreamland of *world view Inc*. what do you get? *Worship information* and you will serve the god of knowledge. *Worship freedom* and you will be at the beckoned call of the lord of opportunity for self advancement. *Worship the country* you live in and you will be under the power of world politics as defined by government Inc. 1Tim.6. 3-5 speaks to our time, as does the Gospel message of our Lord Jesus, when He said, you cannot serve two masters, for you will either hate the one and love the other, or you will cling to one and forsake the other. Read the sermon on the mount again and see if the foundation for your house if solid or not.

Some years ago, in discussing the urgent need for workers for Christ world wide, one of my good friends with medical training as well as academic training in Bible studies, told a large group of young High School students, that they should be well prepared for ministry to lost people. As an example he cited the background he had and training of several years in preparation for becoming a medical doctor. He then went on to ask the group of students, "Who would you rather have operate on you, a well-trained, experienced and knowledgeable surgeon or a young new intern?" Of course to ask this question is to answer it. So the doctor used this to illustrate the need for academic studies to prepare for missionary ministry around the world. Sounds great!

But I saw what was happening here to be another example of mixed messages. For when the students agreed with the conclusion of the fine Christian doctor, all of them failed to follow up in their minds with another obvious question and example. Jesus was the one who most used the tool of 'complete' thinking, yet many miss this point. So later I asked to share with some of these fine young minds, a second illustration related to the good doctors illustration. I simply asked, "and if you are in a war, and on the battlefield and your hand is blown off, who would you rather have come to your aid and stop the bleeding, and save your life, the qualified, well experienced, *trained surgeon who is 8,000 miles away*, or the medic or corpsman in your battalion *who is there near you?* Now put that next to the first question. Because the fact is as follows; we are not the physicians, Jesus is the 'fixer' the savior of mankind He is the physician, so the illustration is not even adequately applicable. Being a witness for Jesus has not the same requirements as being a medical doctor. We can all witness for Christ, but we do not all expect to be medical doctors. We are just the 'runners' (a military term for 2nd world war message carriers from unit to unit).

Secondly, it is obvious that if I am in need of a message that can save me, I'll gladly take the words from the simple (non-academic) Christian who happens to be in my country, at my door, as opposed to the well trained, professor, theologian who is not there, but is in his little school 8,000 miles away. As I have said for years, the first real qualification for mission work is to *show up!* Because no matter how well trained, and well qualified you are, if you are not there, you can't help anyone anyhow, anytime.—But for well educated men, to offer a one-sided illustration to prove a point for the value of academic studies as a litmus test for Christian service, is a bit ludicrous to say the least. Give it your best shot dear theologians, the greatest teacher of all is the one who said, "Follow me, and *I will make you fishers of men! And don't think Jesus is not still in this business, little children sing it, and true Believers accept it, and new souls coming to Christ experience it, If I were you I would not doubt it!*

We have put the emphasis on the wrong syllable, we have in our generation spoken in our churches and circles of Christian education, more about *what we can learn about the Bible*, than we have about what we *can do to get it spread* around the earth.

What about this great task before the church, to go into all the world, not part of the world, to do the whole job not some of it? If we all agree that a job half done is not well done, then how can the American church just float along taking so much of the precious time allowed for reaching all of the world for Christ, keep starting more churches, building more buildings, hiring more staff for each church in this one country, **doing part of the job only—and not feel guilty? How can such a church expect Jesus to say…** *"WELL DONE…*good and faithful servant" to a church that admits the fact that half done is not well done, or that partly done is not well done? Where is the 'well done' you expect to hear?

It is not going to be there if it hasn't happened. Jesus is not only the Way and the Life—He is the *Truth!*

Al Hamilton
Missionary

25

The Rain That Falls

✦

Matt. 5: 45

Perhaps, the rain that falls, and the sun that shines, in this verse has more meaning for this present life in modern America, than we care to attribute to it. If the followers of Jesus are to be the children of the Heavenly Father, Jesus makes a commandment about love and kindness so paramount that we cannot overlook the significance of it's power to place us in 'the family' of God. Treatment of others with love, and in the way Jesus commands is a prerequisite, to being called children of our Father in heaven, because Jesus states it this way, **"that** you may be the children of your Father who is in heaven."

This adds the conditional aspect of the words commanded in verses 43 & 44. The command is, love your enemies, bless those who curse you, do good to those who despitefully use you, and persecute you.

Do this (we could say, in a paraphrase), **so that you may be the children,** who are just acting in the same way as the Father in heaven, because the Father in heaven gives as much sun light and rain to the bad guys, as He does to the good guys. There are some blessings that are available to all of humanity, no matter if they who receive them are right or wrong, good, bad or ugly, and whether or not they are living by faith in the Lord or if they live horrible lives of disgrace to humanity, or whatever. The blessings of sunlight and rain, are there, and the benefit of both sunlight and rain will be the same benefit to all people, believers and unbelievers.

The truth of these blessings (that sunlight and rain provide) as gifts from God**, and** how Jesus uses this example, **reveals more light** than we may want to acknowledge perhaps. There is the blessing of life giving—sunlight (heat and light), and the blessing of life giving rain, available for all of God's marvelous creation. So this scripture reveals that good things from God, which provide the necessary components for well being and for sustaining life on earth, are not measured out only to those living under God's favor. Speaking of light, this verse of scripture sheds a lot of light on how God values the existence of humankind. It also sheds light on the tremendous love and grace that all people of the earth receive daily, from the Creator's handiwork.

So the point is, since God has provided some blessings necessary for life, to all people, therefore the spiritual blessings of kindness, and love that He puts within His followers are to be shared equally as well, under all circumstances, even for the enemies of the elect. Just as a follower of Christ will treat his fellow Christian, he/she must treat even an enemy with the good will and kindness that God has put in the believer's heart. These spiritual blessings of a 'changed' life are not to be reserved only for those who know the Lord, but must also extend to the unkind, the persecutor, the hater of God. Some deeds of life giving care are meant to be shared with all others, even the people considered undeserving. For, as **Jesus stated, if you only love those who love you, what reward is there in that?** Lost people can do that much. The love of Christ that is in the heart of the believer is meant for everyone, just as the sunshine and the rain from heaven is meant for everyone.

This will really make the churches which give help and care **only** to **their own membership**, shrink back and take a second look. That is, if they are honest with the Word of the Lord. There is also the broader application of these words about the rain and the sun's blessings upon mankind, it is an application that reaches into dimensions of life that we seldom consider as being connected to the Christians 'world view'.\

Consider for example, the fact that people, especially in the Western world, who work hard, apply sound principles to their business or activity, live with positive mental attitude and do all the right things after a successful business mind-set pattern, become known as great people of wealth and are therefore viewed as successful people in the world, and become recognized as examples of good business practice. These same people may have no love for God or for spiritual and biblical values.

This too, is the rain that falls. This is the sun that shines on the good, the bad and the ugly. There are principles (we may call them principles) of success or rules of life that will work, for anyone who will use them. The idea of planting and reaping what you sow, the ideas used in many corporate sales meetings, or principles of life that make people succeed at what they do, will work for a lost soul as well as a saved person. **This too is the sun that shines, and the rain that falls.** But it is really not smart to take the example of success that the 'Western

World' has seen come about, (as a result of applying wise principles given like rain to all), and apply these examples and business rules to the church. Just because these principles worked, and made some people wealthy or wise, does not indicate that all who follow these principles will be in favor with God. Just because the rain falls on the unjust, and the just, it does not make the unjust chosen vessels of God. The **rain, or the blessings that fall upon those who apply good rules for success in their business life**, will not just automatically bring them closer to God. The rich man who went away from Jesus, very sad (Matt. 19. 22, lk. 18. 22-23) kept **his wealth, but lost his soul**, (as far as we know, unless later he decided to do what Jesus commanded). The rich man missed it altogether, Jesus said he was not far, but was still not **in.** This is not horseshoes, getting close will not count. **Getting wet in the rain is not the idea, and receiving blessings that God gives to all humanity will not write your name in the Lamb's Book Of Life.** Those who practice great principles of life in this world, and find rules of success that are effective, **are just walking in the rain.** The great strides in business or other fields of endeavor that many business men and women, Christian or non Christian take, and the success attained thereby can be attributed to various causes. A person who wisely applies great skills, natural or learned, can perhaps find success raining down upon him or her, and become popular and wealthy. That rain from above and that sunshine is for them to enjoy, but it does not mean that just because they are in the worlds 'book of successful people' that they are special in God's eyes, because of their success. Real success in life that the Lord Jesus values is achieved by trying to treat everyone equally, with love and respect, and to make no difference between the rich and the poor in this world, because God provides some things for everybody, but He provides life eternal only for those few who love Him, and love others the way He commanded. The rain that falls is for all, but not all people know who sent it, nor does everyone who gets wet in the rain, choose to follow the rain maker, and let Him be their 'new life' Creator.

In the book of James, 2. 1-10, we have a picture of the type of person that God holds dear, in James 2. 5, the Lord is said to choose the poor of this world, but rich in faith, to be the heirs of the Kingdom He has promised, to those who love Him. So where is the commendation and applause from the Lord, for the wise man or woman of the world who knows not Christ as Lord, though that person is a great success in the eyes of the world? Sorry, **no praise from the Lord goes to those who know not the Lord.** So what if you gain the whole world, and lose your soul, what is really gained?

A revelation of the way God sees things, and the way God values the invisible qualities of eternal things, such as, hope, love, kindness, obedience to truth, respect for others and all of the qualities of life that God's Spirit bears as fruit, in the lives of His saints, are not even on the list of **the lost, rich and famous of the world**. And yet the **church in America has placed great value** on such visible and outward signs of progress that even lost people highly value, in the present world system. Perhaps we have not been told the whole truth about the present 'Christian's worldview' of world values.

There is much talk today, about the 'Christian's World View', which is supposed to refer to the believers wider vision of total humanity.

But maybe we need to know what the American church values in it's own social order. **Would someone please explain to the 'persecuted church'** in other lands, what the American Christian really values? The bigger buildings (extravagant of course), the multi-staff ministry programs of the mega church, would be a good place to start. **Or is the American church at a loss as how to explain all of this excess? Especially in a time of such human need and human suffering that runs wild in the midst of all these 'good' Christian seminars, tapes, books and lectures on 'the true meanings of Christ's great sermons'**. It all makes me think of the words of Jesus to His disciples when he told them about the Pharisees, and scribes, "do what they say, but do not follow in line with what they do, for they do not practice what they preach." (My paraphrase). Take a look at the March/April 2004 issue of "**Ministries Today,**" a magazine for Christian Leaders.

Churches seem to seek pastors and leaders with higher academic degrees more now than ever before in the history of the church in America. Why? Pastors and ministers in 'high places' write articles on the necessity for higher learning, as if such academic skills were needed, really needed, to do what? Will this higher(?) learning make the Word of God more effective? Will all of this education make people of great success more motivated to join the church of the affluent? Will the PhD. Degree make the pastor more humble, more holy, more effective among the lost sheep, including those on the highway and the byways?

Today those who write in some of the Christian magazines (Ministries Today, March/April 2004), express the value of higher education, and yet refer often to the lives of great men and women of God who changed history or made history, as we say, but fail to quote statements from these early saints, **which emphasize the same kind of importance** they themselves (as American church leaders) place upon this academic excellence. What about the value of the examples of faith set by Chinese pastors, and house church leaders around the world, who will never have such academic excellence? **Why not use their lives of service and dedication as an example**, rather than the American (having not suffered in a similar way) pastor who knows only the <u>classroom,</u> the <u>sanctuary,</u> the <u>scheduled TV presentation</u>, large <u>audiences</u> and <u>the book store</u> as his *'mountain top' of spiritual expertise*? **Get the education that is needed for effective evangelism** (a Bible translator, or teacher of English Lang. to people who can be won to Christ though that avenue, or whatever skill may be needed **for the sake of others**), but to require everyone who enters a pulpit to have certain levels of education, is simply not biblical.

What is it that we really mean by 'Christian World View?' We might have chosen a term here that will come back to haunt us. **A view of the world is not what we need today** in the American church, **we need a view of the heart of God, the Word of God and the will of God**, a view that is accurate, simple and clear. If the American church had a view of the will of God that is true and clear, the view of the world would be just as true and clear. Only **then would we also see lost souls seeking salvation, not education, people dying without hope, not without seminaries**, souls of the young and the old who cry out for eternal, invisible truth, not for more materials, and lessons <u>about the truth</u>. Is there not a verse in the New Testament that said something about, a form of Godliness, in the last days, but denying the power thereof? **Again I say, let us get real so that we can get right! I like the verses in Romans 12, especially verse 16, in the KJV, when it states, <u>condescend to people of low estate</u> (people of humble means), and be not wise in your own conceits. Perhaps if we <u>get down</u> on the level of the humble, <u>we can see which way is up!</u>** This word surely sounds more like the Jesus of the Bible, than the types of Jesus that are presented in many of the pulpits in America today, (see Matt. 24. 23,24). **And by the way, the real Jesus is already standing up!**

Awh.

26

The Casualties of Convenience

✦

Amos 6. 1-6

In the book of the New Testament, (which reminds the Christian of the need to 'pay attention' to the purpose of the Old Testament), the book of 1st Corinthians 10. 1-11, states that those things that happened in the past, happened to the people then, as a warning to us who live now. It is upon us that the end of the ages has come. The Old Testament events were not just a record of history, but had also the purpose of providing us today with an example. (vs. 11, 12).

Even in the American scene, there is a parallel with the churches of America. The effort to excel and to improve the 'quality of life' in the 'land of opportunity', became an obsession with modern Americans. Not only was life to be enjoyed, it was to be improved in the area of comfort and ease. The more modern the country became, and the more advanced the level of all life style became, the more comfort and ease of life people sought. Now the excess is unquestioned, the advertisers appeal to the desire for ease and convenience. American consumers have become the target for all producers of goods which facilitate the pleasures of the physical existence. There is no need for proof or evidence of this obvious fact. Americans (including Christians) are spending more time and money on pleasure and 'happy hours' than any people on the planet.

This could be expected of lost souls who seek the fulfillment of fleshly desires. But the churches have joined this 'rat race' of pleasure seeking, this 'Disney Land' express which rolls into every youth groups list of activities. What a sad indictment on today's church!

A better knowledge of the 'church around the world' where persecution abounds would be a good study for youth in today's churches. Even when the subject of Heb. 13. 3 is discussed, most members of the church in America fail to see the significance of the admonition to—consider one's self as in the same circumstance' as those who suffer for Christ. In some research on this subject, I have come to the following conclusion. The Laodecian church which is described in Revelation chapter 3, is the church in America today. But there is even more to be considered. For example, how did the churches in America come to this point? Why is the call for repentance the only sound we should be hearing from the pulpits today?

In the close encounter of the most serious kind, where the churches in America and the country of America have come together like some big happy family, we find so many similar attitudes, that anyone doing a little honest reflection can see the problem. The churches in America are, of course made up of American citizens. Those who look back to the history of the country, see **that same national** history—as if it was also the history of the church. Oops, easy mistake, or it seems to be a mistake that anyone who is a citizen but not a Christian, might easily make. Not so! This has been addressed in other pages I have written, how the American dream, was not a dream or vision referred to, or as described in Acts 2. 17. The American dream is known world wide, as a dream of opportunity for freedom to become anything you want to become. But the dream and visions given from God, were not dreams of prosperity, happy times, and simplicity of life, which brings affluence and pride. There is not only a difference in the kinds of dreams that the saints of God have and the children of the world have, there is a great difference in the place that God has in the lives of mankind. Those who know not God, will not have the same desires, or dreams as those who belong to the Lord Jesus. A difference exists between citizens of the world and Kingdom of God people, like the difference between night and day, light and darkness, the kind of difference that must and will exist between those who think with the mind of Christ, and those who enjoy the pleasures of sin for a season.

Now for the problem of Convenience

When the American life style included great amounts of indulgence and the seeking after 'convenience' as a by-product of success and achievement, we saw the rise of the 'convenience store'. This was a result of the constant wish of the American public, to have everything made easy and comfortable. But notice how the idea of convenience entered the church, in the last 50 years, much like the introduction of selfish intent which the Devil brought in as recorded in Acts chapter 5.

Today, churches want padded chairs, or pews, nice basketball courts for their little 'spoiled' darlings to play in, and a large concentration of 'youth and children's ministers, (while nations and countries go without any Christian ministers). The American church wants, the best 'orchestra' the top singers, the nice sound systems, the most extravagant buildings and highly paid 'pastors', not to mention plush accommodations for the spoiled members. This is all, a result of the close encounter of a serious kind, with the American culture. Even though the church leaders know that friendship with the world makes one an enemy of God, this did not seem to hold back the tide of selfishness and indulgence that modern America brought to the shores of 'holy ground'. The prophet Amos warned the people of Israel against their pride and 'life of ease' as he addressed these similar problems. Woe to those who are at 'ease' in the mountain of God (Zion). The casualty of this convenience therefore is the church itself, at least those churches who clamor for more comfort.

Perhaps however, there is another casualty in this craving of pleasure and convenience in today's—modern American church. What has shown up in America among Christians, as pride, self-centeredness and complete narcissism, has also cost the unreached peoples of the world, a chance to hear the Gospel. I know that many would not want to hear this, but what other reason would there be, for American Christians to have done so little in recent years to hurry the Gospel to the dying souls in other lands? The idea that American Christians can do both, the work of reaching into all the world, and still have extravagant and elegant facilities in American churches for personal comfort and ease, is not a logical possibility. The figures make hypocrites of the wealthy churches. It is not a hidden secret that 90% of the money in American churches, given in public offerings is used right here in the USA. So it is that in 2004, as in years past, it remains unchanged that 5% of the world church population 'eats up' 90% of the resources.

This would be a good time to be reminded that in the book of Luke and chapter 17, the account of a certain 'rich' man, clothed in fine garments, ignored the poor beggar man, who was well within his reach, while he deliberated within himself about how to 'hoard his riches'. This account is given as a warning and a lesson for those who would be dumb enough to do the same thing. The problem stated is not the same as the problem solved. Knowing what brought on this dilemma should help any thinking person, to know two things. Thing one, we should see how God feels about covetousness, and thing two, we can see how God in His time, turns things around. Just because judgment is appointed within the timing that God alone decides, does not mean that judgment is overlooked or postponed. Every warning in the Old Testament record, given by the Prophets of God, stands as solid proof that American churches are in great danger of being punished for this selfish hoarding of resources and personnel. Since the church has been built on the foundation of the Apostles and Prophets, Jesus Christ Himself as the Chief Corner Stone (Eph. 2. 19-22) then the message of the Prophets as well as the Holy Apostles of Christ, are the lessons and warnings that stand as the hope of all the Saints.

In the book of 2 Corinthians chapter 8, verses 9 to 15 the subject of equality is clearly set before all believers as a rule of faith and practice in the Ecclesia (body of Christ). As it is written, he that gathered much did not (hold on to) have too much, and he who gathered little, did not do without. The Old Testament teaching was carried over into the New Covenant people, Acts 2-4 are examples of how this holds true. **Today American churches gather much in funds and Christian workers**, and yet, those in need around the world, have suffered without their needs being met. Somehow a little common sense judgment and honesty would be more of a worship before our God in the American church, than all this 'happy hour' hoop-la that passes for worship. Read Isa. 58, and see if our (today's worship or fasting, can apply equally) services in the Sunday meetings, measure up to the standards that God gave His people in this setting. I would like to see a church service on Sunday when the minister calls upon all the members to go to their knees in repentance and call upon the Lord for mercy, and agree to obey the Great commission and find the lost sheep, and expend all efforts, at all costs, to obey this great command. The persecuted Christians around the world are praying for American Christians, to repent and turn to Christ as Lord, believe me, I have been among the persecuted and I have heard their prayers.

Read the books of Hosea, Amos and the other prophets. Notice how the Apostles were forewarned and foretold that suffering would be their lot in walking the path of the Master—Jesus. In both Testaments, there are more warnings for disobedience and disbelief than we are hearing in today's pulpits. When the message of today in churches in America, are not even similar to the messages of the Apostles and Prophets...there is something wrong with the messages of today, because we know the Prophets and Apostles spoke the Word of the Lord.

Where are the tears of repentance in congregations, where are the trumpet sounds that bring people before the Lord of hosts in solemn assembly with broken and contrite hearts? (Ps. 51. 17). God heals the broken hearted, and He respects those who mourn, (Matt. 5. 4), but the proud and those who boast in men, shall be put down. Those who thought they had sight, but were really blind, and therefore could not be helped, were the religious leaders who 'failed the test' (John 9 . 41).

This age of comfort in the flesh, will become the catalyst which sends the proud into their judgment, for our God is a consuming fire (Heb. 12. 29). Not many sermons are preached today about the fierce wrath of a Just God, but the 'hallelujah—happy hour singers' need to revisit the scriptures and see what message made up the majority of the words of the prophets to God's people were in the days of old. Even the apostles of our Lord say, those who refuse to repent and obey the Lord, 'judge themselves unworthy of everlasting life', and bring on their own destruction (Acts 13. 46, Heb. 12. 25-29, 1st Thess. 5. 1-9, Jude 1-25). Be on guard, and watch, for we know not what hour the Lord will return. But blessed is he who is found working and providing food for the household (world—wide) when the Lord does return. But if the servants of the Lord are found to be saying, the Master delays, and begin to have feast s and celebrations, and are not busy caring for others in the household (spreading the Gospel to all the world), the Lord will come at an hour those servants are not aware of, and appoint them a place with unbelievers. This may seem to some, to be a rather liberal paraphrase, but the meaning is clear. We are not in a time of celebration, that will come when the Master's work is done, we are to be in the field of harvest in labor, bearing our cross, weeping and bringing our sheaves with us. Today there is much talk and singing as a celebration of our relationship with the Lord, but I always thought an Olympic team celebrated more when the Gold medals were passed around, than when they just got chosen to be on the team. I think there is something wrong with today's picture of the American church. If you think there is nothing wrong, then I worry about you as well.

Awh.

27

The Last Laugh, and The Last Word

✦

Matt. 7. 21-23 ; 25. 12, 41, Mark . 13. 13, Ps. 37. 13, Ps. 2. 4.

The arms of the wicked shall be broken: but the Lord upholds the righteous. (Ps. 37. 17). In the last day, when all men face their judgment and the Lord divides the sheep from the goats, it shall not matter if we say we know the Lord, <u>what will matter then, is who The Lord says HE knows.</u>

Today, many say they know the Lord, but the reason the scriptures state that it is appointed unto man once to die, and after this the judgment, (Heb. 9. 27),is to give each person a chance to hear the final word from the Lord, and at that time, it will matter if God knows us! For many will say they have done much for God, but **on that one day, only one thing** will be important, and that is, if He who is Truth, the only Lord Jesus Knows us, at that time, the question is not if we know Him. It is very easily illustrated in our daily lives. If a person brags about knowing an important or prominent figure in society, but comes to greet that person and seek a favor, it will only matter if the important person knows the one who has claimed the acquaintance.

What we know today, and who we say we know, seems to satisfy our own company of friends and fellow Christians, but the day of the Lord will reveal many secrets of men's hearts, (Ps. 44. 21, 1 Cor. 14. 25, Heb. 4. 12, Rom. 2. 16), and then it shall be important if the Lord knows us, not what we say we know about Him. **God has the last word**. Many people are deceived, and more will be deceived before the time of the end of all things as we know them on planet earth. The love of many will grow cold, as evil increases, and wickedness prevails in the earth, Matt. 24.12, and there will be a falling away from the faith in these last days, 1 Tim. 4. 1-9. It is important to recognize that these days are the 'last days' spoken of in Scripture. We knew it would come, and we knew that some generation must face those times—called the "...the beginning of sorrows..." Matt. 24. 8.

The evidence of 'last days' events can be seen easily in today's terrorism and world chaos. Not only can Americans see extreme horror and brutality, but nations around the world who have witnessed tragedy as a 'normal' life style, can see even more extreme conditions of suffering than ever before. Think of the American way of life in years past. There was not the evil of abortion, homosexual activity, domestic brutality and heathenism like we see in this country today. Unknown in most of the third world countries, is the fact that America has an agency called "Family Protective Services" or services that oversee the welfare of children who are mistreated, brutalized, beaten and even killed by their own parents. America is probably the only country (with such modern medicine, intellectual capacity etc.) that has found it necessary to create **an agency for the protection of Children who are in danger 'at home.' And all of this in the 'land of the free', and home of the brave**! What a joke this must be to those across the ocean.

America has embarked upon a **'theme of extremism'** with publicity given to that idea of—extreme sports, extreme this and that, which is really only accenting the **extreme evil and wickedness of humanity. We** can see 'extreme' alright, it is all around us, the country most wealthy and most productive in goods, has become emaciated in the social and spiritual context. When parents kill their own children, and attribute it to stress or some other 'social' or psychological cause, then there is present in the American society a wicked departing from goodness, which goodness had in early years made the country great, in the eyes of all the modern world.

"When America ceases to be good, it will cease to be great." This is the statement made in earlier years by a wise and noted scholar from a country overseas. Well, America has ceased to be good, and there is no doubt that greatness will be the next quality to go. A 'good' nation does not legalize abortion on demand, nor try to create a union between members of the same sex and call it marriage. A 'good' country does not need to make laws which give legal privileges to homosexual activity.

It is true in the life of an individual. If there is no goodness or way of truth in a person, there is no greatness either. When sin and disobedience entered the heart of mankind, and was therefore introduced into the present world (Gal. 2.4), it was given only a period of time, then as God designed, His plan to destroy the works of darkness, and to bring into the experience of mankind a new way, that included a new heaven and new earth would come into view. 2 Peter 3, makes the promise of God clear, along with many other scriptures, including the book of the Revelation to St. John the Apostle. The enemy of God, Satan, and those who follow the evil path, will soon come to their end and their reward. Until that day, evil prevails in the darkness of wicked hearts, and deception will hold court in the plans of men with evil intent. An **article in the newsletter** "Jews for Jesus" Vol. 1:5765, Sept. 2004, stated-"**Many think that the way of ministry is to get all the necessary backing, and then begin the work of proclamation. They want years of training and organizational skills before they start to witness. Well, that might be a good idea in running a business, but it's not the way that God builds a testimony or a ministry." (Copied from Magazine—Jews for Jesus.)**

Part of the 'falling away' from God's established pattern for ministry and world evangelization, is seen in the present 'Mega church' method of heavy emphasis on training and preparation for academic acceptance among 'men' rather than spiritual depth of soul in closeness to God and burden for lost souls. Just like the Pharisees of the New Testament, who were pronounced as 'children of the Devil' because they refused to see Jesus Christ as the Messiah,(since Jesus did not fit their academic qualifications and because Jesus told them not to seek the glory of men, but the praise of the Father in heaven)men today become enamored with their own identity. Look at John 5. 31-45, -8; 42-47, John 7. 15. Today's seminaries are filled with those who seek the acceptance of man, and may not even understand the scriptures, nor the need to rather seek the praise of God. You cannot have the praise of the proud, and the praise of the Lord who loves the humble, at the same time.

Jesus called a little child to Himself when asked by the disciples who was considered the greatest in the Kingdom of Heaven (Matt. 18 1-9). Unless this spirit of humility is seen in a church and the leadership of a church, you will not find the Spirit of God in that place either. This is why many churches today do not have the 'power' of the Gospel and the power of the Holy Spirit (1 Cor. 4.18-21,—2 Tim. 3. 5). There is plenty of circus activity, and 'happy hour' family events, but little (if any) real life changing power in the American church today. Look at the emphasis of most churches, they advertise programs and events to attract members. "...we have a program for you and your family..." or "we are the church that meets your family needs..."

In John 6, many ran away from Jesus, because His sayings were too hard for them, and Jesus did not send any disciples after them. In Acts 5, 11, there was great fear when the Lord exercised some discipline against hypocrisy and lying within the fellowship. Today in America, few people fear to join the church because they see great power and serious discipline in the body of Christ, they rather see the church as some kind of social club trying to appeal to their human social needs. **If there was more fear of God in the man in the pulpit, there would be more respect for the things of the Lord in the people in the pew.** As well, people would think twice about being a part of the body of Christ which leads people to 'lose their lives in the present world,' in order to find new life in Christ for eternity. **The only ones who really belong to Jesus are those who chose to no longer belong to the present world.** You can't follow two leaders who walk in different directions.

The wicked souls of this world may laugh at real Christians today, but all the laughing is not over yet. WE live in a time when the decision to follow Christ is clearly a decision to no longer love the present world.

Those who mock the believers in Christ, or rejoice in iniquity shall find that the day will come when God has the last laugh, and the professed atheist will know only the wrath of God which comes upon the children of disobedience. The final lap has not been run, and the final word has not yet been spoken. There is a God in heaven, who shall put all rule and authority under His feet, and bring justice as rain upon the people who are chosen to fill the ranks of citizens in His Kingdom. In John 12. 48-50, Jesus stated that God would have the last word. Those who reject Him, shall be judged by His words, not by what man thought Jesus said, or by what was interpreted, but what Jesus actually commanded and requires. Today so many say the know the Lord, but in the last day, it shall matter not what men say they knew, but who it is that God says He knows. It will be His Word not ours, that decides our eternity. Welcome to God's World, which is the real world, and the only one that lasts!
(Matt. 25. 45,46—Lk.18 . 29-30).

A.W. Hamilton, Missionary

28

The Man of God—and the Will of God

♦

1ˢᵀ Kings 13, Ez. 12, 13 Ez. 34, Gal. 1. 6-20
Also connected to: Lessons From The Garden

<u>**Once you know the will of God,**</u> don't confer with flesh and blood,(seeking the approval of man or the opinion of man about it). There are not many illustrations like the one in 1ˢᵗ Kings, that reveal how serious it is and how important it is, to stand firmly on the revealed word of the Lord. The dealings of false prophets in the Old Testament, are proof of how determined the enemy is to destroy the work of God in the lives of God's people. The example in 1 Kings 22, is evidence that a lying spirit can influence those who are not listening to the will of God. The Prophet Micaiah was the speaker for God in 1ˢᵗ Kings 22, but he was imprisoned by the king because his message, though from God, was not acceptable to the ears of the wicked King, Ahab. However, here in 1ˢᵗ Kings is an example that is unusual, you have a man of God used to test a young prophet of God, to see if he will **remain true to the voice and command of God**. Even if a man of God tells a thing that he says has come from an angel of the Lord (Gal. 1.8), the man of God who has been clearly instructed by the Lord, must not make any changes and believe someone else, **_once he knows what God has said._**

It is clear that there have been and will be in this generation as well, the floating messages of men, which **sound** good, **but not good enough.** Remember, the magic of the Pharaoh's magicians imitated the miracle of Moses when the magicians made their staff's become serpents just as Moses did. But the staff, which had become a serpent, of Moses devoured the serpents of the magicians. The power of God was greater than the powers of Darkness, even though that power or miracle of changing a staff to serpents, was imitated by the wicked witches of Pharaoh, without interruption by the Lord. **The Lord did not forbid the imitation by the** Pharaoh's magicians to take place, **God simply showed that His own power could overcome and destroy the wicked act of the 'copy cat' Satan.** The Bible says, to believers, 'overcome the world through faith.' There is no indication that the world will not have some power, since Adam's sin opened the door to evil and trickery, but there is example and teaching that the imitations and falsehood in the world can be identified and in the **power of the word of God** (Rom. 1. 16) **be overcome**. ONLY the Gospel is the power of God unto Salvation, and that is only for those who believe. The Bible states in 2 Cor. 11, 12-15, that there are definitely false apostles, deceitful workers, transforming themselves into the apostles of Christ…and no marvel; for Satan himself is transformed into an angel of light…" In 2nd Tim. 3, and 4.3, and in 1st Tim. 4. 1, there is warning about the deceitfulness of those who seek personal, selfish and monetary gain, to turn away people to themselves and gather a following. The Devil himself sought to gain followers for his rebellion in heaven when he turned a third of the Angels of God Isa. 14. 12, Ez. 28, Jude 6, Rev. 12. 4, 9, 13-17. This record, like many is for the benefit of the believers, (1st Cor. 10. 11) so that those who follow Jesus will be faithful until death, and not be lead astray nor turn from their own steadfastness, (Heb. 6. 1-11, 10. 38, 2nd Peter 2. Jude 5-7).

Today, it is also difficult for the saints of God to determine when a man who claims to be a man of God is true or false. Having the Bible in our own language gives us truth and light, so that we do not have to be deceived and walk in darkness. The great lesson provided in the book of 1st Kings 13, needs repeating in our present time of religious confusion in America. WE need to first distinguish that the churches around the world, especially in areas where persecution against believers is strong, do not seem to have the continual harassment from mixed messages that the American churches have. In America there are so many different religious persuasions that people have difficulty determining what is really biblical. This is one good reason the example in 1st Kings needs our attention.

In the Old Testament record of the young prophet and the old prophet, is revealed the seriousness of maintaining strict adherence to the revealed will of God. This concept and this teaching is not without example in the New Testament. Everyone who knows the Lord and who has read Acts of the Apostles, knows how God speaks to this seriousness of being faithful to the Lord's will. Acts 5 reveals how Ananias and his wife Sapphira, decided to try and trick the church and lie about their gifts to God's work, so they could look good without acting good, and we see what a great surprise awaited them. Death came swiftly and suddenly, much like the fate of the young prophet in 1st Kings 13. The lesson in both Testaments is clear, God is serious about His purpose in the world.

It is my opinion that the reason for confusion and disharmony in America over Bible teachings, is a result of an over concentration of teaching in the same spot. Since the church is to be the salt of the earth, and the light of the world for Jesus, you can see what happens when you put all the salt in one place, or shine the light continually in one spot. In one case, too much salt in on spot (America is only 5% of the world's population), will ruin the food or nullify the purpose of salt as a preservative. All the light focused in one spot gives you a 'laser beam' affect, not a warm sunlight affect. What has happened when the believers in America concentrated so much teaching, lesson material, tapes, seminars, books, fancy facilities and ministers and evangelists in one country, is exactly the same as pouring all the salt on one piece of food, or concentration of light in one spot. More harm than good is the obvious result. If American churches had **spread out** instead of **stacking up**, and if churches in America had been focused primarily on others instead of local 'church growth' we may not be suffering the kinds of disharmony and confusion we see sprouting up in this country.

If we had known that 'church growth' was going to mean church growth stunted, (as far as spreading to the areas beyond America), we may have thought twice about giving it such emphasis. In the book of Acts and other letters of the New Testament, the growth of the church meant expanding to many places, new areas of the world opened to the message of the Gospel. Since (1 Cor. 3. 6) **God is the one who causes the growth** of the Gospel seed, and since the foundation of the Church is Christ, and all His laborers have to do is lay the foundation and plant and water the seed, we can cover the earth without delay. Church growth was not to be our part of the task, our part is to 'lay the foundation which is Christ, and to sow the seed in all the world, which seed is the Word of God, I don't recall a verse of scripture that says 'go out and grow the church.' Too much emphasis on one country, and **too much time and money spent *on one small part*** of the earth, will not allow for some to have a chance to hear the Gospel.

We know this from the simple fact that there are unreached people in the world, and yet we are in a time when this one country (America) has enough resources and technology **to reach the entire earth**. This problem of selfishness does affect the total work of God in the world. The lesson we should learn is that when God gives a command, (the great commission Matt. 28> 18-20), **He does not expect us to be persuaded to treat it lightly.** The illustrations in the **book of Kings**, and in **Acts 5**, are there to remind us of the seriousness of God's will.

Even if an angel from heaven, or another man of God tells us something that we know is different than what we knew from God, we must not cave in. **Gal. 1. 8.**

In recent years, in America, the church of the Lord Jesus has been confronted with issues which are more political (prayer in school, bad TV programs etc.) than spiritual. **While the church becomes preoccupied with social distress and disorder**, many around the world suffer the lack of Bibles in their language, and any opportunity to know the Gospel of salvation. Here is how I compare this problem with the Bible teaching about the seriousness of the will of God. The young man of God in **1ˢᵗ Kings 13,** who was told by the Lord to follow a certain plan, after his great miracle with the healing of the King (vs. 6), did not hold to the word from God, but **later believed another man of God** who told him to do the opposite of **what God had told** him.

God takes very seriously any diversion from His Word. God has shown more than a few times, in His Holy Word, that His Will is to be done by His people and they must not trust the voice of any who would present a different plan as if it was equally the will of God, **(Gal. 2. 4)**. Again it is important to notice that the things written in the Bible, were written for the followers of Christ (**1ˢᵗ Cor. 10. 11**), so that we today might not fall by the same example of unbelief as those who were disobedient, **(Heb. 3. 12)**.

If the church does not take seriously the command to go into all the world and preach the Gospel to every person, we shall not have the **power** that goes with that command, nor are we entitled to the **promise** of the Lord's presence (Lo—I am with you always…). We must first obey and fulfill the command to preach the Gospel message, to the people around the world, or at least be 'on the way' to these people, or be doing something sacrificial and sincere about sending the Gospel to all peoples. Prayers may be said, and plans and activity carried out, but there will be only a form of Godliness without the power that belongs to the true followers of Christ who carry only the true word of God. Already we see that the plan of salvation has been tampered with, and people give commands to 'raise your hands and be saved' which is not even near what the New Testament teaches.

The Apostles, in the book of Acts, who were given the 'keys to the kingdom' told people who had godly sorrow in their hearts over their sin, to repent and be (immersed) baptized in the Name of Jesus Christ, for the remission of sins, and they would receive the gift of the Holy Spirit. We cannot change the order of these words or substitute other words to replace these simple instructions. But see if you hear this answer to the broken hearted sinner's cry for help, in your church on Sunday. You are more likely to hear a preacher (even one called a man of

God) say, '**you should just say a sinner's prayer and you would be saved** immediately.' It would not matter if that preacher said he had heard this from an angel of God, (Gal. 1. 8), we are not to believe it, since the written word of God is in our hands, and we know what Jesus and the Apostles have told us. Do you want to hear a message that is written in the Word of God by men ('carried along by') inspired by the Holy Spirit, (2 Tim. 3. 16), or one invented in the 20th century by (God only knows who) men long after the Scripture was recorded?

There are plenty of messages out in the religious circles today, especially in America, plenty of TV evangelists with a style and popularity that is second to none, but there is only one New Testament of our Lord Jesus Christ, and witnessed to by His chosen Apostles. The Christians in America had better board the next train **back to the Bible**, before we face the days of persecution that will come upon all the earth *to try those who dwell on the earth.*

There is a statement I read sometime back, that correctly identifies the principle in this great example and illustration in **1st Kings 13**. It is this;'**if I have what you want, I can control you.**' This is proven true in very many examples of daily life. A medical **doctor** can control the patient with a prescribed remedy, at least to the extent that the doctor's recommended prescription is believed by the patient to hold the promise of recovery. A **teacher** controls the student, by simple assignments or required reading, because the teacher has what the student wants, a good grade to take home. **The banker** controls the money of the person who secures a loan, (at least the payment amount that is agreed upon monthly)**, we are all controlled by someone, when an agreement is made about a certain transaction or if we have a desired result that can depend upon someone else's cooperation** for fulfillment.

If God has what I want, then **He** can control me. Whatever God commands or asks of me, I will do (Matt. 4. 4), because He has what I want. **His will** becomes my highest purpose. God has heaven, it is His to share, so I want that, and I want it enough to do whatever is necessary to enter, no matter what God commands I will do it. God provides 'hope,' God gives His love, His forgiveness of sins, all of these things that we need for now and for eternity are in His power to provide, and I want these things He offers. If however, this present life and it's carnal pleasures, hold what a person wants, than the present world, and its evil will control the person who desires those pleasures. Whatever we want, there is something that, or someone who can control our behavior. **Tell me what you want, and I will tell you what or who controls your life and your destiny.**

In the will of God, we must find our greatest joy and desire. **Ps.37. 4** states, "delight yourself in the Lord and He will give you the desires of your heart." **In**

Isa. 26, the Bible states, "thou (oh Lord) will keep him in perfect peace, whose mind is stayed (fastened) on thee, because he trusts in thee." The will of God must be obeyed and honored by the man of God, or the man of God will lose his power with men and his authority as a man of God. He will also lose his position and his place as a steward or servant in the house of God **(Matt. 25. 24-30).** There may be many today going around the country in churches in America without the power and the authority they once had, because they did not understand the seriousness of the will of God as it is designed to govern the man of God. **All that glitters is not gold, and all who preach, have not, by the Lord, been told**, Jer. 23. 25-40.

29

The Mark of Cain

✦

Gen.4. 15

The first 'Hate Crime' was indeed a crime caused by hatred, which **hate—was caused by pride**. Hate had a beginning, just as crime had a beginning. Hatred in the heart of Cain, was the result of pride, and it was a pride so sinister and deep rooted that it's fruit was murder. The Bible teaches and encourages mankind to 'hate evil' and love what is good. Because God has revealed the good, and the enemy of God, Satan has revealed 'evil'—the choice is clear, even though the choice is not easy for man in his natural (carnal) state. The word of God also states, they who are living by the desires of the flesh (Rom. 8. 5) give attention to the things of the flesh (carnal nature). In Romans 8. 7,8, the word of the Lord states, that the carnal (flesh) mind is hatred or enmity against God. So—hatred has it's place, but it's place must be decided by a heart filled with the love of what is good.

In the Bible record, of Genesis 4, it is evident that the two brothers, Cain and Able, were given equal opportunity to obey the commands of the Lord God. In Jude, 7-11, the Bible speaks of 'those who gave themselves over to fornication (fulfilling the lust of the flesh), as people who have 'gone in the way of Cain'. In 1st John 3. 12, it is recorded that "Cain was of the evil (wicked) one, and killed his brother", and why—because his own works were evil, and his brother's works were righteous. Another New Testament reference to the attitude of Cain is given in Heb. 11.4, when speaking of the sacrifice that Cain offered to God. Since Romans 10. 17 states that "faith comes by hearing, and hearing by the word (mouth) of God", and we know that Able offered a 'faith' sacrifice, (Heb. 11. 4) **we also know that they both must have known that God required a blood sacrifice.**

Many people have asked me, the question, "why did God not accept the offering of Cain, when Cain offered the fruit of the ground, since he was a 'tiller of the soil? Cain offered what he had, and Able offered what he had, Able as a shepherd offered a lamb from his flock and Cain brought before God the fruit of the ground. This might seem a normal and acceptable difference, unless there was an instruction which made specific requirements. Since the Scripture clearly states that Able offered a more perfect sacrifice (means complete and fulfilling), we know that the brothers were aware of God's requirement, and Cain simply refused to obey. Had Cain been concerned with pleasing God, he would have traded some of his 'fruit of the ground' for a lamb from Abel's flock, and offered the lamb. But it appears obvious **that Cain was more interested in 'forcing the hand of God' or seeking to bend the rules, and try to get God to accept anything that he wanted to offer.**

God makes the rules, we must discover them and follow them. **Cain sought to make God accept anything he wanted to offer,** and so he did not repent and return the next day with an acceptable offering, which Cain could have done, had he been seeking to please God. But this is the key, in this relationship of God with mankind, **man must find out what God requires, and offer that, not try to make God accept whatever it is he wants to offer.** This is what turned Cain against Able. Since Able was accepted, because of his obedience and his (complete) perfect sacrifice as directed, Cain became filled with hatred toward God. It is my opinion that since Cain could not kill God, he sought out vengeance on the nearest thing to God that he could think of, and tried to destroy that which found the favor of God, even though it was his own brother.

Pride kept Cain from showing sorrow over his unacceptable offering, and pride brought on the hatred he held toward God.

The hatred toward God which entered the heart of Cain, was not a new thing, it was this pride and resulting hatred which Lucifer (that old serpent called the Devil), held against God which brought on war in heaven and resulted in the 'throwing down from heaven' of the disobedient angel and his following (Rev. 12. 7-17, Luke 10.18, Isa. 14.12). Pride, un-repented of and left to swell the mind and heart of a person, will bring forth a hatred of all that is true and righteous. Cain in his anger, over the rejection of his (own rebellious) offering, sought not to be redeemed nor brought back into God's favor, but rather chose to take on the spirit and mind of 'the evil one' and rebel against the will and goodness of God the Creator.

Abel offered a 'faith offering' which means that he knew (faith comes by hearing) what God required, and he chose in humble obedience, to be a child of

God. Cain refused to offer a 'faith offering' but instead of seeking to please God, he tried to get God to please him, and in so doing he became a child of the Devil.

A case of two brothers, two children, and two different fathers, is the case of Cain and Able. Cain could have gone to Abel and asked what the people on Pentecost asked, "what must I do"—to gain the favor of God? Even if Cain had not known that an animal sacrifice was required, once he beheld the favor of God upon Abel, he could, if seeking the favor of God, have discovered what pleased God and made such an offering as God would find acceptable. Mankind today is divided into these two categories even in this time. Those who seek to do the will of God in order to please Him, and those who seek to find a way to make God accept them on their own terms, so that God to them becomes a god that pleases them. A Santa Claus who fills our Xmas wish, (a design that man has created), is not the same as the true and Living God, who has come to seek and save that which is lost.

A Santa Claus type of god (1st Cor. 8. 5,6), will be one which bends to the wishes of mankind, and the result is deception and then destruction for the one who creates or chooses a—'make me special, so I can feel good—type of god'. **But many people invent such a god for their convenience so they might feel good about themselves.** The true God who came to seek man and to reconcile us to Himself through Jesus Christ (2Cor. 5. 18) is the only real God and creator of all things. These two brothers, Cain and Abel, are the very examples of the total destiny of all mankind. We are joined to one or the other, to one by faith and an obedient life in Christ, or we are joined to the other by a **rebellious 'hate crime' attitude which will bring final and utter destruction.**

We, who can have a knowledge of the will of God and the Gospel of Christ the Lord, through the word of God, can and will make this choice, about whom and what we will serve in our life time. If we chose to serve ourselves, or some—made up-god of the world, our destiny will be an eternity without God. God will decide what will be the fate of those who have never had the choice presented to them, but this question is not ours to contemplate or to answer.

We know that Cain's attitude is one that is popular today with those who reject the Lord Jesus Christ. Now since humanity is divided into these two categories, both of which have a person from the beginning of man as an example of each category, it may be interesting to consider another dimension of this 'brotherhood' which became the beginning of the 'war and hate', and the 'love and serve' history of mankind. We could say it is time to see which 'brother' is our own brother. Since all of mankind has the problem of sin, and therefore the likeness of the brother 'Cain' syndrome, and since we only can go from that state to a state of **forgiveness of sin, by faith in, and obedience to Christ the Lord,** to a relationship with the Lord God our Creator, by being like Abel, the other brother, perhaps some insight into the character and condition of this brotherhood between Cain and Abel would be of interest.

MY Theory

It has not been addressed in many commentaries, and very little conjecture even arises about the question regarding the 'mark' of Cain.

The bible simply records the fact that Cain feared he would be slain by any who saw him or found him, therefore (Gen. 4. 15) God put a mark upon Cain, lest anyone kill him, and the Lord said that anyone who killed Cain would incur punishment from God. Consider the physical aspects of crime and punishment in this case.

Perhaps Cain lost his skin color. The fact that Cain was afraid that someone would kill him when finding him, makes me believe that there was something so different about him, he would be a threat to others. It may be that in Cain's disobedience he lost something that visibly made him different from other men. When God made man from the dust of the ground, and since there is not much likelihood there would be any 'white' soil in the land where scholars say we find the Garden of Eden, would it not seem reasonable that the first man and woman had some color to their skin? If there was a change of this kind, it could be an abrupt and sudden change so that the man Cain would be easily recognized as different, and even abnormal. The mark would be easily seen. The changes in man's language at the time of the 'tower of Babel' and perhaps even other cultural changes which would separate the races of mankind are no doubt a part of that scattering of the people (Gen. 11), but we may have overlooked the most obvious change and differences that are in the cultures of the world. All nations of the world, except the European culture, have some degree of skin color. Perhaps the mark of Cain, or the terrible crime he committed, brought upon him and his descendents **a difference quite unlike any other cultural difference.**

For example, in the years of ministry in Africa, (15 years) I found that in the association of African Christians, and the African people as an entire culture, with the white race, there is a spirit and characteristic of servitude and the understanding of service to others, that is unlike the White races have. If an American came to Africa, to work as a missionary or volunteer in some other field—even to instruct the local people in ways technology etc. the African was willing to learn and saw the European or American as the teacher and himself as the student or learner. If you would show an African man a photo of two people, one white skinned and the other dark skinned, standing side by side, and you ask the African which of these two men, works for the other man. **The answer would without question be as follows 'the dark skinned man works for the white skinned man'.** The white man was seen as the manager, or the 'boss' and the black man was seen as the worker or servant. It does not take much review of history to underscore this point.

Abel of the Bible, was a man whose occupation was that of a herder of livestock. Cain was a tiller of the ground. This difference may not seem significant, but what is significant in the difference between the two men's nature's is that **a characteristic of dominance or servitude** seem to permeate the relationship. **In American history alone,** how many cases of 'lynching' of white people did we hear about as compared to the lynching and treatment of black (African American) slaves? In more recent days, do you expect to read in the newspaper an account of two black men tying a white man to the back of a 'pick up' truck and dragging him to death? The 'hate crime' of Cain can be found even today.

These are not cases which I present to prove any points, I simply point out the fact that it has been my experience in missionary work (in 4 African nations) over a period of many years, to **notice the different cultural traits which are dominate in the two races.** Perhaps when Cain disobeyed the command of the Lord God, and became a man 'marked' as different, he also lost something that would have been normal to all other people of his time. **I have walked in African villages where the children ran away in fear, because they had never seen a white man before.** One of the African interpreters smiled and said, "they run because they call you **the man who has lost his skin.**" This was an interesting observation, and since it came from the perspective of a child, it is worth comment. I saw this as something to take light heartedly and so did the African brothers. But perhaps again, from the mouths of babes comes the wisdom and insight of truth. **A mark on Cain, which would be easily noticed and not possible to hide, could well be the loss of his original skin color.**

Notice in the New Testament when punishment is measured out in a parable of Jesus, regarding one servant who did not use his talent wisely, but with disrespect and disregard for his master's wishes, decided to hide his talent (Matt. 13. 12, Matt. 25. 14-30), he lost even what he had. The master in the parable **took something from the disrespectful servant,** and sent the servant into everlasting condemnation. When someone in the Bible is punished, they often lose something or the position which they had once enjoyed. This is simply to say, that the **judgment upon Cain would more likely be the loss of something to show he**

has incurred the disfavor of God. A mark could well be the loss of his normal color. This theory may not go over well with the white race, but all curse and judgment of sin is removed in the cross of Christ and His atoning blood which was shed for the remission of sins. This does not have to be a theory that is accepted, because **you can disagree with a theory,** it is not presented as a lesson from the bible, but simply as a possibility of how it might have been.

When teaching the Bible in Africa, I was often asked what I thought the curse or the mark of Cain may have been. I usually present this possibility because it has merit resulting from the history of the human race in cultural circumstances which reveal dominate traits common to people of color and people without color. Perhaps some of the traits of Cain are more prominent in the white race than in races of people who have color. Perhaps this has no bearing on the behavior of man today, and certainly in Christ, all characteristics come under the control and guidance of the Holy Spirit. So equality can only be a spiritual reality, it will never be a cultural trait in the present evil world (Gal. 1. 4). **But I believe the first man and woman were of color, like the earth. And tracing** your heritage to Cain or to Able, we would still need the blood of Christ to cover our sins, since all have sinned and come short of the glory of God. (Rom. 5. 12 & Romans chapters 5-8).

Abel was definitely of the servant nature. Cain was definitely a man who sought his own will above the will of others or of God. Let us be thankful that in Christ we have the answer for the sin of pride and hate, and **only in Christ is there peace among all men of all races.** To God be the glory, for He alone can make all nations into one Kingdom people, who love one another as He has loved us. We as Paul the Apostle, do not count ourselves to have apprehended, but we press on toward the mark of the prize of the high calling of God in Christ Jesus, to the perfection of the Saints by the power of God, that people of God may be complete, thoroughly furnished unto all good works. **"Unto Him who is able to keep us from falling, and to present us faultless before the presence of His glory, with exceeding joy, to the only wise God our Savior, be glory and majesty, dominion and power, both now and forever, Amen".** (Jude 25).

Although every nation and every nationality has known it's own destroyer, the Idi Amin's, Hitlers, Stalins, conquerors and dictators each culture and each generation of mankind knows that in this world there is war and tribulation. As one has spoken in some years past, as long as there are men, there will be wars. The day of the Lord will come, and the new world will be the last world that is needed (2 Peter 3). **We have this hope only in the God of the Holy Bible, and His Son—Jesus Christ the Lord.** It is Jesus who has died and been raised from death, who has the authority and the power to deliver man from himself. Of His kingdom, there shall be no end, and though heaven and earth will pass away, the word of the Lord will never pass away. On this word hangs all the hopes of all people of all nations.

    <u>Rule for the day</u>—God is not obliged to accept whatever offering we want to bring, **we are obliged to find out what God accepts and bring that offering to Him in faith and submission. Rom. 12. 1—Try this command on the next time you start feeling 'SPECIAL'.**

Awh

30

The Assignment

In the verses which bring us a revelation of the heart of God, and also describe the mind of the Lord toward His people, we can become fully aware of the very purpose of God for all humanity. In John's account of the Gospel, ch. 17, verses 24-26, notice the words of Jesus, about the world and about His followers. "…O righteous Father, the world has not known you but I have known you, and these have known that you sent me."

If the world was a school, *the persecuted church* around the world, would be the **teachers,** the Christians in America would be *students* (learners) and the *unreached people* of the world (those who have not yet had a chance to hear the Good News of Christ—the Gospel) *would be the assignment.* In John again, and chapter 18, verses 32-39, when Jesus appears before Pilate, Jesus identifies the truth, but Pilate asks the question, "what is truth" right after Jesus had just pointed it out in verse 37. Jesus, as the King of a Kingdom that is not of this world, said that He had come into the world **to bear witness to the truth**. And He went on to say that everyone who is of the truth, hears His voice. Jesus had just explained that His kingdom was, NOT, of this world, therefore His servants were not allowed to put up a fight to keep Him from being delivered to the Jews and the Roman authorities. So the revelation of *truth* and what it is, as well as WHO it is, was not accepted by Pilate. That is why Pilate made the statement, (to paraphrase) 'and what is truth?' The common approach of an unbeliever, is to pose the question over and over, as if there is no acceptable answer. I have dealt with this issue in other pages. The important thing is to ask the right question. This question about what is truth, is not the right question, because Jesus had already answered that question. Pilate should have asked, **"what will I need to do to accept this truth you have presented to me?" This** kind of question would have been connected to his life and to his eternal future.

The truth, and the kingdom (that is not of this world), and Jesus are in the same 'house' there is no separation of the three. *Jesus the King*, the realm *or*

Kingdom and *truth*. The Jews and Pilate did not accept any part of the three. Therefore the Jews and Pilate keep asking a question which is already answered, but because it is better for a beaten opponent, to act as if the points of disagreement had not been effectively settled, the enemies of Jesus, (the Jews and Pilate, who wanted to maintain the favor of the Jewish priests and Sanhedrin for political purposes), found that it worked better for them to appear as if they did not understand what Jesus was saying. But since Jesus *'parted the waters'* with these simple words, by stating that only those who were 'of' the truth would have ears to hear what He taught (1 John 2. 21), the Jews and Pilate would have had to open their hearts to a truth that they could not handle in their present state of heart. <u>Jesus brought together,</u> Himself as a King, the <u>type of Kingdom</u> He was King of (from above), and the revelation of <u>what real truth is</u>, which is—Jesus *and* His teachings.

The Jews and Pilate therefore could act as if there were still unanswered questions about Jesus' intentions. The Jews and Pilate could still pretend they did not understand Jesus' reason for all this 'ministry' He had been carrying on. If the Jews and Pilate could appear before the people, as men who really sought truth they would still have some form of reputation in tact. But Jesus just would not cave in and fall prey to their furtive plot by trying to find a way out of being crucified. So the crucifixion would be held, and in this way, the Jews and Pilate could rid themselves of this 'pestilent' fellow and maybe even disrupt the movement that Jesus had started.

Why would Jesus explain further what His intentions were, when multitudes heard His teaching, and saw His miracles? What would Jesus gain by more words of explanation about Himself, than had already been clearly given in 3 years of teaching? First of all, as He stated, only those who are 'OF' the truth will hear His voice anyway. Those who live in falsehood, and gain their position and acceptance among their peers with surreptitious means, will not recognize and certainly not admit that they have been wrong. *This is the power of truth*, it <u>seeks out</u> those who have a heart for it, and who respect and love the revealed will of the God of Heaven; for all real truth must center in Christ as Lord.

If the Jews who wanted Jesus dead, and if Pilate, had really been seeking truth, they would have known what Jesus meant when He said, "...to this end was I born, and for *this cause* **came I into the world, that I should bear witness to the truth**..." The truth is, that Jesus is a King, and He is indeed the Son of the Living God. Now this verse means that everything Jesus did and said, was for one reason, to Glorify the Father in Heaven by revealing the will of the Father to humankind and to carry out the redemption plan, which had been designed from the foundation of the world. The world (as the term is used in verse 36 of John 18) does not want to change, that is why believers are instructed that they must 'not love the world or the things of the world.' (1 Jn. 2. 15, 3. 13, 5. 4-5).

The Jews who sought Jesus' life, were not seeking salvation, nor to fulfill the will of God. This problem lies at the heart of all disbelief in the world today, among false religions, and among those who pretend (the word hypocrisy goes here) to follow Jesus. **If our very core purpose is for our selves**, to gain what we can from the things of God and His teaching, for some personal advantage in this present world, we cannot find the Word of God 'working' for us. The Word of God only works for it's intended purpose, to bring glory to the Lord God, and salvation to mankind. If we don't begin here, with the right purpose, to seek the will of God, on this road to truth as it is here in these verses presented and in the whole Bible, we can easily stumble and fall into confusion. *Jesus lived and gave, that we might give and live.* When Jesus came to earth He came with the purpose of revealing **truth** in its fullness and totality. He lived among us, then gave Himself for the world, so that all people who sought Him and sought truth, would copy or follow this example, to give up ourselves for God and others, and we do that by turning the equation around. **We who want to live** for ever, in truth and in righteousness that He gives, **must give of who we are and what we have** in order **to live**. Jesus already had life, so He came to live among us, and give Himself, that we may do what pleases Him, and that is to give our lives, so we can inherit life eternal (Jn. 17. 2). To discover our purpose in the plan of God, that we must give in order to live, is to discover the *heart of truth.* Jesus who lives, came to give His life, we who learn that we posses life, must give it, so we can go on living for eternity.

This is the very purpose of everything that God created. He made the sun and it gives, (heat, light) to the earth. The earth gives (soil and vegetation) to the animal kingdom and to humans. The chain continues, in all of God's creation. In the case with mankind, this is where a decision must be made to fulfill the purpose of God or not do to do so. All else in creation follows it's designed purpose, because it cannot do otherwise. Mark 10. 45, is one record where Jesus expresses His purpose. The Son of Man came not to be ministered to, but to minister and *to give His life*...a ransom for many. Jesus decided to do that, to give His life for the world. Each believer must decide to do that as well, to give his life for Christ and for the work of ministry (seeking and saving the lost sheep for Jesus), if that believer is to live forever with Jesus. This is called purpose. It is also called Christian living, maturity, growing in Christ, being a disciple, being faithful, etc. etc. To *minister* and to *give* are related. The order here is important, Jesus stated that

His purpose was not to be served, but to serve (or minister to others) and you can't do that without giving. In order to serve we must learn to give. To serve is to give of self, time and possessions. Jesus explained His purpose for our sakes. He came not to be ministered unto, but to minister and to give His life a ransom for many (other people). This is a very clear and exact goal, Jesus set the pace, He became the example to follow. To live as Jesus commanded is to forget our personal worth, and see our purpose revealed in saving others. **This is more important than seeking only our own well being**. *It is in this way that we discover our personal worth.*

A soldier in battle must make such a choice, you cannot save others sometimes, without risking the loss of your own life. Those who watched Jesus die on the cross stated something very fundamental about his own suffering, when they stated, "...others He saved, himself He cannot save..." Matt. 27. 42. That was more true than they realized. I call this, the **'law of the cross'** you cannot die (or at least risk death) for others and save yourself at the same time. We too are commanded to bear our cross and follow Jesus. Jesus could not have saved Himself from death, and still have saved all believing people from the penalty of sin, which is death. So it is, to live like this, to give one's life for another, is the greatest love and the only way to fulfill our purpose. This kind of love, makes us valuable, not just to ourselves, but to all others in this world. And to live and die for others fulfills the purpose God had designed us for, when He created us. To love your neighbor as yourself is the basis for **this kind of life goal.**

This purpose in life is the only true reason to live, as I stated above, it is the same for all of God's creation. To discover this purpose is to discover truth. **Everything God created is intended to give of itself** for the sake of something or someone else. *This is true purpose.* To fail to find this purpose, means to miss the whole target not just the bull's eye. To find the true purpose in living is the purpose of truth revealed. Some of our teachings in the 'name it claim it' or prosperity gospel (which is not really the Gospel), deal primarily with receiving, and if giving is mentioned, it is still only for the purpose of receiving. In other words, we are today often taught in lectures, sermons and books on the subject, **in order** to receive we must give. Look and see how many books are written on this subject the next time you visit the Christian book store. Jesus received the church or Ecclesia, the people for His kingdom, in the giving of his life. But there are multitudes of people who do not receive Him, although He gave Himself *in order* to bring them to His fold as well (1 Tim. 4. 10). Jesus would have died for the world if not one soul accepted Him as Lord, because He so loved the world, and that is what love does. **A church member today who gives for the purpose of**

receiving is missing the point. Knowing that in the principle of sowing we reap a harvest, and in giving we also receive is great news, what is reaped in harvest is the very purpose for the sowing of seeds as a farmer, because in farming we must sow and reap in order to survive.

But there is another principle in giving of our lives that is done whether or not we receive anything in return. To apply this kind of sowing and reaping illustration to our lives without the context is not a complete picture. We give things, and we give time, we do sow and we reap what we have sown, but there is another type of giving that does not have in it, the purpose of receiving in return. Jesus stated, "...Give and you shall receive, good measure, pressed down and shaken together and running over shall men give unto your bosom..."(Luke 6. 38), this is one type of giving, which is rewarded in physical things. But there is a giving of one's life, that reaps a different and eternal reward, in the world to come. **If we learn only of a giving that receives in return something in this life**, we have not seen the whole picture. Jesus said, "my sheep...follow me and I give to them eternal life..." John 10. 27,28.

The sun in the heavens gives light and heat to the planet earth, **but receives nothing from the earth in return**. The sun fulfills it's intended purpose because it cannot decide not to, even as the winds and the sea obey the Lord, creation serves it's purpose. That's what **we were created for**, **to give** our life to and for others, but first to the Lord, (2 Cor. 8. 5) so that our giving of life will be of eternal benefit. Humans have the power to decide if they will fulfill the purpose of God. This is where love comes into the picture, it is the motivation for life, and the motivation for giving. To love God is to keep His commandments, and this is His commandment, that we love one another. **Love will make one give when that giving does not foresee an immediate physical return.**

A saved person cannot love a lost soul without trying to bring that soul to Christ. This may be done with a degree of risk for the believer who goes to lost people who live where it is not safe to openly proclaim the Gospel. Christ is the total truth, and He is all of life which can be known or received (1 John 2. 2-12). If our love is not a love from God which we get from our connection and association with God as His child and servant, then eternity is not in that love and therefore neither is there any power in it. This means that we will not take any risk for the sake of preaching the Gospel where it is not a welcome message. **That kind of love is like faith without works, it is dead.** And a life without truth is dead also, and life without this purpose is dead or ineffective as well.

We can love, without it necessarily being a love from God, because we are warned not to love the world. So that kind of love *of* self *for* self will not bring eternal good or eternal reward from God and please Him. When Jesus gave the *great commission,* to go into *all* the world and preach the Gospel to *every* person this becomes very motivating for those who love truth, and we will take any risk to carry out the Lord's command because the risk of life and the danger is worth the results we shall reap when a lost person becomes saved. It is in knowing that lost people are loved by the Lord, and knowing that loving the Lord will make us seek His will and His good pleasure that we discover *our purpose* (Eph. 1. 9-12). There is no power on earth that can stop the true church of the Lord, from fulfilling *the task He gave.* The labor for God carried out by the believers, is a labor of LOVE, **a love that comes from God** to the believer, and goes **from the believer into the task Jesus gave us.** (See Phil. 2. 30, Eph. 6. 23, 1ˢᵗ Thess. 1. 3).

Those who seek a self-fulfilling role, will never accomplish their true purpose. **We are made to give,** and that purpose cannot be fulfilled for God's good pleasure if we seek only our own pleasure. The meaning of the word covenant even declares that each person in the covenant seeks the good of the other party, not his own ends. We do not have to seek our own good because Jesus who brought into effect the New Covenant is looking after our part, we, in turn, must seek His good pleasure in the covenant agreement. That is how the covenant works. The task of caring for others is the reason we were created. All teachings of the Bible reveal that we are to increase in the fear of the Lord and in the knowledge of the Lord, not just so we can feel good about ourselves, but so we can be useful to God and more effective for the fulfillment of our God given purpose, to serve and to give.

This is why the persecuted church in the world is our teacher. These are the souls that give all to glorify Christ and reveal in their suffering, His power to change lives. These who suffer for the sake of the Name of Jesus as Lord, know the price and cost of discipleship. Those who have died proclaiming this wonderful Savior of mankind, are teaching the church in the 'soft' countries about how the job of soul winning is done and how to bring glory to God and not to self. How well the church in the 'west' learns this lesson, is in itself a question still to be answered. No doubt the lesson has been, and is being, taught. Read 'Foxe's Book of Martyrs' it is a great text in this school of life. As we see the American church, continue to emphasize the value of self-esteem and discovery of personal 'gifts' we would do well to re-evaluate our own direction. We could end up at the beginning, and find that we never really left the starting blocks. To do all this traveling and get nowhere would be the epitome of futility.

Those of us who teach our children that they should be faithful to fulfill their assignments in school, had better look into our own school books and see if we have not only failed to fulfill our assignment, but have flunked other tests as well. There is only one final exam and to fail that will be the end of school and the end of the lesson. This school offers no degree 'on line' and there will be no graduates who have not completed their assignment. Enjoy your education, but remember education is more than classes and study, although churches have given plenty of time to study and gathering of information. **We must also finish the assignment** (in this case, so that the teachers will not have wasted their time, and you and I will not feel like failures). Some have failed the test and made shipwreck (1 Tim. 1. 19), (2 Cor. 13. 5-8) in their personal lives, so keep your eyes on the teachers, follow their example, because there are many millions who await our arrival, with **the news that can set their souls free. We must fulfill our ministry**. When the summer is ended and the harvest is past, let no one say, **"and we are not saved,"** (Jer. 8. 20), **because the church was not there**!

"Your brother William has gone mad!" So said Edmund Carey when he read the letter from William Carey in which William had stated," I must part with a beloved family, a number of most affectionate friends. Never did I see such sorrow manifested as reigned through our place of worship Sunday, but I have set my hand to the plough." **William Carey faced the scowls of brethren**, not heathen, at his church who cried, "What about us?" (P. 71 Heroes of the Faith, William Carey, Barbour pub. Co). William Carey had announced his decision to head for India, and at the most inconvenient time in his family's circumstances. Carey had believed all that Jesus and the Apostles and Prophets of the Scriptures had taught. But now we carry the name of William Carey as the "Father of modern missions." Had he caved in to the wishes of family, church and friends, does anyone think we would know about him?

The heroes of the faith, did not come by that expression without cost. They were the early graduates of the school which taught *The Lesson.* The assignment for these heroes of the faith was clear and the assignment was from the headmaster of the school, Jesus Himself. It is Jesus who assigned to the church, the task of going into all the world to preach the Gospel. The Gospel of Christ is the hope of the world, because it is the message that when believed brings people into fellowship with the Creator Lord. Ignatius, a student under John the Apostle, devoured by wild animals in Rome in 111 AD, said, "My dear Jesus, my Savior, is so deeply written in my heart, that I feel confident, that if my heart were to be cut open and chopped to pieces, the name of Jesus would be found written on each piece." (taken from the book 'Jesus Freaks', by Voice of the Martyrs and DC talk, Bethany House Pub. 1999). In the same book, is the account of 30,000 Christians at one time dying for their faith, refusing to deny Christ at the command of the Communist leaders of North Korea, as the government lists the deaths as the communist way of suppressing superstition. This is a normal event in this day and time.

All of these too, as those in Hebrews chapter 11, refused to be set free, because they held the hope of an eternal home and life in the heavens, not made with hands. And the assignment of these who died and those now dying for Christ, was to carry the Gospel of Christ to all the world. Can those of us who live in America and freely continue in the faith of the Gospel, fail to announce the assignment that has been given to the Lord's people? Can there continue to be an emphasis of more buildings, to be built, more ministerial staff increase and more lessons on 'church growth' while more than one billion people today have no knowledge of John 3. 16? What kind of fair play, does today's American church invent under such conditions? If we wait around for the 'qualified' the person of 'perfect' preparedness according to the scholars of the church, the assignment will not be fulfilled. We will all flunk out of school, because we failed to accept the example and instruction of the teachers, if something does not happen to change this unholy and unbiblical condition.

Where will you be when the bell rings, or should we say, when the trumpet sounds? The time is short, the days are evil, and the work is very great. We do not well, we must go and tell the King's household. (2 Kings 7, Eph. 5. 16, Neh. 4. 19,20), so says our heart, so says the King!

31

The Entire World Against Itself!

✦

Terrorism vs. everyone

When children strap on explosives and run into a crowd of people, whom these children consider to be enemies, there are no winners, only losers!

Matt. 18. 1-10

Perhaps no one in the western world, and certainly not in China, would be willing to consider the possibility that the abortion of babies, unborn and nearly born, in America and around the world, would be the actual cause for the onset of a war that cannot be won and must always be fought, called a war against 'terrorism'. As a person concerned with the eternal value of human souls, and having spent 40 years in missionary work among cultures not my own, but desire to please God and spiritual responsibility to be there, being accepted as my own (on assignment from the King of Kings), I believe there is a real and definite connection.

The first hint of this ponderous consideration was when we learned that children among the Islamic people, took suicide bombing of other innocent souls, as a viable approach to vent the hatred and misguided teaching of their elders. When children are brought into such a war, and when we consider how infants (the unborn) were considered as 'garbage' to so many in this great "land of the free and home of the brave" a land we call by many names, such as "land of opportunity," and 'America the beautiful' etc. is it not ironic as well as hypocritical? We ache for the loss of lives today in countries where children are made to believe that some great reward awaits their soul for rushing into a crowd of people of another culture and language, with intent to die with them and prove what, that their own language, culture and religion are superior? This all happens in a world where laws about acceptance and tolerance are the most valued laws of the world! Where is all of this hideous behavior headed? No doubt to some horrible end. "…They called to the mountains and the rocks, 'fall on us and hide us from the throne and from the wrath of the Lamb! '(Rev. 6).

In a recent 'prayer notice' from Voice of The Martyrs to those of us on their volunteer network list, there appeared the announcement that in Australia two men who were teaching on the subject of Islam as compared to Christianity, were arrested and will be on trail even as I write these words, for violating the laws of Australia which were designed to protect people from religious and ethnic prejudice, it is a law called "Racial and Religious Toleration Act" of Victoria, which allows the Islamic people to bring charges against the two Christian speakers. In the United States such laws are intact under various descriptions, but the age of tolerance and acceptance of all people, religions, and life styles, is a well known fact in today's society.

But is it not strange that in a world with such 'touchy' regulations and laws about religious differences, there exists side by side, the legality of abortion of the unborn? So in this kind of a world and in this kind of America, we see such inconsistencies and such total disregard for life, liberty and the (chance to have life) pursuit of happiness. Smart judges, or at least well educated, and smart lawyers or at least well educated, and smart doctors, at least well educated, cannot see the whole picture here, nor can these people see the terrible injustice brought into play (poor choice of words here) which brings out tears for the children suicide bombers, and no tears for the abortion of the unborn children. But actually abortion is not my main subject here, it happens to be an example of the Supreme court justice (what a contradiction in terms that is), ***which kills on one hand and claims to protect rights of people on the other. Perhaps the Supreme Court*** has too many hands, must be more like a human head on an octopus. These people can enact laws which contradict because they can just put out a tentacle and control whatever suits their opinion of public opinion. If all of these smart (at least well educated)people can be so dumb and so wrong morally and still be followed because they make the rules, perhaps the NRA was right, don't give up your weapons. As the Islamic militants wage war around the world, because they don't like America, Jews or Christians, in America they receive the public support of laws which exist simply to provide the cover and the protection they need when victims of their atrocities bring complaints or retaliation or when sincere people who differ with the Islamic religion try to explain the problem as they see it.

This is a poison philosophy of life, it is like a cancer which eats away at the basic truth and freedom which most of the world either enjoys or at least seeks. This idea that children, and women as well,(all innocent people) can become pawns for the hate filled terrorists to use as they so choose in their battle to control for their own religious, cultural and political ends, the minds of the poor, and the helpless, is not new to human thinking. It goes as far back as Cain and Able. But today the support for such ideology is coming from an educated, (not illiterate) and politically savvy, well-financed body of spiritually bankrupt leaders of nations who are void of human emotion. Take out the heart and brain, and you have no chance of finding common ground for community or peace. When America along with communist nations like China, gave legality to abortion of the unborn and nearly born, we began taking the first steps down the long road to Uglyville and its neighboring city of Nonsoul town. So should the world be surprised that children are today rushed out with others to become the victims of suicide bombings which make about as much sense as jumping off a cliff with your baby brother in arms? Did we see these children as valuable at the abortion clinics, and hospitals? No wonder than that war will take some of them that we did not want to offer on the alter of convenience of lifestyle.

In the book, "The Death of Right and Wrong" by Random House, Forum Prima Pub. Author Ms. Tammy Bruce speaks (on P. 40-ff) of the moral relativism of the Left, and she gives attention to the bashing of Christian symbols and other methods used by the Left wing agenda in America, to effectively distort the countries views of Christians and Christianity, to the point of trying to distort the Christian's view of themselves, to make them doubt their own value to human thinking and behavior. The world will not realize that it is it's own worst enemy. This is why Jesus came into the world to save people from the darkness that is in the world, and to separate unto Himself a people destined for a life that has no end. This world, much like the present time allotted to us in this world, will (according to the Bible) run its course, and it is the message of Jesus and the hope of His followers that the third time is not just a charm, but it is the goal, a world not made with hands, eternal in the heavens. (2 Cor. 5. 1, Hebrews 11. 10,16, 2 Pet.3 12-14,). The first world, due to complete wickedness, was destroyed by water (flood) washed clean, the second one we now have, will be destroyed by fire, (2 Pet. 3).

When Jesus spoke of children, He said, 'of such is the Kingdom of heaven. It is time to hear what God says about man's problems. Mankind has been allowed the awesome and phenomenal responsibility to see the evil in the world, and to see the glories of God's creation as well. We have been given ages of time to understand the value of good men and bad. We have seen war and peace, joy and sorrow. It is not over yet, but we need to understand, that we need no more books on 'why bad things happen to good people' this was adequately answered and addressed in the book of Job. We don't need more 'talk about town' addressing the issue of morality and justice, we have walked down the street of life with every kind of emotion, known to human kind. We need to look at the Bible, and decide to read and believe it, so that we can approach the coming days with understanding from above, and with confidence in God, who created all things good, and will bring into view at the time appointed, the kind of earth and heavens that do not pass away. We have seen the God of heaven cleanse the earth with water, some of us will be here when this earth is burned with fire, and all who believe in Him and obey His word, will witness and enjoy the new heaven and the new earth wherein dwells only righteousness. The world became it's own enemy, and the people of earth wanted a piece of the action, but God will always be mankind's only friend and only hope. When the only way out is the way up, and when the only way in (to the Lord's fellowship) is the way through ("...no man comes unto the Father but through me..."—Jesus), and when there is no longer a "My-way Highway" but only Jesus will lead His sheep along, then we can rest in Him. God has shown us that nothing in life (which is His creation anyway) works well, unless He is in it.

Hello there, World, is anybody at home? No, just us skeletons of life past, and dying dreams of yesteryear, when people were human and law lived around the corner near justice and truth. When these present days have passed, if there is still a world left with people in it, there is no doubt in my mind that the history books will fail to tell the whole story, and the historians will be too ashamed to put the blame where it belongs, at the highest levels of government and in the laps of the clergy who felt that government and church had some kind of unholy alliance which went unchecked and for the most part even unnoticed. Sleep well if you can because we are soon to be awakened by a very loud sound of a trumpet. Guess who is back? And it isn't the spooky guy.

Al Hamilton
Missionary
albertham@sbcglobal.net

32

The Importance of—Nothing!

✦

1 Cor. 2. 6, 2Cor. 12. 11
1Cor. 3. 7

In the day and times when **the self-esteem 'engine'** seems to be running full speed ahead, it would behoove us to consider the seriousness and the relevancy of the term which so well describes some of the man-made and man-invented values placed upon Christians. Jesus told the disciples that 'without Him, they could do nothing', John 15. 5. If followers of Christ can do nothing, without Jesus, and if, as Paul the Apostle states, we are nothing then where did this self-esteem 'engine', (as I call it) get all of it's steam? I think we will find that it all came from the psychology of narcissism, and from the world-minded philosophers of this present 'evil' (Gal. 1.4) world.

There has been so much talk in churches about the same themes that the world echoes, you can hardly tell the difference from a lecture in the avg. University class on psychology and the sermon on Sunday morning. Maybe this is what was meant by a 'world view' which churches and church leaders have been encouraged to take on. Certainly the idea of world view **meant** to encourage a biblical view of the world, as the field referred to in the sermon about the sower and the seed in Mark. 4. I think I would have called this view the **Christian view of God's task in the world**. Why call it a world view? So much for semantics, or whatever it is called. **Simplicity would be a nice word for the scholars to work on, they seem to have such a difficult time applying it**.

Does anyone stop to think about the terms used by the 'Religious Right' and the multitudes of church scholars today? Consider the theme I recently saw written on a church marquee, which stood for all to see, as a statement by the local leadership—**"count your blessings, not your problems"**. Now that is an interesting antidote, especially when you know the bible states, "I count not my life dear unto myself", (Acts 20. 24), "I rejoice in my infirmities, and in my weakness I am strong" (2 Cor. 12. 7-10), not to mention a number of other references to self-denial. Does this church which posted this sign, not know that the persecuted church (their brothers and sisters) around the world, only knows and experiences one blessing—**their hope in Christ? Our problems are—our blessings.** So the thing called a problem to American Christians, could be the very thing that is called a blessing to those who suffer for their faith in Jesus. Either the thinking of an average American Christian is not founded upon scripture, or the American Christian is completely ignorant of what real Christianity is.

In the verses I have listed above, the word 'nothing' is used to show the real value of this present world's wisdom. Today however, most churches and entire denominations, push and promote education and knowledge in the world's wisdom (which is coming to nothing), upon the unsuspecting youth of the day, and even upon the unthinking adult member of today's congregation. In the Nov./ Dec. issue of the magazine entitled, "Ministries Today"—a writer quotes Leonard Ravenhill's statements (p. 53-56), regarding sacrificial living and Mr. Ravenhill's gigantic statements that to his disdain, the followers of Christ in America respect the world and it's opinions, appreciations and qualifications; yet the magazine promotes that very concept of 'acceptability' in the world when presenting the value of 'higher education' as some great tool for spiritual work. Today's church leaders are much like the Pharisees of the New Testament times, whose forefathers killed the prophets, (whom God had sent to warn them), and then (the Pharisees) built tombs to the prophets as if to appease the people. The Pharisees would not follow the teachings of the Prophets (they rejected the words of Moses about the coming Messiah—so they turned down the Lord Jesus as the Messiah), yet because the people respected and accepted what the Prophets said, the Jewish religious leaders—wanting the favor of the people so badly, played the game of acceptance but in their hearts there was pure rejection of the message of the prophets—(John 1. 11-12).

What game is this that the modern American church plays with the present world system (in America), which has rules for engagement in a biblical command from the Lord, yet refuses to take on the issues of self-ism, and exaltation of success in (2 Tim. 2. 2-4), the entanglement with worldly things?

This is really great logic, publish a magazine which advertises the exaltation of worldly wisdom and yet quote a man ("Why Revival Tarries"—by Leonard Ravenhill), who shows disdain for such things as the exaltation of wisdom of men, ...i.e." **we are suffering today from a plague of ministers who are more**

concerned that their heads be filled than that their hearts be fired…" p. 54. Ministries Today. Maybe we can have our cake and eat it too. The American churches should get together and establish a bakery, where the Christian who wants the best of both worlds (this one and the one to come), can believe that such a thing is possible, although the present world has no 'best' it is all bad. They could bake cakes that when eaten stay in your hand too. Sounds impossible doesn't it? Well it is no more impossible than to believe that you can be an accepted success by lost people in a doomed world, and still find favor in the sight of the Living God in Heaven! Try reading Matthew 24. 9 and following. Perhaps today's churches in American can explain how the follower of Christ can be hated by all nations in the world and still be loved by America. Perhaps America is not a nation! Or perhaps it is an exception! May as well build that bakery as believe that. No doubt it will be a tough battle, when American Christians find that the government and a majority of American citizens (of the liberal and the 'baser sort'—Acts 17. 5) begin to bring civil action against Believers who show contempt for wicked deeds and corrupt decisions which will be perceived as 'politically correct' in American courts. Perhaps the church is guilty of loving the country!

The attitude of the Apostle Paul, and the attitude that Jesus told His disciples to have about self (Luke 17.10), is not the attitude that we hear presented in the pulpits of American churches. This hype in the pulpit to be seeing one's self as of great importance, and the exaltation of 'self-esteem' is not a biblical perspective nor is it a biblical teaching. One of the recent notices on a bulletin board in the church I usually attend was an example of **this 'strange fire' offered upon the 'alter of church-ism'. The church ladies were** invited to attend a teaching seminar of some kind, which offered—in bold print—the chance **to "discover the real you".** The theme was entitled, '**Authentic Living.**' Even the thought of such 'Norman Vincent Peal-ism' and Hindu centered philosophy is appalling. This all sounds like a sales meeting of some kind in a corporate 'world' setting for gaining some pointers on reaching the top of the social and financial ladder. **If you discover the real you, all you will discover is a sinner who needs the grace of God for mercy and forgiveness.** And you can be sure this is not the point of that women's seminar.

The only reason a church can sound like the world, is because **the church borrowed the philosophy and goals of the present world, to make it's message acceptable to people, with little or no regard for the Word and will of God! Jesus never tried to gain popularity or acceptance of people.**

There is no reason big enough, no excuse sound enough for this attitude which prevails in todays average American church, which makes people look like some great commodity that would be worthy of the death of the Son of God. **Something is terribly wrong when you see a poster on the wall of the 3rd grade Sunday school classroom which states—"God loves me, so that makes me special."** How ridiculous that is, since the fact is, just the opposite, since **God is the one doing the loving**, it is He who is special, for loving such as us, undeserving as we are. The idea of specialness is exactly as Dr. Aaron Stern has put it in his book, "Me—The Narcissistic American" written in the 1970's, when he stated, **"specialness demands privilege".** And whenever a person demands privilege, he stops being interested in the other person, and becomes interested first and foremost in himself. In looking for words in the Bible which speak of self-esteem, you will find that the subject is mentioned in Romans 12. 10, and Phil. 2. 3, which says, **"Let each esteem others better than himself."** You must know that the American University psychologist loves that one! Not many sermons are preached on how to lose your life, and to hate your life in this world. The preachers of today have let the false gods of Islam have that subject for themselves, and the word martyr no longer refers only to Christians who accept death rather than deny Jesus. But the difference between the 'suicide bombers' of the Islamic religion and Christian martyrs is—**that the Christian forgives and prays for his persecutor, and the Islamic extremist brings death on himself to exalt himself.** So much for the example of self-ism and it's comparison to Biblically true Christianity.

There is also a big difference in attitude **and** in the number of Christians who die for their faith in Christ at the hand of persecutors, and the suicide bombers of the Islamic world. **Around the world** over 5,000 Christians lose their lives every month at the hands of others. Remember, the magicians of Pharaoh imitated the same miracle as God gave to Moses, **but** the serpent of Moses devoured the serpents of the magicians. **Poor imitations always show up in the face of truth and reality!** The effort of Islamic suicide bombers to look like real martyrs for some great cause, does not compare with true martyrdom suffered by the true believers in Christ. The God and Father of our Lord Jesus Christ, who is the Savior of the world, especially those who believe, will not be overpowered by **some weak attempt at 'copy cat' martyrdom.** The test of who is greatest, Satan with his pride and his lies, or God, the only true and living God, was already passed in the time of man's beginning, when Satan was cast out of heaven for his pride and his rebellion. The gates of Hell shall not prevail over the Ecclesia (called out people of God). (Matt. 16. 16-18). May the church of the Lord, be true while being faced with the rising amount of 'tares' which spring up in the midst of the 'wheat' is my prayer. Be thou faithful unto death, and you will receive the crown of life—so said Jesus who Himself faced death, that He may give life to all who believe in Him.

Respectfully,

Al Hamilton, Missionary
(I also have the name—Al, and I am a Christian).

33

The Intertwining

Many strands of twine or cords bound together and intertwined make a strong and durable rope. It is this very thing referred to in the Bible Eccl. 4.12, "a cord of three strands is not easily broken." When the founding fathers of the American constitution put together many good and spiritual teachings with the foundation principals of the new country, they were using good common sense with high and noble intentions. It was a picture of power and influence for the beginning of new opportunities and the establishment of a nation of free people. A people determined, dedicated and highly motivated with high purpose founded the country that would become the leading nation in the present world. (Gal.1:4) But the physical world, would still be only that, the world. No nation **in** the world and **of** the world would be comparable to the Kingdom that God brought from above by His teaching and sending of the Holy Spirit.

Without saying that it was happening, the founding fathers of the American constitution and government, took good Bible teachings and commandments that were given to the "Ecclesia" or church (which comprised the body of people who chose to be saved from sin, and follow Jesus as Lord), and then they incorporated the 'religious faith' they personally had, and these words of the Bible, into their goals for a free and 'new' land. But it was not necessarily their plan to enforce the teachings and way of Christ, the Son of the Living God, upon everyone who desired to be citizens of the new land, or insist that all citizens become followers of Christ. People in this new country, this new land under this new 'free' government, who embraced the teachings of the Bible, found a friend in this material, social and economically sound system of social order.

None seemed to sense any danger in the alliance of social, and spiritual camaraderie, or anticipate any problem, with the idea of Biblical principles being lined up with establishment of a social system designed to promote the general welfare of all peoples. So who would have disagreed with Bible believing people establishing a country—to give freedom and support to all who would follow the new laws of a land that sought the good of all people, and the establishment of liberty and justice for all?

But what was meant for the good of a new social order, became the subtle weakening of the God ordained principles for all followers of Christ. **When the cords of social justice and good will toward all men, as strong as these intentions were, became intertwined with** Bible teachings for those who gave allegiance only to one King, and One Lord of life, there was not a church established with social trimmings, nor was there a country with Biblical basis. The stronger demands of the Creator God, for His chosen people who were redeemed from the earth, (which people would be His representatives to all nations of the world), could not be couched in a framework that would be limited to one nation only. And the new UNION could not 'just pick' the spiritual aspects of the Bible that seemed suitable to its social purpose, and still expect to have the full power of God supporting it.

When the cords of social justice and man ordained laws are intertwined with divine, holy and God ordained—commandments for life, there is a weakening of the latter. No law made by men can equally supply the support and righteous intent that is required by the Lord for His followers. (Matthew 15. 6). This is why Paul the Apostle said to the churches, they should be sure to be found obedient to laws of the land, because the laws of God are so much greater and so much more demanding (ie…".I say unto you, love your enemies…"). It would be an embarrassment for Christians to be found falling short of laws made by men, when they have a greater more demanding law from God.

So herein lays the dilemma. The very separation of these two entities, social justice and spiritual living (Rom.8:6) is evidence that there never was a union of Church and State, so those today who cry for such a union do not understand the Bible. Today the cry goes out, that the framers of the constitution said nothing about separation of church and state. Perhaps that is because they never saw a difference. But there is a vast difference between a nation of the world, or social orders of the world, and the kingdom of God. Jesus said, "My kingdom is not of this world." (The average Christian does not wave a Christian flag at political rallies; he waves the American flag like all other pro-American citizens. Does this not seem a bit ironic to anyone?).

The celebration of citizenship as an American, is only a temporary association. A follower of Christ has more at stake than being a 'model' citizen. And laws made for men, by men, can easily change, but they will always be less demanding than the laws of the Lord God for His people.

For example; the day of political protests has become the age of discontent. People in recent years are accustomed to political protests as well as public dissent, even dissent against Supreme Court decisions, the highest court in the land. We are in an age of individualism that has gone wild, with little or no serious contemplation of the general welfare, or good of the group. Individualism which was taught at all levels in the countries educational institutions, from grade school to Universities, has become the watch-word of the day for human relations, as well as personal development. It is now time for an awakening at least among people of religious faith. Faith is of greater value to people than the legal, political and social requirements of a country.

It is time to awake from spiritual stupor, and see what is happening to the world which is caught up in what has been called, <u>malignant narcissism</u> by author Tammy Bruce. What is more alarming is the fact that the churches of America are not immune to this narcissism, Tammy Bruce in her book "The Death of Right and Wrong," clearly underscores this very fact. With documentation and present day events revealing what I call, the **'left turn' of the 'religious right'**, Tammy Bruce has been boldly warning the American people of the dying heritage that America so proudly hails, and to my knowledge she has not even embraced the teachings of Christianity as her philosophy of life. So she knows the value of high moral standards and their place in the controlling of the State and social order.

American Christians are so into themselves and their own welfare on a social plane, that they cry crocodile tears at each loss in the battle for religious freedom, (prayer in school) and yet they have freedom in Christ, from sin and the powers of darkness forever. What can be better than an eternal and spiritual freedom? *If the Christians preach that all we need is Jesus*, then perhaps we need to be ready to practice that—and not fear what laws man can make and what those laws do to us. In recent days, in the news we have seen Christians mob the Alabama state court house and bemoan the fact that the large marble monument with the 10 commandments of the Bible carved out in stone, were forcibly removed from the public place which was the very heart of truth and justice for the state of Alabama. Other Christians state boldly that Mr. Moore should have complied with the demand to take the monument out of the court house area. This love of freedom has already divided Christians, and now they cannot stand together on this small issue. (Matthew 15. 6).

The noble and wise judge, Mr. Moore, with strong Christian convictions, refused to obey the laws of man and held to his convictions that the laws of God are higher and of greater power than any law made by man, stood his ground and so much as said, if you want the monument removed, dear supreme (?) court, do it yourself. And many church members and pastors (?) took the side of the supreme court of the land against the fine Christian judge. The argument of the pastors was, "we must obey the laws of the land." What a mushy, weak statement, when these men of the Bible know full well, that the laws of God and principles that so reveal the value of the Commandments of God have stood at the heart of the American justice system from the beginning of the country. (It was these principles which were at stake here in this matter). Just read Acts 4. 19, as a matter of fact read the whole book of Acts of Apostles, it is clear that there is a difference between obeying the laws of God and the laws of man. The Christian obeys the laws of any land unless that law opposes the higher law of God.

Is this a clue? Is it hard to decide when God is speaking and man is speaking? As American Christians worry about their land and their physical freedom, does it not stand to reason that the persecuted Christians around the world are embarrassed to call us their brethren? *As I have said, the persecuted church does not need political and social freedom, and they cry not for education and excellence(?) in social achievement, most of them never had any freedom—except in their soul as Believers.*

But American worshippers of the land, the country, the freedom and all that goes with it, have fallen prey to the mystical, and unbiblical **INTERTWINING of God and country**. By the time anyone reads this, it will have become very clear that it is necessary to choose God and His Word and not worship freedom and the blessings that the country of America, (by God's grace), may enjoy. How un-patriotic that must sound. But what about our allegiance to the Lord? For America to fight (which I too would do), an enemy that is trying to overcome the weak of the earth, is a noble cause, but that intent by America's government and military advisors is the desire to bring freedom to people in bondage, and it is *not the same as church members,-trying to drag a country into church and perform a wedding of the two*. If it seems difficult to see a difference between nations of the present world, and the eternal Kingdom of God, His 'Called out people'—than perhaps our preachers have spent too much time on Sunday 'happy hours' and be good to your family sermons, and *left the other 'undone' matters untaught,—(Justice and the Love of God) Lk. 11. 42. ie. Justice toward the unreached peoples of the world, and the Love of God for all people,which makes the real church carry the real message to the whole world, not a twisted religious view of mans idea of how God should accept religions He did not establish.*

When strands of a rope are intertwined with nylon cords, and enough pressure is applied to the rope, the rope will likely break, even though the nylon strengthened the combination and may outlast the strands of hemp. There is something about this intertwining of the church and the government of USA that has **weakened the church even though it strengthened the country**. This might be a good place to be reminded of the verses in 1 Tim. 4:,and 2 Tim. 3. which tell of a 'falling away from the faith'. If the great commission given by the Lord Jesus, had been, 'go into all the world and build a better nation,' or if it had been 'go into all the world and bring freedom to all nations...' then America might have indeed been a 'Christian nation,' acting on the command of God, but that was not the command and commission given by the Lord of Lords, the King of Kings from heaven.

The building of a nation, and a free country was blessed by the Lord, but there were also many blessings that Israel received while under the rule of a king, **but the idea of a king was the idea of the people—not God's**. God said in the early history of Israel, He will be their King...therefore they will not need a man to rule over them—(1 Sam. 12.12), (Hosea 13.4-11), (Isa. 43. 15), (Judges 8. 23**). But the people insisted** and they received their King, even many kings, and the Lord God chose the kings that were any good, for the sake of His people and His own Name, (1 Sam. 8). It should be clear that politics which are designed by men of the world, cannot replace the commands that come from God. From the very history of the people of Israel revealed in the Old Testament, it is continually pointed out, that even a nation that was designed by the Lord had trouble being completely obedient to God. As the Bible tells us, *only one nation was ever designed for man on this earth as a nation that belonged to God and to God completely,—that is the nation of Israel*. No other nation was called the people of God. In Hebrews 11, we of the Faith, are promised a **country not made with hands, eternal in the heavens**, we as Christians cannot cry around trying to make America into some socio-Christian utopia. This is not our goal or purpose. The Lord's church, is the 'Israel' of God today Gal. 3-6.16., Rom.2. 28,29.

God may well have ordained and destined the establishment of America as a country, and used men of spiritual faith to do it, but the country blessed by the Lord was still not the Church of the Lord. When the church was created on the day of Pentecost, and the Church (or actually the 'called out from the world people') was given the Holy Spirit and the Words of the Lord and His Apostles, the Kingdom of God had arrived. AT that time a people of God on earth to bear His Name and follow His leading, had come—*and it is not a political system or a country* where the majority rule, where the **laws are made by the people, for the people, and of the people. No country, no matter how sincere its** purpose or it's beginning can compare with the simple plan of God for his 'Ecclesia.' The true church (Ecclesia—called out persons of Faith in God from the world)—will not be broken, nor will it succumb to the enemy's arrows that fly by day nor the terror by night.

Jesus promised, that the gates of Hell itself cannot prevail against the church (Ecclesia) and this spiritual body has a task to carry it's message to all nations of the world, to bring mankind to Himself, until the task is finished (Matt. 24. 14). When you put new wine into old wine skins, the skins will break as the wine matures, and you will have neither the wine nor the wine skins which contained it. Perhaps in that example, is a picture for us, for it is a fact that a worldly—government social order, cannot contain the church. The parable of the wine skins and the new wine, referred to the power of the new teaching of the Lord Jesus, and the old law of Moses given to the Israelites. It is also true that this world will not survive the coming judgment of God upon evil, but those who do the will of God, will abide forever. The nation of Israel was called into existence by the Lord, and this is different from a nation that called upon God (America) to help in its beginning. **A country may call on the Lord for His blessing, but Israel, and now the Ecclesia, were called into being, <u>by the Lord</u>.**

Now we are brought to a time when people must choose whom they shall serve, as for me and my house we will serve the Lord. Choose you this day, **whom you will serve,-freedom and benefits of a great country, or the King of Kings and Lord of Lords! The time may be now upon us, that the country we live in, may make demands that those who have a country from above, (Heb. 11) cannot bow down to. Two masters, is one to many. The difference is becoming more obvious every day in the 'land of the free.'** The Christians of America can never expect to make all the citizens of America, bow to their God, and accept Bible teachings without repentance and choosing their God one citizen at a time, so to try and make the governing body of America, accept the laws of the Bible today, just because some of the 'Founding fathers' had Christian faith, is not only futile, it is foolish. The history of Constantine should make this obvious. But this is not a day of 'seeing the obvious' it is a time when the eyes of unbelievers have been blinded by the god of this present world.

34

The Miracle of All

✦

Lk. 10. 27. And other verses everywhere

In answer to the question, "what must one do to inherit eternal life?" came the eternal answer, so simple, so clear and easy to understand. One must do that which is written for man to do. There was no better time, no better circumstance, no better person, to ask this all important question than a lawyer, (who knew what the law required), and no better person to answer the question. Jesus, the Son of God, whose purpose on earth was to fulfill the will of the Father, and obey the Father completely, before all human eyes to see. Jesus was the one who held the answer *and He is the answer* to the right questions, if we just ask the right questions. This question was the right question for all mankind, a question asked by one very well educated man, who could well represent all others in that day and even in our day. The lawyer asking this question could well have been before a jury in a courtroom. And in a way this is the court room; the world and the people around us all of the time, when no special setting is arranged and the flow of life with it's questions and answers just rise up before us without planning or structure. **Into the courtroom of life, walks the Son of God,** the Savior of men, the Teacher who is also the Creator God, bringing into the experience of humans, the very express image of the God in Heaven.

Jesus, knew men's hearts, He became a human being so that no one could say, 'God just doesn't understand our lives and our human problems. 'Jesus, put His heart, mind, body and soul at the level of all human experiences, learning to love the disciples as much as men in battle learn to love their comrades upon whom they depend and trust with their lives. Jesus, stepped out of Heaven onto earth, to walk with mankind, understanding the heart of a mother whose only son had died, understanding the heart of children who gathered around Him, this Jesus, understanding the pain of losing a friend in death (Lazarus), seeing the sorrow of men and women with disease ridden bodies, yearning for a better life, this Jesus, telling about a Kingdom that is eternal and about the heavenly Father, God who cares and has been holding all things together, until the time appointed for a new world without end, to be brought into place, this same Jesus comes to meet men face to face. This Jesus, who could obviously have answered questions before they were asked, was ready for those who had sincerely wanted to know **that one thing** which is most important to know, this Jesus was quick to remind the certain lawyer, that he, already knew the answer to his own question. So as Jesus often did, He answered the inquiring heart, with another question. "What is written in the law?" How do you understand that law?

The lawyer knew better than to give the wrong answer to this question, in public his reputation could be on the line. So the lawyer had to be correct and complete. Jesus in reply, complimented him with His own affirmation and added the comment, you do as you have just answered and you will have life. In other words, Jesus said what has been commanded by the Lord God and has been written by the Lord's servants, since long ago, is and has always been there for the honest person to know. The Jewish nation had the advantage that many nations did not have, they had the revealed will of God for all mankind. Those who would choose to be honest about who God is, and honest about their own need for God's favor and mercy, can know how to receive the blessing of life eternal.

The next verses in this great encounter of a normal kind, take a very normal turn. The lawyer, willing **to justify himself**, since he did not think everyone was worthy of his love, had to qualify the statement which required one to love his neighbor. He could do this love thing, if he could just be sure exactly who qualifies as a neighbor. The lawyer needed to know in his own kind of heart, just upon whom it is that this love he is going to pour out, is going to fall. That was the lawyer's only 'loop hole' in the entire discussion. He had to find a way to get out of this requirement to love (certain) others if there was any way possible. When a person questions the Master Teacher, the Lord of the Universe, that person is in for a great shock. ***Because whoever questions*** Jesus Christ, the Son of God, <u>with any real purpose of discovering truth,</u> **will never be able to ask that same question with honest purpose again.**

This matter of questions and answers is in itself a field of study. As we look at the questions men have, and the answers that God's word gives, you find a real library of thought and deliberation; endless volumes of communication pile up which cannot easily be sorted out to everyone's satisfaction, scholar or novice, scientist or layman. But <u>this is the battle field</u> upon which all must find success or failure in the search for truth.

The illustration that Jesus used to define the meaning of the term neighbor, is a very clear to all people of all nations. It is strange to me that in a national missionary convention just a few years back, this very question was chosen for that years theme. "Who is my neighbor?' I responded to some friends, in this way, I said, why are they still asking that question, it has been answered for years? The missionary theme should have been, something like "How are we doing at being good neighbors?"

They could have at least picked, some theme that would deal with the answer, not with the question. It is quite a trick of the world corporate, business exec's., to ask questions over and over, as if more information is required, when in reality it is the aim of the person asking the question, to discredit the answer or the person responding to the question. **This is called in the business world, manipulation for the purpose of discrediting the one who is being questioned**. To keep an opponent continually on the defensive is a way to have the advantage in discussions of a serious nature.

It will make the person asking questions seem very interested in gaining more information, when in reality all he is seeking to do is discredit the answer. This is why, **Jesus often answered a question with another question** or challenge, such as in Matt. 22. 17-21, when Jesus was questioned about the tribute money for Caesar. As I have said elsewhere, **to plow the field with questions, then plant the seeds of doubt**, you can expect to **reap the harvest of distrust**. The Pharisees really made use of this question method, they wanted to reap a harvest of distrust around the words of Jesus, but they never succeeded. Today, mission committees and other seemingly sincere people in the churches, use this old method of manipulation with great success. Just keep asking the same question enough, and some people will begin to doubt any answer given. **Ideas carved out in the Devil's workshop never change their appearance**, only their targets, to protect the guilty and destroy the innocent.

The great answer to this lawyers question, about how he might determine who is really classified as a neighbor, must have left the lawyer speechless, and for a lawyer that is in itself a miracle. The answer could only be understood by humble people who sought to fulfill the very perfect will of God in a perfect way. Jesus was in these great lessons, defining the purpose and value of the commandments of God. It would be made clear very soon, how perfectly Jesus obeyed the will of His Father in Heaven. When obedience is our purpose, our goal, our footsteps are guided by wisdom and courage. The point of the discussion with the Lawyer was to arrive at the truth about who Jesus really is. In the verses just before the lawyers question, Jesus had been saying that all things were delivered to Him, by

His Father and many prophets and kings had desired to see the things that these people standing before Jesus that very day were blessed to see. These words were evidence that this *Jesus of Nazareth was able to talk about and explain—life.* **Jesus had spoken of names written in heaven.** (10 20). Perhaps this motivated the lawyer to ask this question about eternal life. And the lawyer may not have expected to receive the response he did, and then of all things, he had to answer his own question.

Do this, which you have stated about the laws requirement to love the Lord your God *with all* your heart, *all* your soul and *all* your strength and *all your* mind; and love your neighbor as you love yourself. What an answer, to this great question on how to have eternal life. No teacher of the law among the Pharisees, Scribes or the great Sanhedrin would have come up with this answer, unless they knew the Old Testament very well. What does love have to do with eternal life anyway, few would have pulled this command up in place of "worship the Lord and serve Him only."

With this command to love the Lord God with all one's being, there was the following command to love our neighbor as we love ourselves. Notice the absence of the word ALL in that last command. To love our neighbor as we love ourselves is clear, but it does not have the same complete coverage that our love for God compels. It is as if the ALL word is used to give us no place or room for anything else. If we love God with all of our heart, does this need to be first? Is there significance to the heart as leading in this order of the five things mentioned? To love the Lord with all the heart would mean that God holds the preeminence in our heart. There is no heart left for something else. But love includes so much, there is no worry that family, friends etc. would not be loved too. To love God with all the heart one would have to get to know God personally and very well. **There must not be left in the heart, deep feelings for things that are not of God.** If we love God with ALL the heart, then nothing ungodly or displeasing to God will have a chance to take root in our heart. The power of—ALL—to fill every corner and all available space in the heart leaves no room for questions, about what *else we* love as much as we love God. This is no mistake that the word all precedes the words heart, mind, soul and strength nor is it a word to be overlooked for its place is miraculous as well as inclusive. The great work that this word *all* can accomplish is beyond the thoughtless attention it is often given. I believe that the order of these words is also significant. First the heart, then the soul, then our strength, and finally with all the mind, there's nothing left of us to give, nothing left for other gods or other things and other people. We must love God with all we have and all we are but this does not become an exclusive love which eliminates the things that are from God. For example when God gives us a mate for life, or a child or any blessing in life, it brings us back to God, and since He is the source, we have added His creation for us, to our own existence and His plan for us in this world, is connected to our own experiences. Our love for God, when given with ALL of our heart does eliminate the things that are ungodly, and anything that is not from His hands, but it includes all things that are from God. It is no wonder we are commanded to Love the Lord our God with all of our heart.

The heart is the seat and center of deep emotional attachment. If our heart is not in some act or deed of kindness, the act or deed is not well done. All our strength is what the coach of the team asks for, and at work the boss wants all our effort, all of our attention and all of our heart or feeling. But the soul you can only give to God. It is the breath of life that makes us living creatures, and it came from God's own breath. The bible states, "and God breathed into man the breath of life and man *became a living soul.* If a persons heart is divided or given to many things other than the love for God, then only dysfunction, depression, division and destruction will ensue, not to mention a host of other unpleasant results. A heart that is all given, in total surrender and submission will connect a person to the purpose of God for that heart, plus all else that such a purpose will bring forth.

In one of the recent magazines (U.S.News & World report) in the November 10 Issue 2003, an article by Paul Bedard states that bad manners at the White House in Washington D.C. have become atrocious, entertainers and celebrities don't even attend as requested and many do not RSVP on time, one insider during the Clinton era, stated that American manners of those invited to the White House, have become deplorable, and it is even worse under the Bush administration.

There are so many signs and indications that "the increase in wickedness" foretold by Jesus in Matt. 24. 12, which will turn the love of many into ice, is already upon the nation and the world. The power of total love cannot be ignored, although it takes some thought to ponder the value and importance of complete love. When Jesus gave this lawyer in Luke 10 the chance to answer his own question, he was giving the man a doorway to truth and life. The truth would of course have to first be accepted, then the opportunity for life eternal would be available. This command to love the Lord God with total and complete heart, mind, soul and strength is not just a casual request. There is no way a person can have the life at the other end of the journey without the word ALL being a part of the obedience to this command. No one will continue loving God and paying the price that such love will demand, if there is room for other things in the heart, mind or soul. If **the mind** of a person is not ALL given, to the love of God, then the concentration on God's will shall be threatened and compromised. We all know that any worthwhile task must have a certain amount of our mind's concentration, and the amount required is in direct proportion to the seriousness of the task and it's importance to us. So when the Lord Jesus stated that those who will belong to and follow Him and have life eternal, must have a love, a devotion and commitment that cannot be allowed to slide off on other causes or interests. Even in the present world, in any vocation, or endeavor, partial interest and limited activity which accompanies it, is entirely unacceptable.

What coach wants a player who is not giving his or her full attention, or total mind to the training necessary and to the anticipation of victory that must accompany athletic success? What employer wants an employee who is not completely and fully attentive to the business of his position? What teacher enjoys teaching a class of students who have no real desire to learn, what doctor wants patients under his care to be only partially interested in recovery? There is no end to the relationships, in family, business, sports or any other role in this present life that require complete and full support to attain success. When a bride and groom exchange their vows of affection and commitment to one another, there is no vow or pledge which states, "until I please to leave the relationship, or until I feel differently than I do now," or I pledge to give most of my love, or most of my attention, most of my concentration etc. to this my chosen partner for—now.

The same can be said for the strength, or might we put into this love for God. There is a place for effort and strength of body in deeds to be accomplished that will please the Lord our God. It could well be that in applying our strength physically and then with all of our mind's attention and concentration, we will see the fruit of our labor, in a measure that could not have been possible in some half-hearted, half-strength effort. The term 'half hearted' was made for such a connection as this, it is in half-hearted living, that our strength is depleted, our soul is sick and our hearts made sore. It is when our soul or purpose of life is missing from our task that trouble overcomes us and failure floods our spirit and our efforts. No one ever gave his all and received nothing in return. Those souls in the last days referred to in 2 Tim. 3. 1-13, are such people as turn back because they did not count into the equation of their life goals, the miracle of the word ALL. A few years ago a Sunday school teacher in a church (adult class) was using the outline of a renowned professor of a Bible college, on the subject of love. He opened the class with the statement that "God had to create people because God is love, and love requires an object of that love." This statement is false and yet it has been circulated widely. The fact that God had to do anything first of all is ludicrous, and secondly the idea that because God is love, should give the Sunday school teacher a clue, that such love as **the love of God, is a complete love and therefore needs nothing else to make it complete**. The love of man is different, mankind has been made in the image of God,. **Man, to have a complete love or see love in its completeness does have a need for such a thing or person** but man is not God. God's love cannot be compared to the love that man has for God or that man has for fellowman, or even mate or family. **When God's love is spoken of in scripture it must be understood as a love that needs nothing else for it to exist in the heart and mind of God.**

We could even understand this in some measure with the simple example of a mother's love for her son or daughter. If a child becomes a criminal, or for some other reason turns on the mother, and rejects completely the mother's love, this will not necessarily affect the love the mother has for the child. The love of the mother has more 'staying power' than the love of the child perhaps, but one person's love in this relationship of mother and child does not exist simply because of the other persons responding love. It is indeed too bad that people even in the churches, do not see more clearly that God is not a man and man is not God. The book of Job would have been a better study for that Sunday school class I attended, at least the teacher would have come across the statements that God does not need to ask anyone anything to learn something from man nor does He need anything from man. God's love is perfect, that means without a need of some kind to be met or fulfilled in order to be there, but it is a love that exists on it's own, apart from a weakness or lack which can only be filled by some other responding love. It is amazing how much professorship does not teach you, even when some things seem so exciting to learn, there is one more thing to be learned from 'much study' and that is the simple fact that everything there is to know is not in the hands of mankind or in the minds of those who teach others. Indeed, the book of Job has been overlooked even by the teachers of the Book. Man (meaning mankind, male and female) must give all of his love to God, or he will not be able to give all of his soul, strength and mind to God either. God's love is the only perfect love, but man can love God by accepting God's grace which allows mankind to show, in obedience to God's will, the fullest measure of love that mankind has.

Those who recognize the importance of this miracle word, will experience the fruit and results of its power, and will become the people who inherit the earth. Thank the Lord for adding the little word *all* to His great commandment. To love the Lord our God with ALL of our heart and soul, strength and mind, does not mean that God needs it, but that man needs to respond to God in such a way, that nothing about man is left for any other god (as if there was one), or any other object for man to serve. Him ***only shall*** you serve!

35

The Things of God,
And the things of men

✦

Matt. 16. 23

In the context of the scripture verse in Matt. 16.23, Jesus makes it clear that there is a difference in how man thinks about some matters and how God sees them. In the above vs. of Scripture, Peter is trying to help Jesus see a better plan or keep Jesus from making a big mistake and falling into enemy hands. He did not realize that Jesus already had an agenda, and a plan well designed before the foundation of the world. This fact that man has always seemed to have a different plan than God is illustrated again in several other cases, such as Luke 16.15, "...that which is highly esteemed (valued) among men, is abomination in the sight of God..." and of course, I Sam. 16.7, "...man looks at the outward appearance, but God looks at the heart..." KJV.

For centuries now, the world, actually America mostly, has borrowed (maybe stolen is more accurate) from the church, or the Bible, teachings about morals, social values, standards for decency, concepts of right and wrong, etc. (which teachings were given to Believers, by the Lord), and have applied these teachings to the society. People of the world who have not really embraced the full teachings of Christianity, nor accepted in trusting faith a personal relationship with Christ as the Son of God, have still tried to put into place in their politics, and in their laws of the land, some measure of Christian teachings. Because such good teachings were of social benefit and proved to be of sound judgment and a common sense approach to a solid and wise basis for acceptable human relations.

Obviously the opposite philosophy of life, or sin, crime, hate and greed were on the other side of the spectrum and were taking 'equal time' although not desirable for the establishment of a nation of freedom loving people, nor were such avaricious deeds conducive to well being and good relations between human beings, from so many different cultural backgrounds. In other words, it was to the advantage of any human community, to seek out a foundation on which to build a country that would survive it's own existence, therefore Christian faith and Jewish faith, became the standards of the early American people.

As time went on, and laws were put into place, and a system of social justice for the benefit of all the people was devised, the teachings of the Bible were the basis and foundational principles for all laws to govern the behavior of citizens of the 'new world.' It was never the intent of the government 'of the people by the people for the people, to take the 'Lord God of Heaven' personally into the picture. If that had been the intent of the governing body of the founders of America, then sermons would have replaced discussions and plans for framing the constitution would have been dictated by a total adherence to the directives given in Holy Scripture for a life of obedience to God. Today people in America who are religious and adherents to Christian faith, complain when evil prevails. Who should be surprised that a world system, and a government of people by people for people, does not comply with all the Biblical principles given for people of God?

The Kingdom of God is Christ centered, not man centered. It is not of this world, and it belongs to God, it is not a 'kingdom' of people dedicated to the creation of a militarily super power, or a nation of people who are all citizens simply by birth in the country or by adherence to the laws of the land.

America is not synonymous with the Kingdom of God, or with the church that Jesus built (Matt.16.18). If America is different FROM and different THAN the Church (called out assembly of believers), then America as a nation is a part of the present evil world (Gal.1.4). In this beginning we can see that the ways of God and the ways of man are very different. Eph.5.11 states, that the believer is to have no fellowship, (things in common) with the unfruitful workers of darkness,(or works of darkness) but he is to rather reprove (or rebuke) those who engage in acts of wickedness. So the church has been busy denouncing the evil in the world and in America, but the church should never be surprised that the message to repent is not often heard. Nor should the believers in America expect the country (God bless America) to follow the leading of Christ and His word, as a nation when it has never been dedicated, in it's original purpose to the obedience of the Gospel, it has only borrowed the teachings that it liked, and found useful, without any allegiance to the Lord Jesus as King and Lord of all. It is one thing to seek the favor of God for your own purpose, and another thing to seek GOD and His will for His purpose and glory.

A country will not have turned to God through obedience to Jesus Christ, without embracing the total New Covenant demands which provide entrance into the fellowship of Christ. The dilemma for American Christians today is, that they have carried the USA to church with them, and expected to see a wedding of the two. But the Bible is quite clear (I Cor. 6, II Cor. 6.) that light and darkness cannot co-habit. A Christian can be an American citizen, and a citizen can be a Christian, but residence in any country in this present world (Gal.1.4), does not make one a Christian, and being a Christian does not make one a resident or citizen of any particular country. The two kingdoms, one of the world, the other not of this world are not friends, even though they may have some similar rules, but they are also not even related because they have not the same Father. America is either a nation of the present world, or it is in total a part of the body of Christ. As you will hear me say many times in these pages.

Since the governing body (the 'not so' supreme court) of America makes rules that do not comply with the Bible, the country cannot as a nation be a 'joined' branch or extension of the Body of Christ. Either the Christians who live in America have got to get a clear understanding of the differences, between the church (called out people of God) and the nation, (western world countries—but especially America) or we will never see revival in the land. Asking the country to repent and turn to God, as a nation, is like trying to sweep all the dirt off of the earth, it is all dirt, it won't sweep off. Commanding the nation to repent is good, telling the country to turn to God is good and it is right, but as a believer in Christ, trying to hold hands with the nation, with allegiance and commitment equal to that of allegiance to Christ will not work. You cannot serve two masters, or worship two gods. The country seeks the fulfillment of the desires of the flesh, the kingdom of God is destined to walk in the Spirit of God. (Romans 8).

There are two kingdoms, the kingdom of light and the kingdom of darkness, there are two places to spend eternity, Heaven or Hell, there are two worlds, the present one and the one to come (2 Pet.3), while we can live in the world we cannot be of the world, we can renounce evil, but we can't vote it out of office (Matt. 24, Mk.13). America as a country never intended to look to Jesus as Lord and follow His commands, the country we live in was designed to accommodate all people from any country, and give the same people certain rules to live by, rules that were taken from the Holy Bible. This was done perhaps to gain the favor of the God of heaven, but it was not done in order to please the God of heaven. Remember to seek God's favor is not the same as to seek Him.

I believe it is clear that Christians in America have been very confused about the relationship that the church has with America. For one example, while serving as a church camp dean one summer, I placed the Christian flag on the flag pole one morning above the American flag and before the pledges were said I was questioned about it, and I simply replied, "the pledge of allegiance so states 'one nation UNDER God'…etc. so I put them in the right order." I would that every Christian in this country understood which is the 'right' order.

The apostle Peter, in trying to help Jesus make a better plan, and keep Jesus from falling into the hands of the enemy, gave advice from the perspective of human reasoning. Jesus, found that suggestion to be exactly the opposite of what must be done. When Jesus said to Peter, 'you are not thinking as God would, but as a man would, (in his natural mind without conversion to Christ) it was more than just a matter of the statement of Peter or Peter's intent it was a reminder that Peter is now a follower of Christ, he should no longer think as a man who is without the knowledge of God. Scripture reveals how far off human considerations are from the purpose of God for eternity. Human nature is exactly what the term describes; humanness is from our nature not from the Spirit. To think as a man thinks, seems to be a condemnation in this discussion that Jesus and Peter engage in. We might ask, why Peter should not think as a man in this case. Jesus reveals that the things of God cannot be found by using the standards and measuring rod of human and selfish thinking. Herein lays the problem with the church in America. Christians normally believe that there is some kind of joint effort, or connection between the social, governmental, and corporate America system and the spiritual body of Christ in this country. Perhaps more Bible teaching is needed on the relationship of this world and the Kingdom of God. Once the church fell in love with America the country, the Devil could take the country anywhere he wanted to and the church would follow.

So the country USA,(government and supreme court??) and national legislation brings in legal and therefore accepted life styles (more like death styles) that are unbiblical, indecent, unholy etc. etc. and throws it all into the face of the American church people to change the course of religious teaching. Once a nations leaders accept an unholy behavior and make it legal, the next step is obvious, that is to make the accepted not only accepted, but promote it as desirable, then that which was once tolerated, becomes accepted, the accepted becomes (by media promotion and lawfulness), desirable. The most insidious and subtle form of deception is government designed acceptance and legalization of evil. Evil—is first tolerated, then accepted, then promoted, then legalized and finally enforced as law. Do we need examples? I doubt it!

The teachings of Christ and His Kingdom are not for sale, nor can they be appropriated separately from His Spirit. In John 6. 63 Jesus linked His words with His Spirit and with life. When people practice the things that the word of God commands to all of His followers (love, forgive, be unselfish, do not lie, steal etc. etc.) there is no special spiritual connection to Jesus that is generated by those good acts. A man reaps what he sows, and the rain falls on the good, the bad and the ugly, but America does not gain a relationship with Jesus as Lord just because it puts those teachings, which are found in the Bible, into law and into practice in order to have a "more perfect union." There are other conditions which must be met, if a person, or an entire tribe of people or even an entire nation, is to be under the Lordship of Christ, more than just the acceptance of some Bible teachings. And for a country to honor some of the teachings of the Bible, and give true acknowledgment that God in heaven has ordained these 'chosen' commandments as rules for life, is not the same as bowing before the Lord of hosts and becoming His obedient people and surrendering to His authority only and entirely.

This fact is learned in the entire Old Testament record of God's dealing with the people of Israel. It is written, "…if any man breaks even the least of these commandments, he is guilty of breaking the entire law…for the same God who said that man should not steal also said that he should not commit adultery…" if one breaks one of these commands but keeps the others he is still found to be guilty as a law breaker for the same God who gave one command gave the others also. (James 2.10,11). If the founding fathers of America wanted to build a country that followed faithfully the whole word of God, they did not make it very clear, for they would have said, that no other God, than the God revealed in the Bible would be worshiped. And any other religion that fails to follow the Holy Bible would not be accepted in the new country.

Even those who followed in the footsteps of the founding fathers of America, if they had understood that the goal of the new America was to please God, and serve no other God, there would have been rules and laws made that would have tied citizenship to church membership, (Acts 2 .47, 11.26, 1 Cor. 12.12). There is no middle ground. A kingdom that is of this world is not the same as the Kingdom of God which is not of this world.

It is evident from history alone that the founding fathers of the United States of America wanted to borrow from the Bible, not follow the Bible only, they wanted to have favor with God, and have the blessing of God upon their purpose, but they did not intend to belong only to God and become Disciples of Christ as dictated in the Holy Bible and make no law or enact any decree that was contrary to the Bible. Even if the founding fathers of the country had intended to be followers of Christ alone, the years of government since then, have taken the nation far from the Bible teaching. A nation of the people by the people for the people, is not a Biblical purpose or goal, it is a social goal. A nation would have to be the church itself if it's purpose is to honor the word of God completely and the word of God only.

So what does all of this tell us? For sure, we know there is a difference between kingdoms of the world (which will one day become the kingdoms of our God and His Christ~ Rev.), and the Kingdom of God. And this means that all of the good Bible based teachings that the government of the people by the people for the people, have included in the laws of the land, do not create a relationship with Christ as Lord, any more than a mouse in the cookie jar becomes a cookie.

Furthermore the desire of America as a nation to have the favor of God by means of allowing some of His words to hold sway in matters of legislation but seeking the pleasure and will of unholy people in the land when it comes to other matters (which amounts to giving evil equal time and place) is a true course toward destruction. Some things do not mix, so it is with the thinking of man and the thinking of God. God told mankind how and what to think, ("…think on these things…" Phil.) and if a nation or a government will not abide by that directive, that government and/or nation is not going to have even what it may have sought, that is, the favor of God. It does not make good sense to ask God to 'bless America' if we do not even know what it is that America is trying to do. When one person looks at America, he sees something different than what some other person may see. A Christian sees a country founded by men of religious faith, and supported by the Bible verses which state "blessed is the nation whose God is the Lord…" and such verses which in a similar way promise that the Lord desires the healing of the nations and gives commandments which, when followed will bring His blessing upon those who fear and obey Him. A Muslim, who also is an American sees, freedom to follow his own religion and enjoy the protection and same privileges as any other citizen of the country.

In reality, America is for all people (from any origin, race, religious belief or sexual behavior), a country that seeks unity, harmony and peaceful co-existence for evil and good. To the government of America, abortion, homosexuality and many other expressions (the Howard Sterns) of indecency seem equal to church attendance, honesty, bravery and high moral standards. Each behavior and life style is under equal protection of the laws of the land, and each has been given the same freedoms to co-exist. The Christian cannot expect favors from the government because of his religious belief, nor can the deviants of society demand by law that all become atheists. A good definition of what America is cannot be found, it exists only in the mind of the beholder.

America is a land were all people are free to be whatever they want in personal life, but they must obey the laws that exist so that the country can exist as one nation of people without self-destructing.

This goal or purpose for existence is for the glory and benefit of mankind, not for the glory of God. The Kingdom of God is His property, His creation, His business and it is not under the control of another. A country can self-destruct but the Kingdom of God and those in it will go on for eternity…

36

What the Lord Says to Me, That Will I Speak!

◆

1ˢᵗ Kings 22. 1
TO WIT...2ⁿᵈ Cor. 5. 19.
(Whatever It Takes)

Several students at Moberly Christian College, and St. Louis Christian College stated to me, after learning about the number of people groups in the world who have not had the Gospel presented to them, (Rep. an approx. population of 2 Billion), that they were prepared to do whatever it takes, to reach some of these people for Christ. So I called them, the TO—WIT volunteers. Those who pledge to do, 'whatever it takes.' We should also say—only what the Lord says, will I speak.

A student should study, and learn to do what he/she wants, but that student should only want what is needed. In this modern world where American citizens have the advantage of education and information, that citizen, if a Christian, should be careful what they want, because it is possible to have it. So the advise to a person in America who is a Christian, should be, '**get the training you want, but only <u>want</u> what you need**.' This will require that you pay more attention to the needs of others, than you do to the wants of your own. We are often under the 'peer pressure' to take the course of study and the course of action, others are committed to. When a person begins to investigate the needs of all people around the world, not just the wants of those in the modern countries, (USA, Australia, England, New Zealand, and Canada for example), then the term 'mission field' takes on a whole new meaning, a Biblical meaning (Luke 10. 2) like harvest fields.

A persons perspective is based on the 'frame of reference' that he/she has developed from personal burden (vision), personal interest and experiences. Other factors surely enter in to the programming of this philosophy of life we have, but our frame of reference will be determined by many things that have been welcomed into our heart and mind, over many years through environment and instruction

For me to advise you to 'get the training you want, but only want what is needed', for the task you engage in for the Lord, would be a safe suggestion, unless you are deeply narcissistic, or you are seeking to please men. Today in the churches of all denominations who call America their home country, there is a terrible influence from the world without, to have a church of 'bigness,' prominence, and acceptability, that will appease the self-seeking citizen of the USA. One of the problems with the Jewish leaders of the time during the ministry of Jesus on earth, was the fact that the Scribes and Pharisees, loved the praise of men, more than the praise of God. There has not been much change in the problem even during these last days, when religious leaders show such concern for the opinion of other religious leaders. The praise of man by man, has always been a curse on those who walk in the carnal nature, and not in the Spirit of God.

The 'ax' really comes down on those who place education and academic achievement in the last place, rather than in first place, when ministry is discussed. It is no secret that the heavy (and un-biblical) emphasis on education and achievement in the academic field has been an albatross around the neck of the modern student. There is the cost, then the time, and especially the pride that swings it's unseen pendulum in the mind of the student of Biblical studies. What student will not admit that he or she continues to weigh the value of many years in scholastic endeavor, over and over in their mind, only to arrive at the decision that '**acceptance**' among the peers and parents requires some kind of degree for service in Christian fields?

We speak of the Bible as the book that does not put requirements of man on the work of God, but we push the requirements of man and society on the student as if we held the two as equal in value. Big mistake. <u>Man cannot require, what God does not demand.</u> *Only when we get honest can we begin to get right.*

AWH

37

When World Meets Messenger

✦

John 7. 15—I Cor. 1. 17—2. 1-16

The very two things which have made the message of the prophets of God in ages past, and the Apostles of the Lord in the book of Acts unacceptable to the people who opposed them are the very two things that **led to the crucifixion of the Lord Jesus Christ**. My good friend in Indiana, reminded me in a phone call, that his study in the Gospel record brought to his attention a most serious and obvious indictment on believing men. He reminded me that the ridicule and rejection that his message to churches and mine, (which message seemed hard for the elite of the brotherhood to receive), has been not unlike the history of God's message to narcissistic men throughout the ages. **Two most loved** (keep Lk.16. 15 in mind as you read on*) possessions* of man, are at the heart of the cause of hatred toward God's servant messengers. I believe these two things, have taken more money, time and devotion away from the cause of world missions in the modern era,than any other issues. These two are **Temples** and **love of knowledge.**

What was it that the accusers of the Lord Jesus brought (falsely of course) against Him? **One thing** was that Jesus said "…destroy this temple and in three days I will raise it up…" He spoke of course of the temple of His own body. But what infuriated the priests and Pharisees was that Jesus had spoken against the temple. They were afraid that He would literally destroy their temple. This is the place where they did their teaching, where they gathered to decide what was holy and what was not holy, the temple represented all that was dear to their 'religious' hearts and minds. When Jesus spoke lightly and even with no consideration about the importance of the temples they had built, they used this to turn the crowds against Him. If you go back in time a bit, you can recall that when David the King of Israel wanted to build a temple, a dwelling place on earth for GOD, the Lord said to him "…the heavens are my throne and the earth is my footstool, so what kind of temple will you build for me…"? This is quite revealing, the Lord God, Creator of the universe does not dwell in temples made with hands. Later the Lord said the day would come when He would dwell in the hearts and minds of His called out people, and He would be their God and they would be His sons and daughters, saith the Lord Almighty. God allowed Solomon to build a temple, and God's glory was present, but under the **New Covenant God's Spirit** dwells **within** the believer and they are themselves the temple of the Holy Spirit.

Again, as time has shown, man wants a physical evidence of the invisible presence of the invisible God. I have found that in even suggesting that extravagant buildings and requirements of college degrees for ministers of the Gospel are not Biblical requirements for effective world evangelism, brings down the wrath of man. Although I have only made the announcement, delivered the message, these who have opposed me are like a man who wants to kill the 'telegram boy' for being the bearer of such news.

The second thing that turned the Jews against Jesus was revealed in their questions about Jesus and Where He got the authority to do the things He did, (John 7. 15). "How does this man know these things, having never studied (learned). The Jews would have known if Jesus had graduated from their 'school' of knowledge. Today the very informed and knowledgeable church leaders seem to be unaware of how churches grow and the Gospel spreads all around 75% of the world, without either 'high minded' professors of theology, and without stained glass extravagant buildings. The love of knowledge and study so that we may impress each other, is not a hidden agenda, it is the major emphasis in the many schools of theology in America today. All of this emphasis is without any Biblical precedence.

Yet it is thrown out at youth today and adults alike, that without degrees in theology (and that term in itself is ironic, since it means 'God study') a person cannot be an effective witness or teacher in the pulpits of the land. This is strange in light of the fact that God is not a subject to be studied, He is the Lord to be obeyed and loved and served. Acts 4: 20 and vs. 13 are not statements to simply take up space in Holy Writ, these verses teach something, they tell us about the attitude of God's messengers and of God Himself toward the value or necessity of 'formal education.' How can the church today emphasize what the Apostles did not emphasize? It was the well educated Apostle Paul who stated "what things (in this world's values) were gain to me, I counted as loss for the Excellency of the knowledge of Christ…" Phil. 3. 7-15, and we are encouraged by Paul to be of the same mind or have that attitude. **When a high level of academic studies is required for Bible translators**, or other fields which make it necessary to attain skills **which will be for the benefit of the people to whom the missionary goes**, then we have reason for much study and academic achievement. Here the reason for the study is to give others the Bible in their own heart language. This we know is not for self, but **a necessary academic tool** for reaching the lost souls of the world. However in American church settings, many who minister in churches as pastors or preachers, seek high levels of (financially costly) academic standing, for reasons other than being able to lead someone to Christ. We get so much and do so little with it, in many cases.

Many of the missionaries and preachers of past years had good educational skills, and had great respect for those opportunities to study in formal settings. But you read little of the *emphasis of such* an education by these early missionaries, but rather you hear them speak of sacrifice, dedication and love for God and love for the lost. What do you hear today from our theologians and professors? You hear of the importance of study, degrees and formal education, because that is something men can give to men, acknowledgment of time spent in class rooms, letters of endorsement for being able to read something and then go write it down and get a grade for it. These things do not come from scriptural or spiritual motivation resulting from hearts that bleed for unsaved people. We should have learned something from the attitude of the Jews who turned against Jesus because He had no 'formal' credentials that they could accept. Why do men today in religious circles, reflect this attitude of the Pharisees, instead of the attitude of Jesus and Paul?

It is my belief that this unholy emphasis on education and degrees in seminary to prepare for service to God, does not come from above but from the carnal nature. The time and money that is consumed in such occupation with this malignant narcissism in the American church setting, only serves to make people feel good about themselves, which leads to the feeling of specialness which in turn leads to the destruction of self-sacrifce and suffering that is from a broken heart for God. Read the comments of Dr. Aaron Stern, author of "Me-The Narcissistic American" (Random House Pub.) about the serious detriment to the personality that the feeling of 'specialness' can have upon the average person. Read the comments of Dr. Stanton Samenow in his books "Straight Talk About Criminals" or "Before It's Too Late", or read the statements by the man who is probably the leading thinker in the field of 'Emotional Intelligence' Dr. Daniel Goleman about the value of emotional stability as compared to I.Q. Perhaps if we knew more about the things God said and what people who have studied human nature have said, we could see that life does not consist of the mental or intellectual attainments as much as in spirit, heart and soul.

The persecuted church around the world has taken the Gospel into their own regions in recent years *without temples*, and studies, classes, commentaries, taped sermons, lesson booklets, multi-staff churches etc. Persecuted Christians simply depend upon the Word of God and prayer and each other and faithful obedience. It would be helpful if some of the 90% of the money and personnel consumed in churches in America on staff and college, could be redirected to more needy fields, but if this does not happen, only the servants to whom much has been given will *ultimately pay the price for not paying the expenses* to reach the unreached people.

There is a verse in the Bible that speaks about this fact. "...Judgment will begin at the house of God..." As God allowed my family and I to preach the Gospel in several countries over a period of 15 years we witnessed the hand of God lead us into several countries and leave churches started and souls rejoicing in salvation, where previously a knowledge of salvation was not present as Paul said, in 2 Cor 12.11, *though I myself be nothing*. Perhaps being nothing was not the favorite class in seminary, they probably couldn't find anyone to teach it with all that time spent on 'discover your talent, your gift, or how to improve self-esteem. Who is the real enemy of world evangelism? I'll give you 2 guesses.

38

Highway Robbery

◆

Jer. 23. 30, Isa. 35. 8,9
2Cor. 11. 12-15—John 10. 7-10

The Lord is against all those false prophets, who steal His words from their neighbors. Paul the apostle stated in Acts 20, as he warned the believers, that he knew after his departure, 'wolves' would enter in among the flock of God, and try to draw away disciples after them, to make followers and thus, 'steal the sheep' by deception and trickery. This is not a new thing, this idea of taking the word of God out of context, and creating a man-made message for selfish gain and purpose. From the garden of Eden, when the Tempter lied to Eve, in this 'war' of the kingdoms, the most effective tool of the enemy has been misuse and misinterpretation of the words of God. At the time of the temptation of Jesus, (Matt. 4) Satan took words from God's mouth and tried to turn Jesus from obedience to the Father, and tempt Jesus to worship himself rather than God. So the battle rages. Today the words of God are thrown around loosely, out of context and 'tacked' onto pet projects that exalt men and give little if any, glory to God, except to make it appear that God is pleased with these human 'self-esteem', find your gift and purpose messages.

The enemy is a liar and he is a thief. **He lies in order to steal,** and he is stealing that which belongs to God,—that is the hearts of men. Today you can find many churches in America which use the words of God to their advantage, and unless you really know the Scriptures yourself, you may be deceived. You might actually think that because someone opens the Bible and reads a verse of Scripture, that he is correctly applying those words to the intended meaning for which they were written. But using something for yourself that belongs to someone else is not always a sign of honest application of the original purpose of the tool, or in this case, of the words which are spoken. A thief can take another man's car without the keys and without the knowledge of the car owner, and sell it to someone else, or make some other selfish gain from that theft. This does not make the car manufacturer or the owner of the vehicle the responsible party. Only the car thief should be held guilty in such an instance.

The thing that 'Bible verse thieves' do not know is, that the Holy Spirit is not using the power of God in those words when they are used out of context or for man's selfish purpose. This is called, "'form of Godliness, but denying the power thereof' (2 Tim. 3. 5). Even the Devil can quote scriptures and speak the words that God has spoken and written, but only God can put His power and His Spirit into those words to accomplish the purpose that God had for those words (Isa. 55. 11, Matt. 15. 6). **The words of God when used by the servant of God for the purpose of God, will bring forth fruit to the glory of God (Matt. 13.).** But the words of God used by insincere, dishonest, and false prophets, will have no power to accomplish the works of God, for the Kingdom of God is not is word only, states Paul (1Cor. 4. 18-21) but also in power. The Gospel of Christ is the power of God unto salvation to those who believe, but any other Gospel (Gal. 1) does not have the power of God to do the work and ministry of God. This is what must be understood in these last days of the Lord's work on earth.

All that glitters is not gold, and all that's educated is not smart, and all that is religious is not holy. Conference's and lessons may not present the true Gospel of salvation, from the Holy Spirit. Men can speak the words of the Bible, but they may not be men of God. Since America is so full of religious instruction, it would behoove the public to be sure to have a Bible on hand, **to see if what is said is also what is meant (Acts 17. 11,** Matt. 15. 6). Many have made the scripture of no effect, by their (invented) traditions, such as the practice of raising the hand in a meeting, to be saved, when the Bible clearly says, repent and be baptized into Christ—Acts. 2.38, Gal. 3. 27, Col. 2. 12. **There is no scripture which states** that a person is saved from sin, simply by asking Christ into their heart, or telling God what He already knows, that we are sinners, and we want Jesus to come into our heart right now and save us. **NO such command or such idea is authorized in the Bible**, it is a statement and concept invented by evangelists (?) who become popular by making statements which sound good, but have not one scripture to back up such statements (teachings).

If, as Jesus stated in Matt. 15. 6, a command of God can be made of no effect, by a tradition (teaching) of men, then we know that the power of that scripture or command of God does not have the Holy Spirit behind it, so it is only 'words' even though the words are good, yet if they are used **without the intent** of God's purpose, the same words have no power to effect the original meaning. So when used out of context, God is not obliged to fulfill the promise which God connected to those words, even though they are His words. A man working at a bank as a teller, may go out to hire his friend, and use the words of the bank manager which were used to hire him, but since the words are not spoken by the Manager, in the context of hiring an employee, the words are of no effect. An employee cannot just hire his own friend, to work at his company, no matter what words he may use to do so, when he is not authorized to do the hiring. Jesus is the Savior, His servants are only **the messengers**, not the **authors** of salvation. The Words of the Lord have been stolen from the Holy Spirit, or from God, and used by unauthorized persons, so we have in the world today, especially in America, a lot of counterfeit messengers, **who make promises they can't keep and make conditions which are not validated** by the Lord Himself.

As a popular motto of many years ago has stated, 'the Bible only, makes Christians only.' When men and women stand in the public arena and speak 'great swelling words' and expect people to follow them, they should examine the Scripture and their motive, or be ready to be held responsible for their actions when the time comes. Judgment shall begin at the house of God, and if it first begin with us, what shall be the end of those who obey not the Gospel?—1st Peter 4. 17.

The highway robbery will continue, and we are not the police, but the word of the Lord will abide forever, and those who do the will of God will abide forever. It is the task of every believer to test the spirits, for many false prophets have gone out **into the world**—1 Jn. 4. 1-3. **Grace and mercy follows truth, and narcissism follows pride and self discovery**. <u>Jesus never asked His disciples, 'who do men say that **you** are'</u>? He asked, "who do men say that I am"? This idea of finding out who we are, is not from the Bible, we must know who Jesus is, so watch out for the promoters of self-discovery and self-esteem. The bible says, 'let each esteem other, better than himself,' Phil. 2.3, Rom. 12-15, no one can save himself, and we are to die to self, that we might live unto God. The idea that we can be 'as god' and make our own decisions about what is right or wrong, is a raging bull in America today, so don't run with the bulls, or the roaring lion which seeks to devour, may find you a very tasty morsel. Find humility, and forsake pride.

Warning—Use Only As Directed

There should be a warning sign in front of each sincere church meeting place.

And it should say: WARNING-USE ONLY AS DIRECTED. Just as a doctor's prescription for medicinal purposes, on each Bible, we should understand, that the words-

Use Only As Directed, by the Author, apply. Today so many churches and church leaders are robbing the Bible of verses, (which they especially like) and taking them out of their context, in order to prove an agenda that is very much based on a man's opinion, that there should be such warnings sounded.

When Bible verses are used for man's purpose, those verses are not carrying with them the Holy Spirit, since the Holy Spirit empowers only the Holy Words of God. Men who are politicians, preachers, or in any other vocation, may think that the word of God will have the same power when they use those verses, just because they came from the mouth of the Lord, but when used out of their context, they are also without their intended meaning, and therefore their intended application. This is proven when the Devil tried to use scripture 'against' Jesus at the time of His temptation (Matt. 4). The Devil quoted scripture, but Jesus stated "…it is written, thou shalt worship the Lord thy God and Him only, shalt thou serve…" So the words of Jesus from God, gave witness to the power those words have in that circumstance, because they were in context, within the intended purpose. The words of God that the Devil quoted, were not in context and therefore could not be observed, and those words did not have the Holy Spirit inspiration for that circumstance. We must not handle the Word of God deceitfully, but only as it is intended. Otherwise it will not bring about the fruit of it's meaning, or it will not have power from God when used outside of the will of God. Jesus stated in John 6. "the words I speak unto you are Spirit and they are life" **So only when God's words are used for God's purpose, is there going to be God's power!**

Remember, as I have stated elsewhere, the time in Acts when unbelievers tried to use the Name of Jesus to cast out demons, and the demons became victorious over the unconverted charlatans—(Acts 19. 15). Even the Devil knows who is using the Words of God with authority and power in correct context. **When God is using His words through His servants, those words will not fall to the ground. (1 Sam. 3. 19).**

LITTLE JACK HORNER
In Today's Corner

When nursery rhymes begin to remind us of conditions which prevail in the present world, perhaps we need to take a close look at the conditions, and ask some serious questions about our direction in life.

The nursery rhymes were great teaching tools, along with ESOPs fables. In the 'Mother Goose' rhymes, we saw ourselves, or our conditions and pictures of life in a way that could not be as easily expressed, or as simply presented by common people. Most parents need help in explaining the complexities of life and the challenges of life, to their children, and stories told with humor but—with serious meaning, could accomplish the task that the average person who lacked literary skills, (but who had some imagination), could not provide. So the meaning of life, wrapped in appropriate and digestible style came out of hiding and appeared as pleasant propaganda for the young and the young in heart.

When I look at the Christian message as it is presented to the average 'church member' today, in the pulpits of this country, some of the nursery rhyme themes and characters come to mind. One of these little rhymes known as 'Little Jack Horner' makes me think of the ordinary American Christian. The rhyme goes—'Little Jack Horner, sat in a corner, eating his Christmas pie, he put in his thumb and pulled out a plumb and said, "what a good boy am I".

Notice all the emphasis in American Christian teaching on the subject of 'self esteem', and this rhyme comes to mind. I don't think the author of the rhyme meant to describe the present 'church member' but I do think there must have been an awareness of the need for self-approval for children, in the mind of the author of these few words. Regardless of the intent, the words have found a warm welcome in the philosophy-of the American 'religious right', in these present days which author Dave Hunt describes as 'self-ism' in his book, "Beyond Seduction" which was a follow up of his earlier book entitled "Seduction of Christianity." Dave Hunt clearly ties the emphasis of self-esteem in today's Christian circles, to the suggestion of the Serpent in the Garden of Eden, when the Tempter suggested to Adam and Eve that they could be as 'gods' if they would eat of the fruit from the tree of 'Knowledge of good and evil.'

The Enemy wanted the first humans to join his rebellion and in so doing, turn against the God of Heaven, and be their own gods, or as I would say, 'put their thumb in the Christmas pie and pull out a plumb and say, "what a good boy" am I. In truth, our first awareness of our own existence should be couched in the framework of knowledge of our sinfulness and our belief in the Lord God, as the

Creator of life and all things. From this point each person should then see the need for God's mercy and God's forgiveness. Those who believe in the Lord God, also seek to do His will, to have His favor. Ps. 36. 9,....**in thy light shall we see light.**

All emphasis in life on 'self' as the major value and number one person of importance, must lead to excessive narcissism. When we see ourselves as only a part of the human race, **not as the only important one in the human race**, there is hope for us as useful contributors to the good of all humanity, including ourselves. The better and higher aim for self, is to see ourselves as created beings in the image of God, for the glory of God and as the sheep of His pasture and as people who can participate in His joy in eternal relationship with Him and one another. In America, much of the problem finding an 'accurate observation' of our own importance came about when University and College professors began to emphasize individuality and 'uniqueness' of each person's identity, race and culture. In a land where many nationalities became part of the 'melting pot' which makes up the great 'land of the free and home of the brave', people would willingly lose their prior citizenship and roots of early heritage, in order to become simply—an American. To stand side by side with other Americans who had made the same commitment and same decision created a 'oneness' which became the 'watchword' and the mortar to make this country one and provide it with a unique, and unusual identity. Other countries had citizens of mixed culture and language, but no other country provided the same amount of opportunity and authority to each citizen as America did. It was the equality of citizenship and the freedoms included in that equality that helped make America different. The dark pages of history which included driving the natural American Indians from their homes, and importing 'slave' labor from Africa stand out as major hypocrisy and violation of the very foundational elements of the Mayflower Compact and the Constitution. Perhaps this hypocrisy was the beginning of the country's problems.

The parallel that exists between the history of America's progress and it's present dilemma in social disarray, and the changes that churches in America have made over the years, is worthy of special attention. There should be a look of hypocrisy on the face of the Statue of Liberty, and there should be a similar and admitted look of embarrassment on the face of American pastors as well. These two institutions which have for some years now, walked hand in hand (god and country), need to look in the mirror and see today's conditions and then take a look at their own history, and see if there is not a need to 'seek the old paths' as the book of Jeremiah chapter 6 and verse 16 states in reference to Israel's departure from established truth. Take a look at how America has forgotten the 'sodomy laws' of the States, and turned completely into a country tolerating and even condoning 'sodomy' in recent legislation. This is only one example. Then notice the decision of many churches in America to accept homosexual 'pastors' as a debatable issue in the same time frame. Notice how the State Universities and colleges, began in the 60's to emphasize the importance of 'individual—ness' and personal heritage, as more important than 'unity' and self-sacrifice. In the same time frame, the churches in America did a similar thing, by placing ideas of individual 'special-ness' and uniqueness as important, and **the idea of 'self-esteem'** through **the 'find your gift' lessons**. The Church growth theme brought with it the desire for **'bigness' and 'intellectual excellence'** which concepts only encouraged the same narcissism for the church members as the society in America promoted the 'self-ism' theme in their educational institutions.

The parallel between the church and state—societal agenda in America and religious teachings in the churches, is very obvious and very revealing. It is impossible to miss the timing of American social changes, and the pattern which theologians and 'mega' church pastors followed for 'church growth' purposes. Even today in 2005-2006, (time of this writing), the United States faces an unprecedented move toward the **'madam president' mode**, while the churches are 'streamlining' the move to use women as 'pastors' along with their husbands, in some denominations. This is not the only example of common ground for the 'land of the free'—'home of the brave,' and the Christian religion in America. I have not even mentioned the soft touch approach with moral vs. immoral behavior in society and the churches debates over 'sexual orientation' and abortion. The 'God and Country' theme which is a part of the 'Boy Scouts' of America, pledge, has been a 'watch word' of the patriotic as well as religious circles of American thinking for more years than most people can remember. **This God and country theme** in America was not introduced by the Bible teachings—that's for sure, it came into the churches through the window of 'the world that surrounded the American churches'. The term 'world' as used in the Gal. 1. 4 reference, for churches to consider as being the world—in this context is, America itself, **that is our world**. The only world a society can be a part of, or love, is the social structure in which the people find themselves. The American Christian does not have to fear that he/she may love the Russian world, since they don't live in Russia. It is obvious that when the scriptures warn, Love not the world—it is speaking of the world or social order in which one resides.

The American churches continue to separate themselves from the churches in other lands, by this 'god and country' theme, as if they did not even know what was taking place in the spiritual realm. How can you reconcile the emphasis in American churches on 4th of July celebrations and other social events (which are celebrated as if the country and church were one integrated, corporate entity) with a spiritual union enjoyed by all Christians around the world? There is no connection. The American church is an absolutely different fellowship than the churches which we see in the many persecuted lands around the world. There is a difference in **teaching, appearance, behavior, emphasis** and **purpose. The purpose** of American churches is to grow bigger, as in expansion, in the persecuted countries of the world, the purpose is to keep the faith, be an example of Christ's suffering and share the Gospel with others. **The emphasis** in American churches is '**family fun time at the halleluiah happy hour**' to **draw in followers after themselves**. The **behavior** of the American churches is seen to be a—spend money on sports, entertainment, nice 'things', please the kids, and a hundred other 'Disney-Land' experiences, just like the lost people of the country. The behavior of Christians in other lands is not self-centered, self-fulfilling, or self-esteem teachings. The **appearance of** the churches in America and their persecuted brethren around the world, is obvious and it goes without saying, 'we just don't look anything alike. Somebody's car has left the track, and I don't think it is the foreign brethren. If you have spent any time at all in countries where persecution of Christians abounds, you know exactly what I am talking about. Heb.13. 3 is a scripture that most American pastors can't even explain in context since they have no idea of the present condition that exists for most Christians in the world. The average pastor who dares to share this scripture will miss the point so far, that his/her fellow members will not get a true picture of the meaning of this verse from today's pulpits. **The teaching** of American churches becomes a "form of Godliness,' without the power thereof. Teaching overseas is just the opposite, the Gospel is the power of God unto salvation, no forms are paramount.

To consider ourselves as 'bound' with others who are in bondage for their faith, (since this was a common condition in the church at that time) would mean to think on the suffering of our brethren, with prayerful contemplation, and to be willing if possible to minister to their families, to see ourselves as bearing the burden and the experience in our own surroundings. It would certainly be a far cry from today's American church scene of 'prosperity is the rightful experience of all believers.' If your brother or sister was imprisoned for their faith, I don't think your 'Disney-land' happy hour would complement a kindred experience. Our churches should be busy planning and praying for a way to carry on world-evangelism and ministry to the needs in foreign lands, not checking out the new car or new house deal in order to see how we can use 'good stewardship' without touching the savings account. Seems like there is more similarity between the American socialite and the American church member, than the Christian abroad and the Christian at home! Oops.

The age of specialization became a part of the American church agenda as well. About this same time, in social change in this country, the churches began to have 'youth' ministers, music ministers, education ministers etc. etc. all of which were peculiar to the American church scene. Some of us can remember when 'a' church had 'a' minister. One church, one preacher was the norm. There was not enough money, or personnel to go around, so everyone did their share and perhaps more. **When specialization hit the scene**, the church, being heavily influenced by the country, began to adapt methods and means to make Christian service and ministry look easy, this is why the American fields of science, medicine, and other major service providers began in look for ways to be more efficient and also become more profitable. **The American church seemed to think this was a great idea,** without looking at the Bible as it's only rule 'of faith and practice' which it bragged was a motto, the church began to employ methods used by the 'world' or country of America, and soon, more ministers were needed, more schools of higher learning had to be built, more money had to be spent, and everything started with the 'big bang' (I call it), **when the creation of affluence and ease for the Christian elite**, became the source of the evolving, *religious education machine of the 'new age.'*

Of course a little bit of missions had to be designed to make the American church look 'viable' to any good bible student. But these days (1960's-1990's) were the years of what I would call 'religious—political correctness.' **Do little, but look good!**

Perhaps the 40 years of testing are over, and the last days are about to include the trials which even the American Christians will find difficult to bear. No matter what Hal Lindsay says about the return of the Lord, there is a verse in Matthew 24. 14 which will be fulfilled before Jesus returns. The Gospel will be preached in **all the world** for a testimony to all nations, then the end will come. First things first. Even Oswald J.Smith preached that this verse is an obvious 'time frame' reference, that is why the word THEN is used, when it states, then will the end come, after the Gospel has been proclaimed in all the world.

Today mission research specialists list at 1200 language or people groups who are unreached. If any are listed as unreached, then the Christians of this generation have not finished their task. It seems hypocritical that church members can claim to have a **'fulfilled life, and yet face an unfinished task.'** That has got to be a real dilemma for any thinking Christian. All the famous Christian authors address the idea and need for a **'fulfilled life'** (whatever that means), yet they say little if anything about the **unfinished task! There has to be something wrong with that picture!**

Onward Christian Sissies
(One mistake—but many consequences)

The Bibles says, "Thou shalt have no other gods before me…" Make the mistake of disobeying this command, and the results or consequences have far reaching effect. **When the church in America became weak, the forces of evil in the country became stronger.** Many of the indulgences of the American society (much like Sodom and Gomorrah of the Bible), are the result of weak teachings in the Christian religion in this country. There have been Christian congressmen, and Senators for many years, but it has not seemed to stem the tide of evil influence in the land. Perhaps we need to re-write the words to a favorite church hymn—'Onward Christian Soldiers.'

If we wanted to be honest, it would come out more like this rendition which I have used at many summer youth camps in this country, as the missionary speaker;

> *"Onward Christian sissies, running from the war, with the cross of Jesus, on our minds no more. We have climbed no mountains, we have crossed no seas, and when Jesus comes again, we'll be doing as we please. We are all divided as anyone can see, some in glass Cathedrals, and some in poverty."*

There are several other verses, but this gives you an idea of what I mean. These two stanzas reflect more of the tone of behavior and thought in the average church in America than the original version. **I have personally looked into the eyes of the persecuted Christians around the world, and I have faced only a small amount of the trials they face. But when I compare the American church with the rest of the world, they look very different.**

One most recent example of the 'sissy' status in America is probably one of the most well known or obvious. Recently I read, **a statement by Evangelist Billy Graham,** on the subject of death and dying. He stated to a certain news person, that he "hoped that he would die before his wife died" because he did not know how he would survive or 'get on' without her. I am sure he took this approach to bring some great noble accolade to his fine wife, but it is probably one of the weakest statements an educated man of 'the cloth' could make. MY question right away when I saw that statement was, 'what did he **want her to do,** go through the pain and suffering of the loss of her loved one, so he would not have to do the same? What in the world is he thinking of? A man who has preached to millions around the world for 50 years or more, can't bear to think of being without his wife? **This is not a noble commendation** for her, it is a ridiculous expression of his lack of ability or willingness to 'take the hit' of such a loss himself. Perhaps all of his preaching these many years have not prepared him for death and dying? If that is the case, where is all this faith from the Bible he has been telling the rest of the world about? I have seen families separated by persecution, death and terrible pain, but I have (in Africa and other lands I have served), never met a real Christian who did not willingly forgive the persecutors and stand prepared to say farewell to their loved ones.

This to me is an indication that walking the walk and talking the talk is very different. It seems to me that Mr. Graham's last words are his worst words, if this is where he leaves the death and 'dying' ssue. He shows fear not faith, and I could not imagine walking behind him, as Paul the Apostle invited his hearers, **"be ye followers of me as I am of Christ"**. Sorry, Billy, I think, you did not think that statement through very long, or you let the cat out of the bag! But whether in pretense or in truth, <u>Christ is preached, and therein do I rejoice.</u>

With much ado about fine (extravagant and eloquent) church buildings in America, and fancy cars, homes, multi-purpose buildings and staff—**to go with the comfortable life style** that the proponents of "prosperity Gospel" continually find enormous crowds to get 'hyped' about, it would seem only sensible that real believers in the Holy Bible would get wise! **<u>The Lord Jesus and His disciples did not promote this kind of extravagance, comfort</u>** and ease, so where did all of this come from? It comes from selfish indulgence in the modern American 'pipe dream' that **really belongs only to the country** and social environment, and belongs not to the real, elect people of God, message. Is anyone going to speak against all of this hullabaloo? The Prophet Ezekiel addressed this very thing, in Chapter 16, verses 48-50, when he warned the people of God (Israel) about their selfish indulgence at that time, he even likened them unto Sodom, a city destroyed for it's wickedness. But you will note, if you read that text, that the real sin was not their lustful debauchery, **that was the result** of their sin. The sin was, "affluence, idleness and caring not for the poor and needy." That was the sin. In like manner I believe the weakness of the churches of America has brought on the terrible conditions in the social fabric of America which we see today. Had the churches been humble, and obedient to taking the word of God around the world to those who have not had a chance to hear that message of Hope and salvation, and not 'stacking' up on each other from town to town in the USA, then we may have had more time before God let the Sept. 11, 2001 tragedy strike. We can't sit and blame the social agenda of politicians, when the spiritual fabric of the country became un raveled, and selfish, narcissistic life styles hit the pulpits and pews of the land. The church mission research specialists in California, list over 12,000 unreached people groups in the world, comprising an estimated 2. Billion people.

In this day and time there should be no 'unreached' people groups, the job could well have been accomplished, if the money spent on 'extravagant, elegant, multi-purpose (that's a laugh, there is no multi-purpose—it is **single purpose—our own**) buildings.

We do not have missionaries in this generation like—William Carey, Hudson Taylor, David Livingston, what we have today in this generation is a host of 'Rip Van Winkles' who need to be awakened from sleep, before the Master of the house returns. We are wrong, and we have a serious problem that needs to be corrected. Sacrifice must replace affluence, Jesus and others must replace self. I hope I do not become your enemy by telling you the truth! As for Billy, when is Mr. Graham going to address this issue of narcissism and selfishness in American churches—perhaps he has, I may have missed that sermon…

When world wide concerts are held (as there are at the moment of this writing), for raising the awareness level of poverty and starvation, and the leading nations (8 in particular) and the leaders of those affluent countries, are told about poverty in Africa, and the church stands around and keeps making plans for 'parking lots' and bigger buildings, I see a problem. It is not the church in America that has led this promotion to alleviate world wide hunger, (millions of children dying daily of starvation), **it is the lost people of these affluent nations,** with humanitarian motives not necessarily a Biblical directive which has turned the heads of nations on this 4th of July 2005. How embarrassing this is. Unless the churches are like those in the Old Testament, who did not know enough to feel shame over their condition.

If we are not embarrassed, we should be.

May God have mercy on such as we, in that day;

Al Hamilton
albertham@sbcglobal.net

39

The 8ᵗʰ Day

In the book of Genesis, right and wrong, truth and lie faced each other. After God had created all things, and pronounced that it was good, (Gen. 1. 31) God rested. The day of rest, was the 7ᵗʰ day. From that day on, history was in the making. The 8ᵗʰ day, would prove to be the longest day in man's existence on earth, I call it the 8ᵗʰ day, the beginning day of history for man.

Mankind began the great leap into existence and life on planet earth, became the future for humanity, the rules for playing the game were laid down. The Lord God commanded the man (Gen. 2. 16) what he could and could not do. The rules were simple, and the stakes were high, but the enemy was very subtle and very determined, and the man—who now also had been given a woman as companion and helper, became the prize which Satan sought to capture and destroy, as a vendetta against the Lord of Creation, because of Satan's expulsion from heaven.

The rules for maintaining life in communion with God, (as Adam knew himself to be created in the image of God), included a command from God, which was both possible to heed and easy to understand. Adam and his wife Eve were not burdened with a difficult task of some kind that would be designed for destruction of their relationship with the Lord their Creator, but rather **they were instructed to avoid the indulgence which would bring about a separation of themselves from the good relationship with their Creator that they enjoyed,** since their beginning. A warning is always present in the Bible when danger is present. The Lord God placed the couple in a garden and gave specific instructions, so that Adam and Eve would know how to fulfill their designed function and please God as well as bring complete joy to their lives, as they worked and brought into the world, a human race which would glorify God and establish divine purpose and human joy—to be established as one condition! We can only understand what God has revealed for our understanding. But reading the bible and learning of the work of God in the lives of His creatures, can give us ample insight into the plan of God for human beings. **So let the games begin!** Although we cannot find this 'game of life' told in such 'light' and simplistic terms, perhaps such a 'hyperbole' will be acceptable for the establishment of one great and important truth—Life is from God!

This important truth which I believe is paramount to understanding (to some extent), the dilemma facing the American church of today, in this 21st century, is the truth that life is from God, and one lie, told by Satan in the garden of Eden has been responsible for the destruction of souls in the present world just as it was in the lives of Adam and Eve. If we can understand the power that one lie can have in man's history, and if we can understand that this same lie, not some newly devised strategy of the enemy, is the source of today's dilemma facing the great company of believers in America, perhaps we can overcome this deception that clouds the minds of most of the American Christian population in 2006. Although we must add, that the lie was not totally responsible, it was also **the decision by Adam and Eve to embrace that lie**, which led mankind down the path to separation from God.

Today, in 2006 AD, it has become apparent that **mankind seeks a way to see himself as able to make his own way out of this 'darkest night' of spiritual despair**—which prevails in the land of the free and home of the brave. I for one, do not believe that the American Christian is aware of the fact (as I call it fact—and it is an observation I believe others share), that departure from the Truth of Bible teaching in this country, is the result of taking on the role that Satan suggested to Adam and Eve, which meant they should make their own decisions. And this they promptly accepted as a viable option to the simple and direct command of God. **Here is my theory**; it is simply this—that it is quite obvious that American 'Christian' teaching in today's religious circles, has evolved into a self-help agenda of 'self-ism' as Dave Hunt expresses it. I call it—A self-esteem engine that pulls a string of 'rail cars' much like a train. **The common and prevalent idea that Christians need to see themselves as being able to bring about, through 'successful' personal effort**, some kind of 'super Christian' persona**. And it is also becoming the theme of songs (often called contemporary Christian music) as well as pulpit messages by pastors of 'mega' churches. It is also my perspective that this lack of humble obedience, and this constant push for narcissistic prominence in the world, is the result of failing to recognize that truth and lie must be separated—and seen for what they are as revealed in the Bible. According to what I have seen in American religious teaching today, and in the society in which Christians in America find themselves for the present, there is the commonly accepted **view that 'right and wrong' each deserve equal time in the public and the religious circles of society.**

This is evidenced by the recent History Channel (2-8-06) presentation of the program it called, 'Decoding the past', in which one episode dealt with the subject of the 'Resurrection of Jesus Christ. In this episode scholars (?) were addressing both sides of the issue. The evidences for the fact of a literal, bodily resurrection were given, then other (so called scholars) speakers represented the idea that the bodily resurrection of Christ was a 'vision' or mentally construed scene in the minds of those who surrounded the event. Equal time was given to both the evidences of a bodily resurrection (as the Bible presents), and the conflicting view that there was really no actual bodily resurrection of Jesus from the dead. In doing this, the History Channel was not giving favor to the Biblical or Christian view, they were doing what Satan did in the Garden of Eden. They were presenting both sides of an issue that has only one side, the side that God states is true. **When God speaks—there is no reason for discussion of another view.** This is how Satan presented his lie. In making it appear that other options should be considered, Satan tempted Eve, with the option that would be seemingly pleasant and desirable, even when it went against the command of God. **Now do you get the picture**? Consider this observation: I believe that if American social and educational institutions (Washington University i.e.—to which I shall refer later), continue to spout the lie that we are all victims, and that we are all oppressed, we will soon begin to believe that there is no one at fault for any 'wrong doing' and that will lead to the belief that there is no right or wrong. This is very well addressed by author Tammy Bruce in her book, 'The Death of Right and Wrong.' **And if there is only right and there is no wrong, then you have neither right or wrong, because you cannot have one without the other**.

If you believe there is no wrong, you must believe also that there is only right, and the idea of 'right and wrong' is lost. Each of these is the opposite of the other, **and therefore you cannot describe one without the other**. The fact of right and wrong, are reality and are obvious to the honest observer. Each of these-'right and wrong' values, is of moral and spiritual design, each is described by definition as—the absence of the other. When Satan tempted Eve in the garden of Eden, he began by stating the words which Adam and Eve heard from God, as rules to live by, simple and logical conditions. God had commanded the pair, that they were not to take any fruit from the tree in the midst of the garden, (the tree of the knowledge of good and evil) or they would die. So to disobey God would be wrong, because it would violate the condition which makes a behavior acceptable, and this acceptable behavior is that which God approves of and requires.

When Satan brought this matter before Eve, he stated it as a question to Eve, "…has God said…?" Then the tempter went from that statement to provide Eve with an option, which was really a way of lying to her. The lie was, that they would not die from eating the forbidden fruit, and secondly, they would in eating of it, become like gods. The lie is the same today, it is the idea that anything that one wants to do, is right, and in making any choice one wants to find desirable, he/she will also find a 'god-like' power. Along with this concept—(anything forbidden must therefore be wrong), is the belief that we as humans, make the final decision about what is right (desirable) and what is wrong.

When any decision or act, is defined as undesirable and it is therefore also understood as being wrong because it does not please us, then what is right is pleasing to our nature or passions, and what is wrong is displeasing or undesirable. So in the final analysis, the idea seen more closely is this, that nothing a person wishes to do or chose should be forbidden, and everything is right if you want it to be so.' The knowledge of good and evil, when discovered, brings with it, the assumption that someone must decide when something is good and when something is evil. But if mankind decides (as the liberal element in American society has done) that nothing should be forbidden, or seen as evil, and that all things and/or all emotions and life-styles are to be acceptable, and in this way we eliminate all wrong doing, it means having the knowledge of what is good and what is evil and having the power to make this decision, when determined by man alone, (at the suggestion of Satan in the garden), about what is good or evil, turns out to foster the idea that—nothing is evil, if it can be perceived or accepted as good according to man's wishes, on his own conditions, apart from what God has said.

This comes through today in several ways. Our modern professors in colleges and universities (in America at least) have continued to present all philosophies of life as relative. There is no absolute, no basis or foundational truth upon which to establish as fact, that something is either right or wrong. But if we accept God's rules, as He is our Creator and spiritual Father, as the only rules which are to be accepted as absolute, this gives honest perspective and purpose to life. As well We are not 'driven' by the nature, but guided by God's command and His Spirit, if we obey God and (Acts 5. 32) have received His Spirit.

If mankind is to be led by the 'will' of God and if you want to call that idea 'purpose driven' no one will argue the point, but you still lose something in that choice of terms because being led is different than being driven. It is simple and understandable even to a child, that God's will, being our true purpose in life, is still based on love and guidance, not just seen as a driving force. We must see God's love for man, and mankind's willingness to love God as a relationship of leader and follower. You do not discover the whole truth of the relationship if all you see is a 'driving purpose'. Children are able to love God, but they may not be able to understand a 'driving force or purpose' in life, at an early age. I prefer to see our relationship with God from the perspective of a child. (Matt. 18. 1-6). In a recent (Feb. 2006) radio broadcast, on the one of the popular talk shows, the host, or his guest on the program referred to the fact that Washington University, was introducing a new teaching tool which they called the 'tunnel of oppression', and if I understood this correctly, the idea is to make obvious to all students that America as well as other nations are all living under oppression. This concept is such a strong position of the 'liberal left' wing of American politics that it now holds a position in a prominent University curriculum. This is not surprising since the Universities have become in the last 40 years, the spring-board from which narcissism and relativism enter the American and the world scene.

When the concept of 'being an oppressed people' is presented in a country like the USA, it is obviously an effort to make all citizens of the country feel they are victims and that the social structure of America is the culprit. In this 'walk way' down the hall of American education, students will begin to fight their own country, and the democracy which spawned their very social existence will be seen as their enemy not their friend. Soon, they will consume themselves in this mental, and emotional, philosophical battle of brains without thought, and they will destroy the very democracy which spawned their social existence. They do not know that they are their own worst enemy and that the social structure they are fighting is the one their forefathers established. Much of this chaos and may-hem in society today in America, is the result of false modern thought churned out by the professors of atheistic philosophy. This is a true picture of consuming ones self by fighting against truth and justice. It is truth and justice as established by God as He used God-fearing people, which has given rise to social equity. The nations under oppression and following atheistic philosophies are the ones who experience deprivation, constant war and suffering. **As soon as the American liberal left can achieve their goal of victimizing all of America and placing blame on sound religious faith and biblical absolutes,** they will have turned the corner and will have led a great country into moral and social destruction. That path will not be pretty and there will be no turning back, since they who embrace this philosophy have already departed from the road which was filled with hope and peace. Few nations return to truth when they leave it, if they have blamed the truth and justice for their problems. The latter end is worse for them than the beginning. (II Peter 2. 21,22). If social injustice, not sin, is considered to be the guilty party in this American dream, then those who embrace the 'American way' and even democracy itself, will be seen as a system or government 'gone haywire', and those who oppose it, will be seen as the heroes not the villains.

No doubt you can see this looming upon the horizon. Already the liberal 'media' and agencies such as the ACLU are pushing the envelope of moral standards beyond any logical and reasonable limits. If the American churches get completely wound up in this fracas, you won't be able to distinguish 'church' from country, and that will be an eye-opener for many people. The logical conclusion to this mix-up will be found to bring the country against all 'Christian' effort to restore justice and truth.

We might well say, in this context which I have suggested here, that the 8th day will be man's last day on earth to discover that tomorrow will be the end of man's time on earth, and the new day that dawns will be the day the Lord has called in the Bible, the Day of the Lord! Man will destroy the earth this time, by bringing down upon himself the wrath of God, and the end of things as we know them today. The Day of the Lord will come, as a thief in the night…(1 Thess.5. 2) suddenly, unexpectedly.

Let not that day overtake you, as a thief would, without your readiness, but awake and stand in the Light. The number 8 in the Bible, or in Hebrew I believe, is the number of/for 'man' and the number 40 it the number related to 'testing' for proving, such as the 40 years in the wilderness, and the 40 days in which the Lord was tempted after His baptism in the river Jordon. Perhaps we are in the 8th day, in a sense of the use of the number, one thing is certain, mankind is now in a day in the world, which will determine the destiny of many. Let us walk as children of light, in the day, not as those who sleep in the night.

40

The Fish the Flag and the Hope-chest Chronicles of—The American church

✦

(apologies to the author of Chronicles of Narnia)

Intro.

The old nursery rhyme—'Little Jack Horner' is a good reminder of the attitude of today's American church movement. The rhyme as I recall, goes like this...'little Jack Horner, sat in the corner, eating his Christmas pie, he stuck in his thumb and pulled out a plumb, and said,' what a good boy am I.' Perhaps the **self-esteem 'engine' of the American religious right**, could use this as their motto. There has never been, in the history of Christianity in America, a more self centered religious body than we have in this country today. I will deal with the 'Little Jack Horner' mind-set in another article. At this point I **want to deal with some mistakes made by the religious establishment**, (evangelicals included), which can be identified by the following statements—revealing some problems of the American church—as I have observed the American religious groups of today.

1. Exaggerated importance of Education—(M.DIV)?

2. Narcissistic leadership—(Prosperity gospel)

3. Fighting small fires, while the world burns-(politics)

4. Exalting political issues—(Religious Right)

5.   Ignoring world-wide opportunities-ie—(unreached people)

6.   Hypocrisy—love of the world—(Disney-land saints)

7.   Division—and deception; as seen in—denominations.

In contrast we have: The Persecuted Church in the World which more correctly identify with the Bible verses:

Lk. 9. 48, Matt. 5. 19.

Whoever will do and teach **these things**, shall be called great—in the kingdom of heaven.

The Characteristics of Greatness
In The Persecuted Church
Around the World
Matt. 5. 19
1. **Faith** that is strong
2. **Humility** That is genuine
3. **Suffering** that is Real

◆   ◆   ◆

In seminaries and Bible colleges of America today, the emphasis from the classes and professors is—" get your M.DIV."

Which translated means—become as educated as you can, in the theology of your denominational position, so you will (like the Pharisees of old) appear acceptable, presentable and knowledgeable to your peers, (for your own glory). No need to look for a Biblical reason for such academic attainment, you won't find such a 'critter'—but you certainly will be proud and pompous (just like the tune that's played at graduation ceremonies—pomp and circumstance...duh). The big—unanswered question however, is this...**just whose Divinity are you master of?** In 25 years no one has answered that question for me.

As Nero fiddled, and watched Rome burn...the blame fell upon the innocent, who happened to be—the Christians. As the world today burns, (figure of speech) the church in America continues its celebration services which are mostly about their own salvation and excitement over the great gifts God has given them, along with the prosperity and affluence that goes with it. **95% of the**

world outside of the American church...suffers innocently at the hand of per-secutors who hate the Bible.

About 2 Billion souls without a knowledge of God's Word and without a way to call upon the rich American church for help, still wait to hear the gospel of the Kingdom of Heaven (since this Billion + souls doesn't even know that their hope lies within the confines of the great mega church 'glass' cathedrals) so they lan-guish in poverty and war. It must be repeated for emphasis and for sake of clarity, that the affluent church in America has looked in the mirror of God's word, and seen (Rev. 3. 14-22) the church of Laodicea staring back at it, and still does noth-ing to show sorrow, remorse or repentance. For the most part, there are no ser-mons in the pulpits of the land calling for repentance.

Are the American churches, ignorant, uneducated, or just plain unwilling to call 'a spade a spade.' You attend such a church, perhaps you should ask your preacher! Then maybe you can ask him (or her) where he or she, went to school. By this time, that question would be appropriate, because it was the school that taught them, not to think about Revelation 3. 14-22, as if it had any relevance to them. The average pastor (using the term loosely), speaks of the 'last days' (2 Tim. 3,4), and winks at the idea that we could possibly be living in that time now. The church leadership in America and her members, seem to be of the opinion that the country (USA) can be fixed. As I have often stated, that **is like trying to sweep all the dirt off of the earth**...you can't...its all dirt. While the 'religious right' is busy with concerns of what is wrong with the political scene and the American social condition, the real task the church of the Lord was given, goes unfulfilled. And strangely enough, the books, the seminars, the religious messages of the day, keep focus on the Christian 'self' and all the goodies that come from being a Christian, and knowing the Lord. In America, **the liberal left,** does verbal battle with the **'religious right'** and it is obvious that neither of these two social 'groups' have any intention of dialogue that is meaningful, or that is likely to bring harmony between the two camps. This is because **common sense** is not the **common denominator** in their attacks upon each other. Today, in the news, the liberal left, TV commentators were discussing the fact that when Harriett Miers stepped out of the race for consideration as a supreme court appointee, and a qualified and respected man of legal skills was chosen to become the next choice of President Bush, Mr. news man, asked "...couldn't they find another woman to step in..." Well Mr. news man, under what tree were you sleeping? They just had a woman who was washed out of the race (like you see the ACLU accomplish so many times), and she took so much personal attack by the liberal-'left' and Flack, that no average person would have continued to make themselves available, for <u>any political position</u>, even this one.

So the News Man, asks the dumb question, "why couldn't they find another woman<u>,"? As if the whole appointment to the Supreme Court was a game of 'tag team' in which the most important thing is—whether the appointee is man or woman</u>! And the social weird-o's wonder why the country looses faith in the established government's decisions, and has no faith at all in the 'liberal left' position! You can bounce back and forth between the discussions of America's plight in the present world condition, and the religious, Christian church member's plight, in his social agenda, and if you look closely you will see the same dilemma that both face. The connection is unbelievable, the Christian and the Jew in America, both seem obsessed with not only world social issues, but primarily America's social agenda. And the agenda of the country is not intended (by Washington D.C) to have any bearing on religious issues or religious positions. In all of this the Christians in America (for the most part), cry "there should be no separation of church and state." What we have is a strange phenomenon, we have churches pushing the idea of "live a fulfilled life"—have the right goals, purpose…etc. etc., and the message of the hour for the churches is, 'being a fulfilled person'**. Now answer this for me—how can you as a Christian have a fulfilled life, and yet you have an unfinished task?** Is not the Christian life fulfilled as it finds itself having accomplished the task given her by the Lord? Is a fulfilled life separated from the work of the Lord in this earth?

And is not **the task**—that of taking the Gospel of Christ into the whole earth? Maybe Matt. 28. 18-20 is not understood today.

Or perhaps the many 'so called Bible scholars' studied and taught the meaning right out of it! Don't think that such a thing does not happen. This is exactly why you have over 300 different denominations, all using the same Bible. You cannot have in the true sense of the terms, (in Christendom), **a fulfilled life, and yet have an unfinished task** The Apostle of the Lord, Paul, stated in 2 Tim. 4, he had fought a good fight, and finished his course, and kept the faith. His task was to fulfill his ministry, and that was to take the Gospel to the Gentiles. It is obvious today that the task of the church now on earth, is to take the Gospel to the rest of the world, which has yet to receive the opportunity to hear it. Rom 10. "…how shall they hear without a preacher and how shall they preach except they be sent…?" Since the present opportunity for American Christians includes the potential to reach in this day and time, the rest of the 'unreached people' of the world, this becomes our duty and our task. If we have that potential and fail to accomplish the same, we in America will be held accountable. We happen to be in that very position, and we have knowledge of the locations of the unreached peoples. In the book of Ezekiel, the Lord had made the prophet whom He called, a watchman over the house of Israel. In the 3rd chapter of the book bearing his name, Ezekiel is made a watchman whose task it was to warn Israel from the coming judgment of God upon them for their disobedience and their idolatry. To be a watchman for God is to know the will of the Lord and to warn the (unruly 1st Thess. 5. 14) wicked to turn unto the Lord. This should be done in America, there should be a warning sounded to the church members that it is their duty to seek the lost sheep of the world, and bring them the knowledge of the Lord and His salvation.

To further prove this point, look again at the message of Jesus to the disciples, in Luke 12—which is the command that the steward of the Lord's house must be faithful to his duties, so that the Master will find things in order when He returns. The servant **to whom much is given** will find that much is required. This will include the great amount of technology, opportunity, resources (personnel, financial) and methods for reaching all parts of the world. We know that the nations shall hear the word of the Lord (Matt. 24. 14), and we know that it is the will of God that all mankind comes to a knowledge of the truth (1 Tim. 2. 3,4), and we know that God is not willing that any should perish, (2 Peter 3. 9), therefore we know what our task is. If the American churches have overfed themselves, at the cost of leaving other people unreached, we shall find these words in Luke 12, being brought to our attention in the day of judgment. And we also know, it is appointed unto man once to die, and after this, the judgment. We also know that we shall be judged according to our works done in the body (Rev. 20. 13, 2nd Cor. 5. 10).

Knowing these things, it behooves us to respond to the needs about us, not the desires of the flesh within us. We must work while it is day, for the night comes when no man can work. The night may well be upon the church in America, with the government becoming less enchanted with the alliance that the present churches have with government and social issues. It will be soon that this love affair of church and state will become a nightmare of discord and discontent. A truly spiritual body cannot bring the world of evil to it's knees, just because of a few years of friendly cooperation. Soon, the tide will turn and government will become restless and rebellious at the constant prodding from the religious right. The conservative 'talk show' hosts of radio and television, will not be able to get the 'liberal left' to make 'sense' because there is no plan or agenda in the camp of the political left of America to find sensible solutions to social conditions in America since they have no absolutes upon which to base their position. **Free-**

doms glory is success, and the glory of success is popularity. There is no fear of God in the minds of those who love the world and the things of the world. No one can serve two masters.

I have mentioned the love of the world, as a problem with American Christians. This can be illustrated in several examples. One example was my experience while attending a church service in Dallas Texas, some years ago. At the close of a message during the 11 AM service one Sunday, right after the invitation time, the minister asked for special prayers, one of which was a request (in all seriousness) for the members of the church to pray for the 'Dallas Cowboys' football team, because if they would win that day (A game was scheduled for that Sunday aft.) then the football team would be 'in the play offs'—Duh. If you think that things of this world are not loved by church members, think again. The university you attend, the state you live in, the football team you favor, the favorite things about the country, have become idols which draw the devotion of church members to things temporary and therefore makes many fall away from the eternal and invisible realm where God is. The Bible states, 'set your affection on things above, not on things of the earth.' (Col.3. 2-11). **A fulfilled life is—a finished task, a job well done!**

The leaven of the Pharisees was hypocrisy, and Jesus warned the disciples to be wary of this condition. The idea of 'putting on a mask' to play a role is for stage and screen only. The Bible teaches us that the appearance of good character is not enough, Jesus said of the Scribes and Pharisees, they love the greetings in the market place, in public they appear righteous before men, but are inwardly—empty graves, they honor the Lord with their lips, but their heart was far from God.

For church leaders, pastors and prominent theologians, in the fundamental churches and most denominations, we have an obvious problem that **stems from public acceptance of the religious position**. The magazine "The Week" in the Nov. 11 2005 Issue, on page 17 advertised a program on PBS from 'Religion and Ethics" newsweekly, a forthcoming four part series on Faith and Family in America. There is such an intertwining of moral ethics and family values, in the 'God and country' mind-set that no one separates the religious teachings from the political scene in America any longer. There will be even more issues debated in days to come, while the country and the churches (not to discount the Jewish religion in it all), find common ground for dialogue. In the days of the 'first Christians'—from the years 60 AD to 160 AD, there was no such intermingling of the church and state. But today the church and state (in America) seem inseparable. There are those (the majority of Christians) who would say there should be no separation of church and state. Then there are those who will fight to maintain such a separation.

The reality is, there has never been (at least by Divine decree), a union of the two. There is no such thing, Biblically speaking, as the church of the Lord Jesus, (see Matt. 16. 16-18), being united with any world government. And the verse in Ps. which states "blessed is the nation whose God is the Lord…" is a **reference to the people of Israel**. They were the only nation on earth that was divinely established by the Lord God. They were the people, (a nation), and a culture in the present world, which **was called into existence by the God of Heaven**. Acts is the **only other time that a people were called by the Lord, for His NAME AND FOR His purpose—this was the**—(Ekklesia), on the day of Pentecost which was brought into being and created. In Acts 11. 26 it is stated that the followers of Christ were first called Christians—in Antioch. The word 'called' here is a Greek word meaning, a Divine Calling. It was from above that the name of Christian was given to the followers of Christ. They are the spiritual household of God, this is the church that Jesus said He would build (Matt. 16. 18), and it is a word which means a people 'called out' from the world, to belong to Christ, as followers of Christ. Israel, as a physical nation, and the 'Ekklesia' the spiritual body of Christ, are the two nations, one physical, one spiritual which God called into being. American Christians seem to discuss the kingdom of God, and write books on it, but few seem to be able to define it accurately. The Bible states that Jesus will say to His followers who are **faithful to their task,** those whom He will welcome into His eternal Kingdom, "well **done,** thou good and faithful servant, you have been faithful over a few things, I will make thee ruler over many things, enter thou into the joy of thy Lord." Matt. 25. 21. **Even physical Israel, must come to Christ**.

There is, in American churches more talk about **blessings received from the Lord**, than there is about need **to do the work of the Lord**. As if the task given by Jesus was already accomplished, and all we wait for now is 'homecoming.' How much is said about sacrifices made by American churches, to reach into all the rest of the world in order to please God? When you can be told at church services to take your work or your education into the harvest fields of the world, for the sake of lost souls, then you can believe **that** message—**is the** message!

The scripture in Acts, which records the time when the Apostles reported all that **God had done through them**, is not to be misconstrued to mean—**'things which God has done for them.'** There is a great chasm between these two concepts. There is the constant need for missionaries to report what 'God has been doing through them' and their ministry, but the erroneous assumption that what

God does THROUGH His people is synonymous with what God does FOR His people is very, very dangerous to the context of Christian ministry today. (Acts 15).

Here is the danger: When the report of activity and fruit from a Christian missionary's labors, is received it can bring with it the idea that accomplishment and success is paramount, and this reported success and/or accomplishment may be seen to be result of human ingenuity, financial strength, good planning and a number of other components, many of which are attached to man-made efforts or genius, rather than simply, the result of the hand of God leading in these works. It is obvious that the promise of God is—"the effectual, fervent prayer of a righteous man avails much," and when people have prayed this way for mission projects and ministries, we know that God has brought about the fruit for those labors, (1 Cor. 3. 7) **and God has given the increase**. But we must know also, that what men see when results are viewed through the normal human eyes of the church, without giving the concentrated effort to continue looking to the fields which are untouched as a part of the task which is our unfinished business, we have the tendency to think—all the work is being done. Simply because much is being accomplished in the world, we must not be deceived into assuming that every soul who seeks to know the will of God is being reached. Many (1.8 billion souls still listed as unreached people) sheep are wandering and not found. If a Shepard will leave the safe and secure 99 to find one which is lost, how much more should a caring shepherd leave the one that is safe and seek the 99 lost ones?

Because the USA has 90 % of the pastors and ministers of any given denomination, and yet America makes up less than 5% of the world's population, we can reverse the numbers in the parable of the 'lost sheep' in Luke 15, since there are more who are lost and out in the wilderness than there are those who are safely in the fold.

One very possible reason why the American church spends so much income and time on itself, could be found—in the theory—that the heavy amount of promotion and awareness of existing mission work has led people in the church assembly to believe that this enormous amount of mission work, the number of mission agencies and this mesmerizing flow of information which results from the same—has created an incorrect picture of world evangelism.

When hundreds of mission agencies in America, and thousands of mission teams, report their work and present the needs of their work to American churches, through the means, and media of advanced technology (i.e.—e-mail, power point presentations, movies, television, seminars, conventions, video etc,) and personal appearances of national workers, we not only learn of the particular ministry or mission, we also become mesmerized with a possibly distorted 'picture' of evangelistic 'outreach' and conditions that exist in only—some parts of the world. We may then create a **mental and emotional frame of reference** for our own view of WORLD MISSION CONDITIONS which does not truly or completely include the plight of 2 Billion souls who have not been given an opportunity to know the Lord or His Word. As the minds of American church members become **saturated with information** about 'the work of God' going on in many places and countries around the world, it is highly probable that they will assume that the work of reaching all nations is being done, and therefore the pastor can stay home, the missionary can be sent to help other missionaries where work is already going on, and the church can make decisions about evangelistic efforts with the idea in mind—that there is no hurry, any place the missionary works is as good as any other need which has been presented. All foreign work becomes less urgent and is seen as a matter of particular choice or 'desire' which comes from the heart of the missionary and his/her sponsoring church.

I believe this theory deserves attention, because we see the continual emphasis of American Christians placed upon the 'seriousness' of political conditions in the USA making these **political conditions consume the attention** of the American church member. A Christian with a **truly "world mission view"** would be looking at the unreached people groups in all parts of the world, which represents those who **are without any opportunity to hear the Gospel** and **who have no churches, no bible and no evangelists.** The few Christians in America who are so burdened with the unreached people, are not given the place of prominence in the conventions and 'workshops' of mission seminars, they receive instead, a slight mention or some 'token' attention, while the 'church growth' enthusiast is marched up to the front to explain the latest 'plan' for attracting more members (probably from other church fellowships), and how to make those who refused to obey the Gospel yesterday, look deserving of another 'shot' (since they have made the wrong decision for years), and because they are in close quarters and easy to reach **we do not 'shake the dust from our feet' and move on** as Jesus commanded, instead we simply 're-write' the script and try to continue our efforts to persuade people who have already heard the Gospel—through more subtle methods.

The 'Hope-Chest' scenario:

What I call the 'Hope-Chest' effort of American Christians is the idea of—building a box or mental 'hope-chest' into which a person places their favorite Bible verses—and then saves those verses to be pulled out at convenience and observed when the chosen occasion merits such action. When American Christians, so possessed with the idea of 'national' freedom and political freedom, begin to see the work of God as if it was to be accomplished at their 'own discretion' or in their own way, we have taken the freedom of choice and applied it to the Bible and to the great commission of Matt. 28. 18-20, as if this liberty and the many freedoms that life in America affords it's citizens, is to be extended to the church's work of evangelizing the world, so the sense of urgency and emergency is missing.

For this reason, people can spend years in academic preparation for a task that God has given to His followers, and the God Himself will carry out, even after all the study and academic 'preparations' are made. If God brings about the increase, and the work of His servants—is to sow the seed and water it, then apart from acquiring necessary skills for Bible translation, and literacy, what is all of this other time consumed in religious academia doing for the lost souls? It is not done for the Lost souls-who only need the word of God and encouragement, support and prayer, it is done to make the 'pastor', missionary or other Christian worker feel qualified, and to make the sending churches feel confident in the 'sending' of the mission team. God does not need our academic skills, He needs the available hearts and bodies of the worker, that is how He has arranged it. **One of the greatest needs of human kind,** is the need to be needed.

So the Lord made a plan to 'make His people feel needed' by commanding them to go into all the world and preach the Gospel of the Kingdom of heaven. This is indeed a true and existing need. But men continue to teach men the things that men think they need to know, based upon American (Corporate) success standards. And the lost souls of the world still go on waiting for a drink of the 'water of life' and the simple knowledge of the word of God, and religious institutions are busy 'baking cookies and cakes.'

If the American church is busy putting favorite and special verses of the Bible into it's personal 'hope-chest' of salvation, that church will not fully understand it's role, nor it's purpose in the will of God. The Bible states, '…be not unwise, but understanding what the will of the Lord is…" Eph. 5. The churches and the American society, have borrowed bible verses and taken certain teachings from the scriptures, and applied them and used them—expecting to have the power of God from these verses as well, but without planning to do all that God has commanded and without teaching—within context, the words of the Lord, the country and many churches have found themselves as having a 'form of godliness', empty of power and effectiveness. Therefore denominations spring up, new schools of 'thought?' appear constantly, and most American church members are understanding neither what they say nor whereof they affirm, so they wander in the dark as the blind leading the blind.

The country of America, (the citizens and government) have been using Bible verses from time, to time, to establish laws, to provide guidelines for socially acceptable behavior and for most every other suitable plan developed for public harmony. There must be laws, so that lawlessness can be stopped from bringing chaos and mayhem into full bloom. Every society must have governing powers and rules to live by, if it is to survive it's own existence. The fact that America happens to have used the Bible as the guiding principle of government and law, is commendable, but in doing so, the government sought no real surrender to the total will of God, or sought to make each member of society a full blown 'follower' of the Lord. The general rules of government or society were not applied to the citizenry as commandments to live by—for the sake of bringing honor to God and surrender to His Son, Jesus Christ the Lord. The rules for acceptable social behavior were borrowed, or taken from the Bible, but the Bible was given to mankind by the God of Heaven, 'holy men of God' wrote and spoke as they were 'carried along' by or directed by the power of the Holy Spirit. This was—in order to bring mankind to the foot of the cross of Christ in repentance, so that salvation would be the result.

Scriptures (or the Holy Bible) are not in a book form, simply written by the imagination of men, as their own design, as their own carnal nature might dictate. So you cannot take God's words and subtract His Spirit from those words (John 6. 63) and expect to have God's blessings upon 'how these words of His' are used. If you take the words of a judge in a court of law, out into the street after the case is decided, and use those same words to apply to other people and other cases, the words of the judge will not apply nor stand up as 'rule of the day' for any situation you wish to apply them to. Neither can you take the words of God and make them fit your own personal agenda, or use them out of context and expect the Spirit of God to honor the meaning of those words you have 'stolen' from His book.

Churches have done this same thing, just as the government of America has used the Bible when it wants to, or refused to follow it as it so decides, churches and religious leaders do the same thing with the Holy Scripture. It is called handling the word of God deceitfully, (2 Cor. 4, Acts 20. 27-35) and drawing away followers after themselves. Satan himself used Scriptures out of context, to try to tempt the Lord Jesus to turn aside from His course.

The form of godliness that accompanies the conditions prevalent in the last days, which form denies the power of the Lord, comes about because the power is missing (1 Cor. 4. 20) and that power is the 'Gospel of Christ' this is the power of God unto salvation, to everyone who believes it, and this word 'believes' is a word meaning belief accompanied with obedience to that word. When someone takes the words of the Bible to use for his/her own purpose, without a mind to become submissive to the total will of God in His covenant with mankind, then that word is empty of power, not being accompanied with the Holy Spirit. The Holy Spirit will use the word of God and give it fruit and power, but only when it is applied with the intent to please God and serve His divine purpose. "Thy kingdom come, Thy will be done" will have to be the intended use of each word that God has spoken and had recorded in written form. Man shall not live by bread alone, but by every word that proceeds forth from the mouth of God. **The words <u>of</u> God, can only be <u>empowered by the Spirit of God</u> when given in context to be used <u>for</u> the <u>will</u> of God.**

Man may organize, operate and promote a church (religious assembly) in America, but only God and His Spirit will bring power to Scriptures as they are preached according to God's will and taught by Holy Spirit led servants of God. A nation can use, borrow, or steal truths found in the Holy Bible, but a nation cannot use these truths for its own purpose and call it the will of God. God is not subject to the will of man, but as Cain in the book of Genesis found out, man is to be subject to the will of God, if he expects to have the presence and blessing of God. We as humans cannot offer to God what we want to, and expect God to accept it, we must find out what God accepts and offer that, as people who seek to please Him, not as people who expect to 'create' and god that pleases them. America is finding this out and the church in America will also discover this in time.

The Fish and The Flag

American Christians often place the sign of the 'fish' on their car, to make the statement of Christian faith, and present a testimony to the public of that religious position. In a country where peace and freedom are of great value, and yet a country that is also fighting wars to bring about democracy to others around the world, there are a lot of questions this multi-dimensional, social position raises.

America is a country which can engage in military conflict for the good of others, and yet be found by many voices (inside the country and outside the country) as 'the guilty party.' **America is about the only country (along with Britain perhaps) that can fight a war for someone else's sake and be called 'wrong' for doing it. But in this <u>world it is not</u> unbelievable that someone can try to do the right thing and look wrong for it**. America's 'type' of social structure and moral standard of right and wrong, has always been under the microscopic view of other nations in the world. There have always been, and always will be, those nations which, under dictators and atheists, view the American way, as the wrong way. And even the 'good guys' can have in their own camp those who try to swing the vote, and the agenda in the opposite direction. In America the liberal element has been the wheel that squeaked the loudest, carried the most $ in their pockets to sway the crowd, and thus inhibit the plan and direction of the well meaning citizens. The 'far left' is by nature, far from right—in all moral judgments, bible based absolutes, and concern for the general 'good' of the people. No wonder they accept the nomenclature of 'THE LEFT'—they don't even want to relate to the word 'right' with the agenda they have. The idea of a 'one world government' to be led by or directed by 'who knows what or who'—would be better to the liberal left than to allow the so called 'right wing' political side of the spectrum to have any voice at all. It is a lot like the 'Hippie Movement' of the 60's—they did not have anything to offer, they only knew that they did not like the present 'establishment' so in their rebellion and riots they were against anything that people with strong conservative views were favoring. **To be against something only makes sense if you have something you are for!** What Liberal America, (the far left) is against today is—all the things that the 'far right' are for! The issues are not the issue, there is nothing the far left can offer the American citizen, except the destruction of the American way of life as it has been defined in the constitution of the United States of America.

With a country like America, coming soon under the complete control of what we now see as the 'liberal left wing' leaders, what we do not need is the Christian position to be torn asunder by remarks from 'Pat Robertson' representatives, or mega church leaders who cry out 'save the country' at all costs. The true Biblical position of a follower of Christ, is not supported by, or well represented by these who wear the Name, but cannot handle the shame of sacrifice and suffering that must come to those who truly follow Christ the Lord. **When Christians** in any country seek social favors, and social freedoms, and churches with good intentions, **make the right statements** about the wickedness of abortions, the legality of homosexual behavior, and show good judgment about what is right and what is wrong, and then **those same believers** spend more money on themselves and their 'administrative staff' and buildings than they do on caring for the poor, the starving and dying people around the globe—**who is going to believe their message?**

What **is** believed by the citizens of the country (and the rest of the world, which is watching closely), **is that the American church is going to be most**

angry when the American political scene does not give high favor to the views of the majority of American citizens, which just happens to be views that belong to people of Christian Faith! The Churches in America seem to be ignorant of the fact that many people around the world, and many in America who have not embraced Christianity, still know what the Bible teaches, and they (who do not believe the Bible) **know when the churches are being selfish and when they are not**. Even though the 'lost' unbelieving souls of many nations, and many in this nation, do not believe or follow the teaching of the Holy Bible, they still know what the God of that Bible says to His followers. The world may be lost, but it is not ignorant. **The person who says that there is no God, is a fool for taking that position, but he is not ignorant of what that position requires of its followers.**

America is on the door step, I believe, of turning a deaf ear to the 'talk' of the evangelical, Christian leaders. This will not be far from the decision to work against the Christian religion in America, even to the point of bringing pressure against the Christian evangelicals. I believe that when a liberal (probably a woman) president takes the seat in the White House, as the Commander in Chief, of this country, there will come the new laws which will govern the activities of the 'evangelical Christians' legal activities in this land 'of the free.' Why do I see this as the scenario? **Reason one**—the talk that—all religions are equal is not a message accepted by the average evangelical Christian church, **reason two**—tolerance will be the name of the game, and many Christian churches will find that position 'intolerable' to their beliefs.

Then the rope around the neck of the Fish, will be the American Flag. The liberal church will hang itself with it's own insistence that the country continue to provide the freedoms, and the liberties that the church has 'always' enjoyed in years past. Perhaps at such a time, the emblem of the fish and the flag displayed on the 'pick up' truck or car seen daily in the streets of America will conjure up a whole new image, and the 'accepted' church member will be, by most un-Christian American citizens a despised member of society. Then maybe American Christians will be fortunate enough to feel what the persecuted church around the world feels—when the social acceptance of Christian faith, becomes socially unacceptable. That experience of social un-acceptableness is, what is known 'world wide' as—**the normal Christian condition.**

I foresee in just such a case as this—the church buildings which cost millions $$$, being of less importance, the multi-purpose buildings and staff, becoming ineffective for 'luring' the American into the little 'hallelujah happy hour' service, and I foresee people finally looking to the Bible, not the seminary professor's class, as the hope for discovery of the—reason for the season. If you see this personal vision I have presented as a good thing, you are probably already a saved person. If you are bewildered or negative in your response to such events as I have described, you probably need to re-evaluate your spiritual condition. Since the Bible teaches, 'all who will live Godly in Christ Jesus, will suffer persecution.' Persecution usually means that you are now listed among the 'undesirables' of society. Of course this definition is designed by the 'ruling elite' of the 'new society or in our case, "The New World Order." When you are listed among the truly, Biblically persecuted for the Name of Christ, don't be afraid, just realize you are finally 'Far Right.'

When the Lord God in Heaven, called Abraham to be the father of the nation of Israel, it was the beginning of the physical 'chosen people of God' on earth, to usher in the Messiah, Jesus the Son of God. Just as we have a physical Adam, then a spiritual Adam in Christ, the physical then the spiritual. Jesus is the 'first begotten from the dead' the spiritual Adam, the Captain of our salvation. The physical will pass away, but the spiritual people of God will live eternally. We have the first heaven and earth, then the second heaven and earth (Rev. 21. 1), we have the physical body, then a new spiritual body, like that of the Lord Jesus ("…we shall be like Him for we shall see Him as He is…" 1 John 3. 3,—1 Cor. 15. 44). These things are clearly described in the Bible. **Two Adams**, one physical, one spiritual, two heavens and earth,—physical, then the one to come, eternal, different and not made with hands, and the New Jerusalem, a city prepared for the Bride of Christ. **We have the two nations**, the physical people of God, Israel, then the Ekklesia (called out people of God who are a spiritual body—born again people, born from above), the household of God, the bride of Christ. Even the people of physical Israel (Jewish people) must come to Christ for the new birth, and new citizenship in the eternal Kingdom of God.

This is why it is so important for the believers in Christ to see the physical Israel today, as the shadow of the spiritual Israel, not to see it as the 'eternal spiritual body of Christ' church or ekklesia (Romans 1-4). For even Abraham was justified by his faith, which is the spiritual blessing that Christians are joined to, even though they are not physical Jews. Abraham was justified not by the works of the law, which included circumcision, and which 'rite' made people a physical Israel, he was justified by his faith, trusting in God's promise. Abraham is both the physical father, and he is also in a figure the spiritual father-Gal. 3. 7 of all who believe—for we are all children of Abraham by exercising the same faith, for it is the faith that relates us to Abraham, the first to show faith which was accounted as righteousness to him......Romans 4. **Abraham was a physical and**

spiritual part of the plan of God. Jesus came into the Jewish nation as a man, but He is the Spiritual Adam, bringing many sons into glory. We become children of God by faith in Jesus Christ, Gal. 3. 26-29.

In baptism into Christ, we take off the lst Adam and put on the new 'man'—the second Adam (the spiritual) which is Christ. But our faith unites us to the inheritance or promise that was given to Abraham, which is the promise of life eternal. Our hope is in Christ, not in just a few chosen verses which we 'hide away' in our hope chest of religious views. This brings us to the difference between the nation of Israel and the Church (or biblically the ekklesia, kingdom of God people, who are called out of the world unto Him). The physical Israel is not under the New Covenant in Christ Jesus the Lord (Rom. 2. 28). Circumcision is that of the heart, not that of the flesh. Our hope is in Christ not in any government or freedom provided by any government. We have here, no continuing city, but we seek one that is above, not made with hands, eternal in the heavens (Heb. 11). This world is not our home, so we should not act as though it is, either in America or in any other 'homeland' which is physical. If we are citizens now of a heavenly Kingdom, let us so live and so act as those who do not place our **eternal hope** on **a temporary location**. Our task is to announce the coming King, and to announce our trust in Him, so all who know us, will see Him in us, as the one who controls our every goal on earth and destiny. **To God be the glory.**

978-0-595-40572-5
0-595-40572-X